PHP & MySQL®

Your visual blueprint™ for creating dynamic, database-driven Web sites

by Janet Valade

WILEY

Wiley Publishing, Inc.

PHP & MySQL®: Your visual blueprint™ for creating dynamic, database-driven Web sites

Published by
Wiley Publishing, Inc.
111 River Street
Hoboken, NJ 07030-5774

Published simultaneously in Canada

Copyright © 2006 by Wiley Publishing, Inc., Indianapolis, Indiana

No part of this publication may be reproduced, stored in a retrieval system or transmitted in any form or by any means, electronic, mechanical, photocopying, recording, scanning or otherwise, except as permitted under Sections 107 or 108 of the 1976 United States Copyright Act, without either the prior written permission of the Publisher, or authorization through payment of the appropriate per-copy fee to the Copyright Clearance Center, 222 Rosewood Drive, Danvers, MA 01923, (978) 750-8400, fax (978) 646-8600. Requests to the Publisher for permission should be addressed to the Legal Department, Wiley Publishing, Inc., 10475 Crosspoint Blvd., Indianapolis, IN 46256, (317) 572-3447, fax (317) 572-4355, Online: www.wiley.com/go/permissions.

Library of Congress Control Number: 2006925879

ISBN-13: 978-0-470-04839-9

ISBN-10: 0-470-04839-5

Manufactured in the United States of America

10 9 8 7 6 5 4 3 2 1

1D/ST/QY/QW/IN

Trademark Acknowledgments

Wiley, the Wiley Publishing logo, Visual, the Visual logo, Simplified, Master VISUALLY, Teach Yourself VISUALLY, Visual Blueprint, Read Less - Learn More and related trade dress are trademarks or registered trademarks of John Wiley & Sons, Inc. and/or its affiliates. MySQL is a registered trademark of MySQL AB in the United States, the European Union and other countries. All other trademarks are the property of their respective owners. Wiley Publishing, Inc. is not associated with any product or vendor mentioned in this book.

LIMIT OF LIABILITY/DISCLAIMER OF WARRANTY: THE PUBLISHER AND THE AUTHOR MAKE NO REPRESENTATIONS OR WARRANTIES WITH RESPECT TO THE ACCURACY OR COMPLETENESS OF THE CONTENTS OF THIS WORK AND SPECIFICALLY DISCLAIM ALL WARRANTIES, INCLUDING WITHOUT LIMITATION WARRANTIES OF FITNESS FOR A PARTICULAR PURPOSE. NO WARRANTY MAY BE CREATED OR EXTENDED BY SALES OR PROMOTIONAL MATERIALS. THE ADVICE AND STRATEGIES CONTAINED HEREIN MAY NOT BE SUITABLE FOR EVERY SITUATION. THIS WORK IS SOLD WITH THE UNDERSTANDING THAT THE PUBLISHER IS NOT ENGAGED IN RENDERING LEGAL, ACCOUNTING, OR OTHER PROFESSIONAL SERVICES. IF PROFESSIONAL ASSISTANCE IS REQUIRED, THE SERVICES OF A COMPETENT PROFESSIONAL PERSON SHOULD BE SOUGHT. NEITHER THE PUBLISHER NOR THE AUTHOR SHALL BE LIABLE FOR DAMAGES ARISING HEREFROM. THE FACT THAT AN ORGANIZATION OR WEBSITE IS REFERRED TO IN THIS WORK AS A CITATION AND/OR A POTENTIAL SOURCE OF FURTHER INFORMATION DOES NOT MEAN THAT THE AUTHOR OR THE PUBLISHER ENDORSES THE INFORMATION THE ORGANIZATION OR WEBSITE MAY PROVIDE OR RECOMMENDATIONS IT MAY MAKE. FURTHER, READERS SHOULD BE AWARE THAT INTERNET WEBSITES LISTED IN THIS WORK MAY HAVE CHANGED OR DISAPPEARED BETWEEN WHEN THIS WORK WAS WRITTEN AND WHEN IT IS READ.

FOR PURPOSES OF ILLUSTRATING THE CONCEPTS AND TECHNIQUES DESCRIBED IN THIS BOOK, THE AUTHOR HAS CREATED VARIOUS NAMES, COMPANY NAMES, MAILING, E-MAIL AND INTERNET ADDRESSES, PHONE AND FAX NUMBERS AND SIMILAR INFORMATION, ALL OF WHICH ARE FICTITIOUS. ANY RESEMBLANCE OF THESE FICTITIOUS NAMES, ADDRESSES, PHONE AND FAX NUMBERS AND SIMILAR INFORMATION TO ANY ACTUAL PERSON, COMPANY AND/OR ORGANIZATION IS UNINTENTIONAL AND PURELY COINCIDENTAL.

Contact Us

For general information on our other products and services, please contact our Customer Care Department within the U.S. at 800-762-2974, outside the U.S. at 317-572-3993, or fax 317-572-4002.

For technical support, please visit www.wiley.com/techsupport.

Cathedral of San Vergilio, Trent, Italy

From its modest origins as a fifth-century chapel marking the grave of St. Vigilius, the martyred Bishop of Trent, this cathedral began its evolution to glory at the hands of artisan Adam d'Argogno in 1212. The project outlived d'Argogno, and his descendants faithfully carried it on for centuries. In 1545, the expanded cathedral hosted the historic Council of Trent, which was convened in response to the Protestant Reformation and disbanded in 1563. Modifications and renovations to the cathedral have continued virtually unabated, with the most recent interior restoration having been completed in the early 1990s.

Learn more about Italy's historic treasures in *Frommer's Italy*, available wherever books are sold or at www.frommers.com.

WILEY

Sales

Contact Wiley
at (800) 762-2974
or (317) 572-4002.

About the Author

Janet Valade has 20 years experience in the computing field. Her background includes experience as a technical writer for several companies, as a Web designer/programmer for an engineering firm, and as a systems analyst in a university environment where, for over 10 years, she supervised the installation and operation of computing resources, designed and developed a statewide data archive, provided technical support to faculty and staff, wrote numerous technical papers and documentation, and designed and presented seminars and workshops on a variety of technology topics.

Janet currently has four published books — *PHP & MySQL For Dummies,* Second Edition, *PHP 5 For Dummies, PHP & MySQL Everyday Apps For Dummies,* and *Spring into Linux,* and has coauthored *Master VISUALLY Dreamweaver 8 and Flash 8.* In addition, she has authored chapters for several Linux and Web development books.

Author's Acknowledgments

I want to thank my mother for passing on a writing gene, along with many other things. And my children, always, for everything.

I wish to express my appreciation to the entire open-source community. Without those who give their time and talent, there would be no PHP and MySQL for me to write about. Furthermore, I never would have learned this software without the lists where people generously spend their time answering foolish questions from beginners.

And, of course, I want to thank the professionals who make it all possible. Without the people at Wiley, this book would not exist. Because they all do their jobs so well, I can contribute my part to this joint project.

TABLE OF CONTENTS

4 CONTROLLING THE FLOW OF THE SCRIPT 74

5 REUSING PHP CODE 98

TABLE OF CONTENTS

TABLE OF CONTENTS

HOW TO USE THIS BOOK

PHP & MySQL: Your visual blueprint for creating dynamic, database-driven Web sites uses clear, descriptive examples to show you how to create dynamic Web sites. If you are already familiar with PHP and MySQL, you can use this book as a quick reference for many Web site tasks.

Who Needs This Book

This book is for the experienced computer user who wants to find out more about programming dynamic Web sites with PHP and MySQL. It is also for more experienced PHP and MySQL users who want to expand their knowledge of the different features that PHP and MySQL have to offer.

Book Organization

PHP & MySQL: Your visual blueprint for creating dynamic, database-driven Web sites has 12 chapters and 2 appendixes.

Chapter 1, "Setting Up Your Development Environment," shows how to set up the environment in which you develop your dynamic Web site. The chapter shows how to install and configure PHP and MySQL. It also shows how to install Apache. In this chapter, you write and execute your first PHP script.

Chapter 2, "Learning PHP Basics," describes the basics of writing a PHP script. You learn how to add PHP sections to your Web page source files, how to output HTML code that is displayed on your Web page, how to work with variables, how to handle different types of data, and how to troubleshoot errors.

Chapter 3, "Using Arrays," explains arrays, a useful tool for building dynamic Web sites. You learn how to create, modify, remove, sort, compare, split, merge, and perform many other operations on arrays. You also learn to create and manipulate multidimensional arrays.

Chapter 4, "Controlling the Flow of the Script," provides instructions for using complex PHP statements to control the flow of your script. You learn to use conditional statements, such as if statements and switch statements, and loops, such as for loops and while loops.

Chapter 5, "Reusing PHP Code," shows how to write code that you can reuse wherever it is needed in your scripts. You learn to store code in separate files and include it in your script where it is needed. You also learn to create functions that you can call to perform a task whenever necessary.

Chapter 6, "Some Useful PHP Built-in Functions," provides information on using many functions that are provided by PHP to assist you in writing your scripts. Built-in functions that manipulate and modify strings, format numbers, send HTTP headers, and set configuration options are included.

Chapter 7, "Using MySQL Databases," shows how MySQL databases work. You learn how to create the database structure; how to insert, update, and delete data; and how to display data on your Web page that you retrieve from the database.

Chapter 8, "Administering MySQL Databases," explains the MySQL administration tasks. Adding, modifying, and removing MySQL accounts, setting and changing passwords, stopping and starting MySQL, backing up the database, and other administrative tasks are described.

Chapter 9, "Adding HTML Forms to a Web Page," shows how to output the HTML code that displays a form on your Web page. You learn how to display various form elements dynamically, building the form fields from data in your database.

Chapter 10, "Processing Data from Forms," provides instructions for processing the information that users enter into a form. You learn to validate and clean the data. The chapter also discusses storing data in the database.

Chapter 11, "Managing User Sessions," shows how to move users and information from one Web page to the next. You learn to create and use cookies and PHP session features.

Chapter 12, "Object-Oriented Programming in PHP," describes the PHP object-oriented programming features. You learn to create and use objects and classes, add properties and methods to classes, use PHP magic methods, copy objects, use exceptions, and many other tasks.

Appendix A, "Programming Editors and IDEs for PHP," describes some useful editors and IDEs.

Appendix B, "Troubleshooting Tips," covers several common mistakes that can produce errors in your scripts.

What You Need to Use This Book

The use of PHP and MySQL requires a computer that is connected to the Internet. You can install PHP and MySQL on your own computer for hosting your Web site, or you can house your Web site on a Web hosting company computer where PHP and MySQL are already installed. In many cases, you do both, developing your Web site on your own computer and then transferring the completed Web site files to a Web hosting company computer to make it available to the public. You transfer the programs using FTP via your Internet connection.

PHP and MySQL are available for all popular operating systems and require very little in the way of resources. To write the PHP scripts, you can use a text editor available on your operating system, such as WordPad or vi, but you will be more efficient if you install a programming editor or IDE, as described in Appendix A.

WINDOWS REQUIREMENTS

Windows 98/2000/NT/Me/XP. Windows 98/Me can run PHP and MySQL for development, but are not suitable for a production Web site.

MAC REQUIREMENTS

Mac OS X

LINUX REQUIREMENTS

Any Linux computer. Many come with PHP and MySQL already installed or available on the installation disks.

The Conventions in This Book

A number of styles have been used throughout *PHP & MySQL: Your visual blueprint for creating dynamic, database-driven Web sites* to designate different types of information.

```
Courier Font
```

Indicates the use of HTML code such as tags or attributes; scripting language code such as PHP statements, operators, or functions; and SQL queries.

Bold

Indicates information that you must type.

Italics

Indicates a new term.

Apply It

An Apply It section takes the code from the preceding task one step further. Apply It sections enable you to take full advantage of PHP code and MySQL features.

Extra

An Extra section provides additional information about the preceding task. Extra sections contain the inside information to make working with PHP and MySQL easier and more efficient.

What's on the Web Site

The Web site accompanying this book contains the sample code files for the book. Go to www.wiley.com/go/phpmysqlvb and there will be a link for the code.

Introducing Dynamic Web Sites

oday's World Wide Web (WWW) is a dynamic, interactive environment for transactions of many types — commerce, research, forums, and so on. In dynamic Web sites, HTML forms collect information that is used to build additional Web pages or is stored, or both. If the Web site stores information, a back-end database is required. For example, most online catalogs are databases of product information. Customers select

the type of product that interests them via an HTML form, and the Web page displays only the requested product information. HTML alone does not provide the functionality needed for dynamic Web sites. The most popular dynamic Web site technology is the PHP scripting language with the MySQL database. PHP is currently installed in over 20 million domains, as shown at www.php.net/usage.php.

PHP

PHP is a scripting language, with many of the same features found in any scripting language and syntax similar to C. PHP can output text, execute conditional actions, perform repeated actions, and so on. However, because PHP was developed specifically for use on Web sites, it includes features that simplify building dynamic Web sites.

PHP is open-source software, which means that you can download and use it without paying a fee. PHP runs on almost every operating system, including Windows, Linux, Mac OS, and most flavors of UNIX. PHP is particularly strong in its capability to interact with databases and has built-in features for working with MySQL.

PHP works in partnership with your Web server software, which is required on every Web site to deliver Web pages to users. PHP code is embedded in HTML source files, enclosed by the PHP tags, `<?php` and `?>`. The Web server sends the code enclosed in PHP tags to PHP, which executes the code and returns the output to the Web server, which in turn sends the HTML code and the output from the PHP code to the browser. The browser displays the Web page.

MySQL

MySQL is a small, fast RDBMS (relational database management system) that is popular for use on dynamic Web sites. The term *database* refers to a file or group of files that contains the information needed by your Web site. The database can contain information that you want to display on your Web site, can store information collected from users, or both.

You can download an open-source version of MySQL, called the *Community* version, which you can use without paying a fee. An *Enterprise* version of MySQL is also available with a commercial license. MySQL, like PHP, runs on almost every operating system, including Windows, Linux, Mac OS, and most flavors of UNIX.

The MySQL software consists of the MySQL server, several utility programs, and some supporting software. The MySQL server handles all your database requests. You send SQL (structured query language) instructions, called *queries*, to the server, which creates databases, stores information, retrieves information, or performs other operations according to the instructions in the query.

Before you can send queries to MySQL, the server must be running and waiting for requests. When used as a back-end database on a Web site, the MySQL server is set up so that it starts when the computer boots and runs all the time, listening continuously for queries. The MySQL server does not need to be installed on the same computer with PHP. PHP can send queries across a network.

How PHP and MySQL Work Together

PHP includes functions designed specifically to access MySQL databases. You use functions to connect to the MySQL server, select a database, execute a SQL query that saves or retrieves data, and perform other needed database operations. The PHP functions handle the details of accessing the data in your MySQL databases. You do not need to know the details.

MySQL can store very complex information. PHP can perform complicated manipulation of data. Together, PHP and MySQL can be used to build a complex and sophisticated Web site.

Help for PHP and MySQL

Both PHP and MySQL provide very comprehensive manuals on their Web sites. The first place to look for answers is the online documentation at http://dev.mysql.com/doc/refman/5.0/en/index.html or www.php.net/manual/en/.

Open-source software, such as PHP and MySQL, does not provide a phone number that you can call when you have a question. Instead, open-source software users help each other through discussion lists and forums. Because PHP and MySQL are popular, discussion lists hosted on their Web sites include hundreds of people who are experts. When you post a question on a list, the answer often shows up in your email box within seconds. You can join discussion lists at www.php.net/mailing-lists.php and http://forums.mysql.com. You can search archives of the discussion lists to see if your question has been asked and answered previously.

PHP and MySQL Versions

Because PHP and MySQL are open-source software, new versions are released often and sometimes without much warning. Sometimes new releases include changes in the way the software works or the installation procedure that require changes to your application — not often, but occasionally. Consequently, you need to be aware of versions and keep informed about PHP and MySQL versions, changes, and problems.

The PHP Web site www.php.net currently provides PHP 4 and PHP 5 for download. When PHP 6 is added, three versions will be offered for a period of time. The MySQL Web site www.mysql.com currently provides three version of MySQL — 4.1, 5, and 5.1. Version 5 is currently the stable version recommended for most users. If you are creating a new Web site, install the newest version of PHP. PHP 4 does not support some of the features added in MySQL 4.1 and newer versions.

PHP communicates with MySQL using functions. Beginning with PHP 5, PHP provides two sets of functions for interacting with MySQL — the `mysql` extension and the `mysqli` (MySQL Improved) extension. If you are using PHP 4, the `mysqli` functions are not available. You can interact with MySQL 4.1 or newer versions using the `mysql` functions, but you may not be able to use some of the advanced MySQL features added in newer versions. With PHP 5, you can use the `mysqli` functions that better support MySQL 4.1 and later. When you install PHP 5, you activate `mysql` or `mysqli` functions. PHP and MySQL installation instructions are provided later in this chapter.

Set Up Your Development Environment

A Web site is basically a collection of files, stored in a location that visitors can access from the WWW. You can locate your Web site on a computer provided by someone else, such as a Web hosting company or your employer, or you can install and administer the Web site yourself, on your own computer.

Each solution has advantages and disadvantages. Housing your Web site on a computer administered by someone else is much easier, in terms of work and knowledge. You do not need to know how to install or administer any Web site software. You just upload your Web site source files. The disadvantage is that you lack control over your environment. The administrator of the computer where your Web site is located provides the environment that works best from his or her point of view, which may not be the environment you prefer. When you run your own computer to house your Web site, you can install hardware and software with your preferred configuration and settings. However, running your own Web site requires more work and more knowledge.

Design Your Development Environment

Whether you build your Web site on someone else's computer or your own, you need to set up an environment that facilitates your development. In most cases, you want to build your Web site in a test location — a site that you can view but the public cannot. You need to view the work in progress, but you do not want visitors to see your half-built pages, with coding errors and design flaws. So, you need two Web sites — a development site and the final site where the Web pages are available to the public.

Your test site can be located on the same computer with your public Web site or on a different computer. Many people who use a Web hosting company set up a test site on their own computer, installing PHP and MySQL locally for the test Web site. Only the finished Web pages are copied to the hosting company computer.

If you locate your development test site on the same computer with your public Web site, you can set up a subdirectory in your Web space where you develop Web pages. You can access the URL, such as www.mywebsite.com/testsite, to test Web pages, but the test site is not available for public access.

Select a Web Hosting Company

A Web hosting company provides everything you need, including computer space and Web site software. You create the Web site files and move them to the location indicated by the Web hosting company. This is the easiest way to publish a Web site, but you need to choose your Web hosting company wisely.

Many companies offer Web hosting services for a reasonable monthly fee, which usually depends on the resources provided. For example, a Web site with 1 megabyte of Web space would cost less than a Web site with 20 megabytes. To build a dynamic Web site, as described in this book, you need a Web hosting company that offers PHP and MySQL. The reliability of the Web hosting company, the speed at which Web pages download, and the availability of backups are important considerations. You want access to technical support when problems arise. Other factors to consider are the MB/GB of disk space you need for your Web site, whether the hosting company charges for sending Web pages to users, how many email accounts you receive with your Web site, what supporting software the hosting company provides, and whether you can collect statistics on Web site traffic.

If you search with Google for **"Web hosting company"**, you will get several million hits. You cannot research this many Web hosting companies. Asking for recommendations from peers and colleagues is a better approach. You can compile a list of recommended and to-be-avoided Web hosting companies, based on the experience of others. You can then research the recommended companies to find the host that best suits your needs. As of this moment, GoDaddy.com is the world's largest Web hosting company, according to the Netcraft survey at www.netcraft.com.

Register a Domain Name

Every Web site needs a unique address on the Web, called a *domain name.* A system of registering domain names ensures that no two locations use the same domain name. Anyone can register any domain name as long as the name is not already taken. Many Web sites, including most Web hosting company Web sites, provide a form that you can use to register a domain name. The standard cost is $35.00 per year, but bargains can be found.

Some Web hosting companies assign a domain name to you, rather than allowing you to use your own domain name. Some assign domain names that are subdomains of the company Web site, such as yourcompanyname.webhostingcompanyname.com or webhostingcompanyname.com/~yourcompanyname. In most cases, you want to find a Web hosting company that allows you to register and use your own domain name.

Find Supporting Software

Your work environment includes the software that you use to create your Web pages. Although you can certainly code in a simple text editor, such as WordPad on Windows, an editor with more features makes your life easier. Programming editors and IDEs, which have features that help programmers, are described in Appendix A.

Software for administering your MySQL databases is also useful. The MySQL Web site provides two packages on the download page: MySQL Administrator for database management and MySQL Query Browser for adding or retrieving data. PhpMyAdmin, written in PHP, is another popular database management tool and is available at www.phpmyadmin.net.

Run a Dynamic Web Site on Your Own Computer

To host a public Web site, your computer must be connected to the WWW. The ISP account that you currently use to access the Web may not be fast enough to provide access to a Web site, or it may not provide domain name service (DNS), which is needed to allow the public to access your Web site using your domain name. Contact your ISP and discuss your Web site needs. Your ISP may be able to provide the services you need, or you may need to find a new ISP.

A Web server is required for every public Web site. If you are hosting your Web site on a Web hosting company computer, the Web host handles the Web server and WWW access. However, if you host the public Web site on your own computer or if you want to develop the Web site on your local computer and upload only the final files, you must install a Web server on your own computer.

The most popular Web server is Apache, which powers almost 70% of the domains on the Web. Apache is open-source software that you can download and install for free. Obtaining and installing Apache is described later in this chapter. Microsoft Internet Information Services (IIS) is the second most popular Web server, powering slightly over 20% of the domains. IIS is included with Windows 2000/XP.

You must install PHP on the same computer where your dynamic Web site resides, including your local development and testing computer. Your dynamic Web site must also have access to MySQL, either on the same computer or on a computer that can be accessed via a network. Instructions for obtaining and installing PHP and MySQL are provided in this chapter.

Obtain Apache

The Apache Web server is open-source software that you can download and use for free from http://httpd.apache.org. For Windows, you can download the Microsoft Installer file, which has an .msi extension. Most Mac and Linux computers come with Apache already installed. However, you probably need to start the Apache server, which is described in the section "Install Apache."

Apache is available in three versions: Apache 1.3, Apache 2, and Apache 2.2. All three versions are supported and upgraded. Apache 2 changed considerably from Apache 1.3; Apache 2.2 changed from Apache 2. Third-party modules that run on 1.3 will not work correctly with Apache 2, and modules that work on Apache 2 may not work correctly with Apache 2.2. Therefore, only modules that have been modified for Apache 2 or 2.2 can run on Apache 2 or 2.2.

PHP runs with Apache 2 or 2.2. However, some PHP third-party modules may experience problems. If you plan a simple Web site without third-party PHP software, use the most recent version of Apache 2. Apache 2 runs better on Windows than Apache 1.3. However, if you plan a large, complicated Web site, on which you may use a variety of third-party PHP software, it may be best to stick with Apache 1.3.

Apache runs on almost all operating systems. It runs on Windows 95/98/ME/NT 4/2000/XP. However, running a production server on Windows 95/98/ME is not recommended. For Windows XP, you need to download and install Service Pack 1 before you install Apache. The Apache Windows installer file requires version 1.10 or later of the Microsoft Installer (MSI). MSI is built into Windows XP/2000/NT, but you may need to upgrade it by downloading it from the Microsoft Web site.

Obtain Apache

① Type **httpd.apache.org/download.cgi**.

② Scroll down to the Apache version that you want.

③ Click Other Files.

Note: For Apache 1.3 on Windows, click Win32 Binary and skip to step 7.

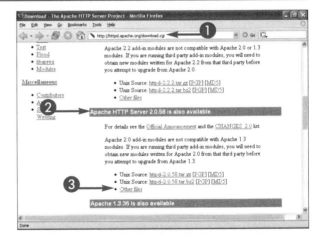

A list of download links opens.

④ Click the link for the binaries/ subdirectory.

Note: The appearance of this page may vary with different mirror Web sites, but the list of links will contain a link to binaries/.

The binary download page opens.

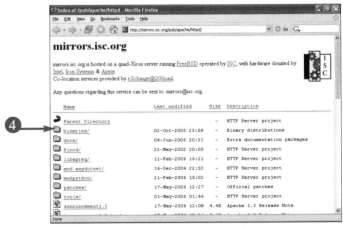

⑤ Click the link for your operating system.

A list of files available for download is displayed.

⑥ Click the file that you want to download.

In this example, the Windows Binary Installer, with the filename apache_2.0.58-win32-x86-no_ssl.msi, is selected.

The file download dialog box opens.

⑦ Click Save to Disk.

⑧ Click OK.

The Save As dialog box opens.

⑨ Navigate to the folder where you want to save Apache.

⑩ Click Save.

The Downloads dialog box opens and reports the downloading progress.

A message appears when the downloading finishes.

Note: Your browser may or may not close the download dialog box when finished downloading, depending on its setting. You can change this option in your browser.

Note: After downloading Apache, scroll down the Download page to the Verify the Integrity of the Files section and follow the instructions.

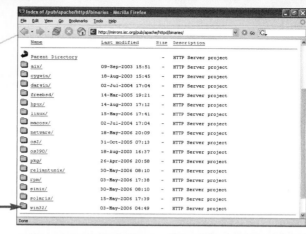

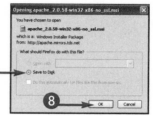

Extra

The Apache Web site provides a method to verify the Apache software after you download it. Because Apache is provided on many mirror Web sites, it is possible that the legitimate Apache file has been replaced with one that has been altered. Verifying the downloaded file is a security precaution to make sure that the file is the correct file.

Most Apache files must be verified using the PGP method. The PGP software is installed by default on Linux and Mac. On Windows, you must download and install the software. For more information on PGP software, see www.gnupg.org.

To verify with the PGP method, you must download the file named KEYS and the file that ends with .asc, as well as the file containing the Apache software. The KEYS file is the same for all operating systems, so it is in the binaries directory, not in the individual operating system directories.

TYPE THIS	RESULT

`pgpk -a KEYS`
`pgpv apache_2.0.58.win32-x86-no_ssl.msi.asc`
or
`pgp -ka KEYS`
`pgp apache_2.0.58.win32-x86-no_ssl.msi.asc`
	An output line that contains a line similar to the following:
	`httpd-2.0.58. win32-x86-`
	`no_ssl.msi is signed by`
	`William Rowe 10FDE075`

The MD5 verification method is simpler. This method is available for the Apache 1.3 Windows installer on the download page — the first page that opens in the steps in this section. The MD5 method, as well as the PGP method, is also available to verify MySQL and PHP files. The MD5 method of verification is described in the Extra area of the section "Obtain MySQL."

Install Apache

Apache is installed when Linux or Mac OS X is installed, but not when Windows is installed. On Windows, you must download and install Apache by running an installer file that you download from the Apache Web site, http://httpd.apache.org. Downloading Apache is discussed in the previous section, "Obtain Apache."

When you double-click the downloaded installer file from Windows Explorer, an installation procedure starts. You see several screens, one after another, that request required information, including your domain name, your server name, the email address of the Apache administrator, and the folder where you want to install Apache. Then, when you have provided the information, Apache is installed.

The Apache Web server must be both installed and started. Apache can be set up so that it starts automatically whenever the computer boots or so that

you must start it manually. During installation, select For All Users, on Port 80, As a Service to set up Apache to start automatically.

On Mac, Apache is usually installed, but you need to start it. Open System Preferences and click the Sharing folder. On the Services tab, check Personal Web Sharing.

On Linux, Apache is usually installed, but may not be started. To start the Apache server, type

```
/usr/local/apache2/bin/apachectl start
```

At times, you will need to stop or restart the Apache Web server. For example, when you change Apache or PHP settings, you need to restart Apache before the new settings go into effect. On Windows, you can start and stop Apache from a menu item in the Start menu. On Linux, use the `apachectl` script, as shown above, with `restart` or with `stop`.

Install Apache

1. Double-click the Apache installer that you downloaded.

2. On the Welcome screen, click Next.

3. On the License Agreement screen, click I Accept . . .

4. Click Next.

5. On the Server Information screen, type your domain name.

6. Type your server name.

7. Type your email address.

   - Leave this selection to have Apache installed as a service that starts automatically.

8. Click Next.

9. On the Setup Type screen, click Typical.

Note: Custom should only be selected by users with system administration experience.

10. Click Next.

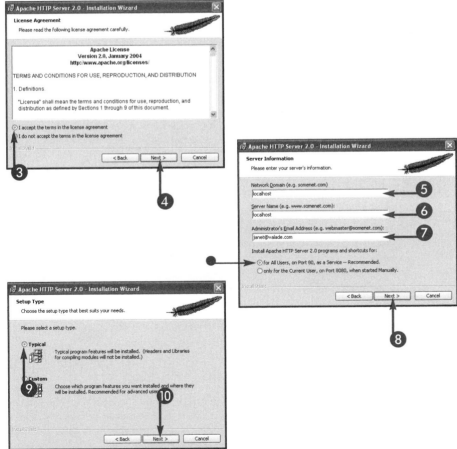

The Destination Folder screen opens.

- A default destination folder is selected.
- You can change the destination folder if you want.

Note: Maintaining and upgrading Apache is easier if you install in the default directory.

⑪ Click Next.

The Ready to Install the Program screen appears.

⑫ Click Install.

The wizard shows the progress of the installation.

A message appears when Apache is finished installing.

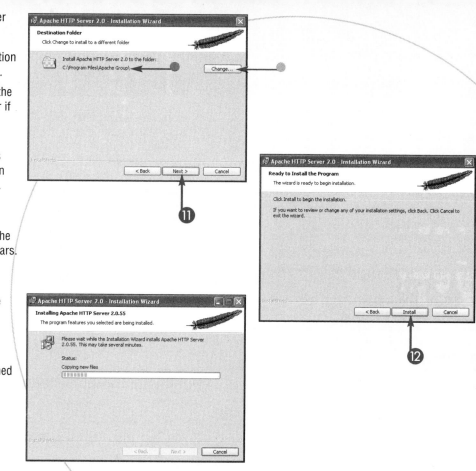

Extra

You can determine whether Apache is running on Windows by checking whether it appears in the list of services on your computer. Click Start ➔ Control Panel ➔ Administrative Tools ➔ Services. An alphabetical list of services is displayed. If Apache is listed, it is installed as a service, but it may not be turned on. Check whether its status is Started and its type is Automatic. If you need to, you can click Apache in the services list and change its status and/or type.

If Apache is not listed, it is not installed as a service and will not start automatically when your computer boots. To install Apache as a service, first open a command prompt window.

TYPE THIS

```
cd c:\Program Files\Apache Group\apache2\bin
apache -k install
```

If you did not install Apache in the default directory, substitute the path to the directory where Apache is installed.

RESULT

The Apache Web server is installed as a service. It will automatically start whenever your computer boots.

Obtain MySQL

MySQL is a small, fast database, particularly well suited for use with a Web site. MySQL provides open-source software, which you can download and use without paying a fee. MySQL also provides an Enterprise version that you can purchase.

MySQL currently offers versions 4.1, 5, and 5.1. Version 5.1 is not stable and should be used only for trying things out, not for production. The current stable version is 5, which is the version most people should download.

The MySQL free download is available in binaries — machine files that are already compiled for specific operating systems. If a binary file is available for your operating system, you should download the binary. MySQL may be already installed on your Macintosh or Linux computer. If not, it may be available for installation

from the operating system discs, although you may want to install a more recent version. Binaries may not be available for older operating systems, such as versions of Mac OS X older than 10.2, in which case you can download source code that you can compile and install.

The Windows download is available with an installer. You can download Windows Essentials — a smaller file and sufficient for most needs — or Windows Complete, a larger file with more optional software, such as the embedded server and benchmark suite.

The Linux download is available in an RPM file for downloading and installation using the RPM command. RPMs specifically for Red Hat Linux and SuSE Linux and a general RPM for other Linux flavors are available. The Macintosh download is a disk image in PKG format, available for specific versions of OS X.

Obtain MySQL

① Type **www.mysql.com/downloads** and click the link for the version that you want to download.

The download page opens.

● Here, the link for version 5 was clicked.

② Scroll down to the section for the operating system that you need.

③ Click the Pick a Mirror link by the version to download.

Here, Windows Essentials is clicked.

④ Scroll down to the list of mirrors.

⑤ Click HTTP by the mirror that you want to use.

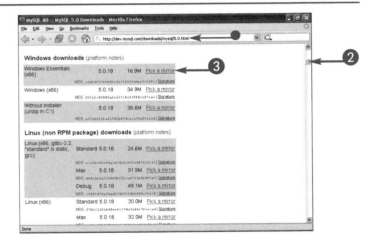

The File Download dialog box opens.

⑥ Click Save to Disk.

⑦ Click OK.

The Save As dialog box opens.

⑧ Click here and navigate to the folder where you want to save the file.

⑨ Click Save.

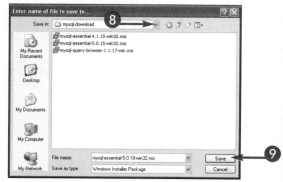

A window shows the downloading progress.

A message is displayed when the download completes.

Note: Your browser may or may not close the download window when finished downloading, depending on its setting. You can change this option in your browser.

Extra

The MySQL Web site provides methods to verify the software after you download it, as a security precaution to make sure that the file has not been altered. You can verify using either the md5 method or the PGP method. The md5 method is simpler. The PGP method is described in the Extra area of the section "Obtain Apache."

On the download page by the file that you downloaded, a long string, called a *signature,* is displayed, similar to the following:

```
MD5: 6112f6a730c680a4048dbab40e4107b3
```

TYPE THIS		RESULT
At a command-line prompt, such as in a command prompt window in Windows, type `md5 mysql-essential-5.0.22-win32.msi` Use the name of the file that you downloaded.		A signature is displayed. The signature here should be the same signature displayed by the filename on the download page of the MySQL Web site.

You can verify the downloads for Apache and PHP with a similar procedure.

If md5 is not installed on your computer, you can download and install it from www.fourmilab.ch/md5/.

Install MySQL

MySQL may be already installed on Linux or Macintosh, but must be downloaded and installed on Windows. Downloading is discussed in the previous section. You can start an installation wizard by double-clicking the file that you downloaded. The example in this section shows installing MySQL on Windows.

In general, the MySQL defaults are the best choices for beginners. The default folder where MySQL is installed is similar to C:\Program Files\MySQL\MySQL Server 5.0. You can change the default, but do not change it without a compelling reason.

MySQL also needs to be configured. You can start the configuration wizard directly from the final installation window or from the MySQL menu item at any time; for more information, see the following section, "Configure MySQL."

For Linux, if MySQL is not already installed or you want to install a newer version, use the rpm command to install the RPM files downloaded from the MySQL Web site. You need to install the server, client, and headers and libraries RPM packages. MySQL is installed in /var/lib/mysql. The RPM creates entries in /etc/init.d/ so that the MySQL server starts automatically. A login account named mysql, required to run the MySQL server, is created if it does not already exist.

Mac OS X 10.2 and later includes MySQL. If you want to install on an older Mac OS X or upgrade to a newer version of MySQL, download the PKG file from the MySQL Web site and double-click the package icon. The Mac OS X Package Installer guides you through the installation.

The RPM package installs MySQL in /usr/local/mysql-*versionnumber* with a symbolic link — /usr/local/mysql. If a directory named /usr/local/mysql exists, it is renamed to /usr/local/mysql.bak first.

Install MySQL

1 Double-click the MySQL installer.

The Welcome screen for the installer opens.

2 Click Next.

The Setup Type screen opens.

3 Click the type of installation that you want.

4 Click Next.

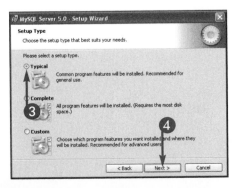

A summary of the settings is displayed.

5 Click Install.

A window shows the progress of the installation.

When the installation is complete, the Sign-Up screen opens.

6 Click Skip Sign-Up.

7 Click Next.

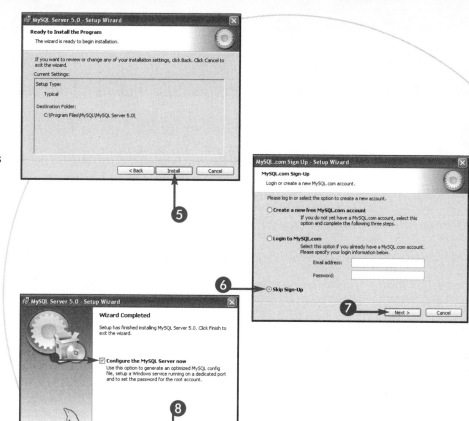

A message states that the wizard is complete.

- Check Configure the MySQL Server Now to begin the configuration now.

Note: Configuration is discussed in the following section, "Configure MySQL."

8 Click Finish.

The Configuration Wizard starts.

Extra

The MySQL server must be both installed and started. In some cases, the server does not automatically start after it is installed. In such cases, you can start the server manually.

To check whether the server is started in Windows, check your list of running services, as described in the Extra area of the section "Install Apache," earlier in this chapter. To check whether the server is running in Linux and Macintosh, check your processes for the MySQL server process.

To start the server in Windows, open a command prompt window and change to the bin directory in the directory where MySQL is installed. Type **mysqld**. To start the server in Linux or Mac, run the script `mysqld_safe`.

TYPE THIS

To start the server on a Mac from the shell:
```
cd /usr/local/mysql
sudo /bin/mysqld_safe
(Cntrl-Z)
bg
```

RESULT

The MySQL server starts running, waiting for queries.

Configure MySQL

On Windows, MySQL must be configured after it is installed. If MySQL is installed from an RPM file or a Macintosh PKG file, the configuration is performed during installation. Otherwise, MySQL on Linux and Mac must also be configured.

MySQL on Windows includes a Configuration Wizard that you can use. You can configure many details of your server operation, such as the number of simultaneous users, or you can accept a MySQL typical installation setup. If you accept typical options, your configuration only involves some account settings and startup settings.

MySQL includes a security system that protects your data. No one can access the data without a valid username and password. An account is created when you install MySQL called *root.* You should use this for your major

administrative account because it is installed with all privileges. You need to set a password for this account.

Also, installing MySQL sets up the software on your system, but does not start the MySQL server. You can start it manually whenever you want to use it, or you can set it up to start when the computer starts.

The Configuration Wizard starts immediately after installation if you check Configure the MySQL Server Now on the final installation screen. You can also start the Configuration Wizard at any time using a Start menu item.

On Linux and Mac, if you did not install MySQL from an RPM or a PKG file, you must run the script `mysql_install_db` to set up the initial privileges and accounts.

Configure MySQL

Note: If the Configuration Welcome screen is already open because you started it at the end of the installation procedure, go to step 5.

1. Click Start ➔ All Programs.

2. Click MySQL.

3. Click MySQL Server *versionnumber.*

4. Click MySQL Server Instance Config Wizard.

   The Configuration Wizard starts.

5. Click Next.

   The configuration type screen opens.

6. Click Standard Configuration.

7. Click Next.

   The Instance Configuration Windows options screen opens.

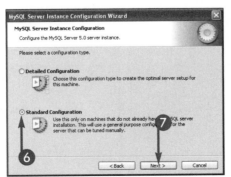

8 Click Install As Windows Service.

9 Click here and select a service name.

10 Click Launch the MySQL Server Automatically.

11 Click Next.

12 Click Modify Security Settings.

13 Type a password for your root account in both fields.

14 Click Create An Anonymous Account.

Note: If this MySQL server is going to be used in a production environment, do not create an anonymous account.

15 Click Next.

16 Click Execute.

The window reports the configuration progress.

A message is displayed when the configuration is complete.

Note: You may need to unblock port 3306.

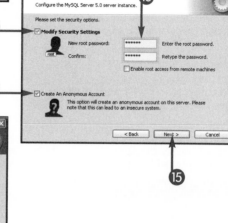

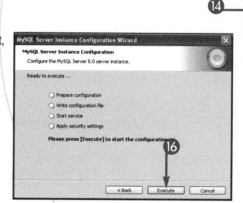

Extra

In most cases, you want MySQL to start when your computer boots and continue running all the time. On Linux, you can add the script `mysql.server` to the directory that your system runs at startup. The MySQL RPM does this for you during installation.

On Mac, you can install a separate MySQL Startup Item package. The Startup Item starts the server by invoking `mysql.server` whenever your computer boots. The Startup Item needs to be installed only once, not during MySQL version upgrades.

The Windows Configuration Wizard can set up MySQL as a Windows service, or you can install it as a service yourself.

TYPE THIS
| ```
cd \Program Files\MySQL\MySQL Server 5.0\bin
mysqld --install
``` |

→

RESULT
The MySQL server is now a Windows service. Its type is automatic, so it starts when the computer boots.

15
```

Install MySQL Administration Programs

Two programs that you can use to administer your MySQL databases are available on the MySQL Web site: MySQL Query Browser and MySQL Administrator. These programs are not required for your development environment, but they provide features that facilitate the creation and use of MySQL databases. MySQL Administrator and MySQL Query Browser run on Windows, Mac OS X, and on any Linux system with the GNOME desktop.

MySQL Administrator provides the features that you need to manage your databases. You can add and remove MySQL accounts, add and manage passwords, add and remove permissions, start and stop the MySQL server, view MySQL logs, make and restore backups, and perform other administrative tasks.

MySQL Query Browser provides a graphical shell, designed to resemble a browser interface, where you can execute

SQL queries on your databases. You can build SQL queries using buttons and drag-and-drop features. The results are displayed in a tabbed window. You can compare the results from various queries. Queries are stored in a history list, so you can execute previous queries.

In Windows, the software is provided in Windows Installer files that you can download. After downloading, double-click the .msi file that you downloaded, and an installation wizard starts. For Linux, the software is provided in generic RPM files that you can download and install with the `rpm` command.

On Macintosh, the software is provided in Package format files that you can download. After downloading, double-click the .dmg disk image file and wait for it to be opened and attached. When a window containing the software icon opens, drag it to your Applications folder. After the copy is complete, you can eject the disk image.

Install MySQL Administration Programs

DOWNLOAD AN ADMINISTRATION PROGRAM

1. Type **www.mysql.com/downloads**.

2. Scroll down to the section labeled MySQL Tools.

3. Click the link for the software that you want to download.

   The download page opens.

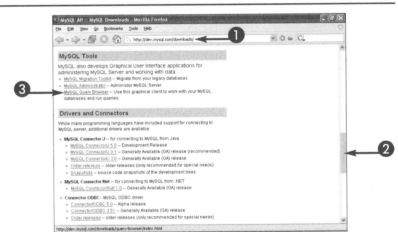

   Here, the link for MySQL Query Browser was clicked.

4. Scroll down to the section for the operating system that you need.

5. Click Pick a Mirror by the version to download.

   Here, the Windows file is clicked.

   The Pick a Mirror page is displayed.

6. Finish downloading the file, as shown in steps 4 to 9 in the section "Obtain MySQL" in this chapter.

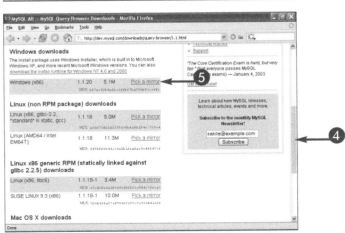

INSTALL THE PROGRAM

7 Double-click the file you downloaded.

8 Click Next in the Setup Wizard Welcome dialog.

9 Click I Agree.

The Destination Folder screen opens.

10 Click Next.

- You can change the destination folder, but the default is preferable.

The Setup Type screen opens.

11 Leave Complete checked.

12 Click Next.

A Summary screen opens.

13 Click Install.

A message appears when installation is complete.

- An entry for the software is added to the Start menu.

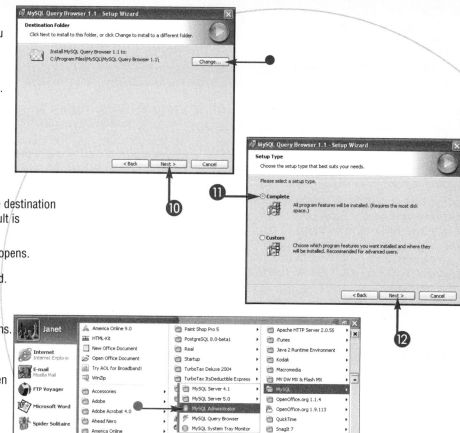

Extra

If you are unable to install from the RPM, you can download the installation `tarball` and install it.

TYPE THIS

After downloading the file, in the directory where the file is located, type

```
tar --directory=/opt -xzvf mysql-query-
browser-nn-linux.tar.gz
```

or

```
tar --directory=/opt -xzvf mysql-
administrator-nn-linux.tar.gz
```

The *nn* string is the version number, such as 1.1.9.

RESULT

The application binary is installed in /opt/mysql-query-browser/bin or /opt/mysql-administrator/bin. Change into that directory and run `mysql-query-browser` or `mysql-administrator` to start the application. You can install the software in a different directory by changing /opt to your preferred installation path.

Create MySQL Accounts for Use in PHP Scripts

MySQL provides a system of accounts, passwords, and privileges to protect your data. No one can access the data in your database without using a valid account. Each account has a set of privileges that define what the account can do — create a database, retrieve data, insert data, delete data, and so on.

MySQL is installed with a default account called *root*. The root account may or may not be installed with a password. The root account is intended for MySQL administration and has all privileges. If the root account does not have a password, you need to add one immediately. The root account is powerful and access to it needs to be restricted.

To protect your data, you should not use the root account when a less powerful account can accomplish the task. In general, create accounts for specific purposes that have only the privileges required to perform the needed tasks.

When your dynamic Web pages need to access the MySQL server, the PHP script must provide a valid MySQL account and password. Using the root account for this purpose, in a script accessible from the WWW, is a major security risk. Consequently, your development environment should include one or more MySQL accounts created explicitly for the purpose of accessing the databases from PHP scripts.

You can create or remove accounts, add, change, or remove passwords, and add and remove permissions using a SQL GRANT query or using the MySQL Administrator software. SQL queries are explained in Chapters 7 and 8. The example in this section shows how to create a new account using MySQL Administrator.

Create MySQL Accounts for Use in PHP Scripts

① Start MySQL Administrator.

② Type the connection information.

③ Click OK.

The program opens.

④ Click User Administration.

The User Administration screen opens in the right pane.

⑤ Click New User.

● New User is added to the account list.

⑥ Type the new user account name and password.

⑦ Type additional optional information.

⑧ Click the Schema Privileges tab.

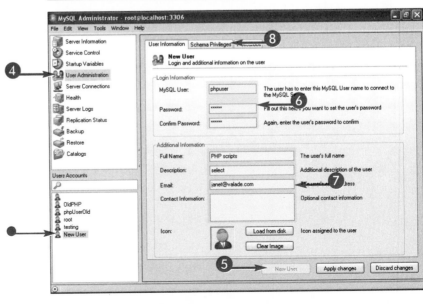

● The account is selected.

9 Click a database.

10 Click one or more privileges.

11 Click the add button.

The selected privileges move to the middle pane.

12 Click Apply Changes.

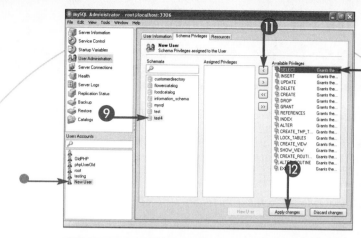

● "New User" changes to the account name that you assigned.

● The username appears on the top of the pane.

The new account is created with only the privileges that you chose in step 10.

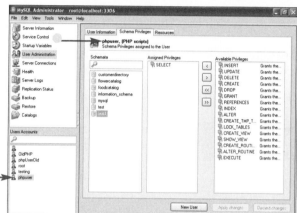

Extra

You can create an account with a GRANT query. You can send the query to the MySQL server with the MySQL Query Browser. Using the Query Browser is described in Chapter 7.

You can also send the query from the mysql client, a command-line client that is installed automatically with MySQL.

TYPE THIS

```
cd c:\Program Files\MySQL\MySQL Server 5.0\bin
mysql -u root -p
```

When the mysql client starts, it displays a prompt. Type the following GRANT query.

```
MYSQL>GRANT SELECT ON *.* TO 'php'@'localhost'
IDENTIFIED BY 'secret';
```

RESULT

→ Creates a new MySQL account named php that has SELECT privileges on all databases.

Obtain PHP

Two versions of PHP are available: PHP 4 and PHP 5. When PHP 6 is released, three versions of PHP may be available for a period of time. If you are installing PHP for the first time and creating your first Web site, you should download PHP 5, or PHP 6 if it is available at the time you read this book.

Although a Windows installer file is available for PHP 5, the installer is not the appropriate way to install PHP for this book. The installer does not activate MySQL support. Therefore, you need to download the zip file. The files that allow PHP to communicate with MySQL are in the zip file.

On Linux and Macintosh, PHP may already be installed. You can determine whether it is installed by testing your environment as discussed in the section "Test Your Development Environment" later in this chapter. Even if

PHP is installed, it may be an older version that needs an upgrade.

The easiest way to install PHP on Linux is with RPM files provided by your Linux distribution. Check your distribution Web site, using the procedures specific to your brand of Linux, to determine the most recent version of PHP available. If the latest version is older than you prefer, you can download the source file tarball from the PHP Web site to compile and install the most recent version from source.

An up-to-date file for the Mac can be obtained from www.entropy.ch/software/macosx/php/. The file is a Mac OS X Installer package that includes all the required libraries. The PHP package is designed to be installed on a Mac running the Apache software that comes installed on a Mac. If the Mac package does not work on your system, you can download the tarball and install from source.

Obtain PHP

① Type **www.php.net/downloads**.

② Click the file that you want to download.

Note: For Windows, download the zip file.

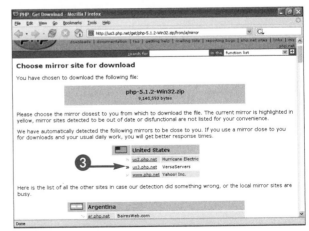

The Choose Mirror Site for Download page is displayed.

③ Click the mirror site that you want to download from.

The site highlights a mirror, which is usually the best choice.

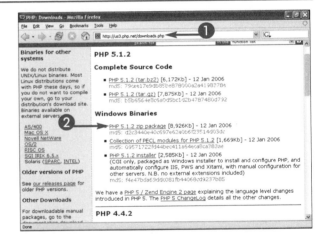

The file download dialog box opens.

④ Click Save to Disk.

⑤ Click OK.

The Save As dialog box opens.

⑥ Navigate to the folder where the download should be stored.

⑦ Click Save.

A window shows the downloading progress.

A message appears when PHP is finished downloading.

Note: Your browser may or may not close the download window when finished downloading, depending on its setting. You can change this option in your browser.

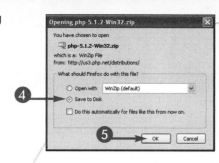

Extra

The PHP Web site provides a method to verify the file after you download it. Because PHP is provided on many mirror Web sites, it is possible for the legitimate PHP file to be replaced with one that has been altered. Verifying the downloaded file is a security precaution to make sure that the file is the correct file.

A long string is displayed below the filename, similar to the following:

```
md5: b5b6564e8c6a0d5bc1d2b4787480d792
```

The string is an md5 *signature*. You should test the md5 signature of the file after you download it. If the signature of the downloaded file does not match the md5 signature on the Web site, the file is not valid.

TYPE THIS		RESULT
In a command prompt window on your computer, type md5 php-5.1.2-Win32.zip Substitute the name of the file that you just downloaded.	→	A signature appears. The signature here should be the same signature displayed on the PHP Web site. If md5 is not installed on your computer, you can download and install it from www.fourmilab.ch/md5/.

Install PHP

PHP may be already installed on your Linux or Macintosh computer. If not, you install PHP from files that you download from the PHP Web site or other Web sites. Obtaining PHP is discussed in the previous section.

Although you can install PHP on Windows from an installer file, the PHP 5 installer does not activate MySQL support. The files that allow PHP to communicate with MySQL are in the zip file. Therefore, you can install PHP more efficiently from the zip file when you want to use PHP with MySQL databases. The example in this section shows how to install PHP from the Windows zip file.

On Linux, if PHP is not already installed, you can install PHP from an RPM file downloaded from your Linux distribution Web site. However, be sure that the RPM

includes support for MySQL. For example, on Red Hat Linux, you need to install a package called php_mysql. If you cannot obtain an RPM file for the PHP version that you want, you can download and install from the source code tarball.

On Mac, you can install PHP from the disk image file that you downloaded. If you are unsuccessful with the PKG file, you can download and install from source code.

PHP works together with your Web server. Therefore, your Web server needs to be configured to expect PHP code. Configuring is discussed in the section "Configure Apache to Process PHP Code," later in this chapter.

PHP has many configurations settings, stored in a file named php.ini, which you can edit. Setting up and changing your php.ini file is discussed in the section "Configure PHP," later in this chapter.

Install PHP

① Open the zip file in zip file software.

In this example, the software is WinZip.

② Click Extract.

The Extract dialog box opens.

③ Type the path to the directory where you want PHP to be installed.

Note: Installation, maintenance, and upgrades are easier if you install in C:\php.

④ Click Extract.

Several files and directories are unzipped into the main PHP directory.

⑤ Navigate to the folder where PHP was installed.

⑥ View the PHP folder to see the folders and files installed.

Note: In this example, the files are displayed in a command prompt window. You can also use Windows Explorer to view the files.

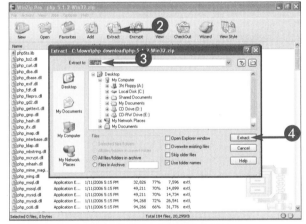

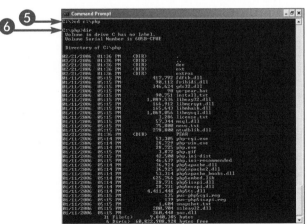

7 Change to the ext folder, located in the main PHP directory.

8 View the files in the ext folder.

- The files php_mysql.dll and/or php_mysqli.dll are required for MySQL support.

9 Copy the `mysql` DLL files from the ext folder to the main PHP folder.

Note: After installing PHP, you must configure Apache, as shown in the section, "Configure Apache to Process PHP Code," later in this chapter.

Extra

On Linux, in order to install the most recent version of PHP or to install with the extensions you need, you may need to install PHP from source code. The procedure is similar to all source code installations.

TYPE THIS

```
gunzip -c php-nn.tar.gz | tar -xf -
cd php-nn
./configure --with-mysqli=DIR --with-apxs2
make
make install
```

nn is the PHP version number that is part of the filename you downloaded, such as php-5.1.2.tar.gz. DIR is the path to the directory where a MySQL file named mysql_config is located, such as /opt/mysql/bin/mysql_config.

RESULT

→ PHP is installed as an Apache module. You still need to configure Apache to process PHP code and configure PHP.

Configure Apache to Process PHP Code

pache reads a configuration file when it starts. It will not start if it cannot find the file. The installation procedure for Apache creates the configuration file — `httpd.conf`. It may be located in the /conf folder in the folder where Apache was installed or in /etc. You can open the file in any text editor, or, on Windows, from a menu item created when Apache was installed.

The Apache configuration file needs two lines to process PHP code correctly: a `LoadModule` directive and an `AddType` directive. The `LoadModule` directive links the PHP software to the Apache Web server. The `LoadModule` directive provides the path to the shared library that is loaded into Apache at runtime. The format is similar to the following:

```
LoadModule php5_module "c:/php/php5apache2
.dll"   (for Windows)

LoadModule php5_module modules/libphp5.so
(for Linux and Mac)
```

The module name is `php5_module`. When PHP 6 is released, its module name should be `php6_module`. The Windows shared library for Apache 1.3 is php5apache.dll. For Apache 1.3 on Linux, the PHP module is `libexec/libphp5.so`. In PHP 4, the PHP directory is organized a little differently.

The `AddType` directive maps one or more file extensions to the type of content that can be expected in the file — PHP code. The format is similar to the following:

```
AddType application/x-httpd-php  .php
```

The `AddType` directive shown tells Apache to expect PHP code in files with a .php extension. You can set any extension for files containing PHP code, but the extensions most frequently used are .php, .php4, .php5, or .php6.

You must restart Apache after editing `httpd.conf`. Apache can be restarted on Windows from a menu item in the Start menu. On Linux, type `apachectl restart`.

Configure Apache to Process PHP Code

1. Click Start.

2. Click All Programs.

3. Click Apache HTTP Server.

4. Click Configure Apache Server.

5. Click Edit the Apache httpd.conf Configuration File.

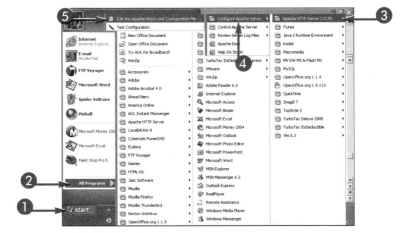

`httpd.conf` opens in a text editor.

6. Scroll down to the `LoadModule` directive section.

7. Add the `LoadModule` directive for PHP, **LoadModule php5_module** *pathtomodule*.

Note: The module name may also be `php4_module` or `php6_module`.

If the line is already in the file with a # at the beginning, remove the #.

24

⑧ Scroll to the `AddType` directive section.

⑨ Type the `AddType` directive for PHP, **AddType application/x-httpd-php .php**.

If the line is already in the file with a # at the beginning, remove the #.

Note: You can use a different extension or set of extensions.

⑩ Save the file.

⑪ Close the file.

⑫ Click Start.

⑬ Click All Programs.

⑭ Click Apache HTTP Server.

⑮ Click Control Apache Server.

⑯ Click Restart.

A small window opens for a few seconds and then quickly closes.

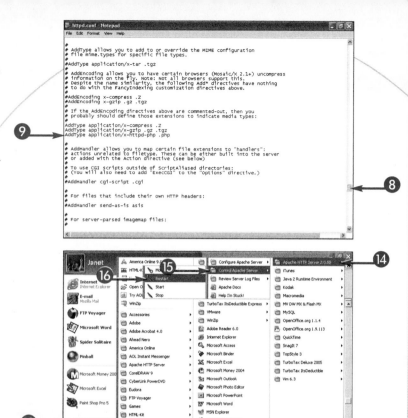

Extra

Whenever you change your Apache configuration, by editing `httpd.conf`, or your PHP configuration, discussed in the following section, you must restart Apache before the configuration goes into effect. You can restart Apache on Windows from the Start menu. How you restart Apache on a Linux system can vary. You may be able to restart from your init.d directory. You may also be able to start using a script named `apachectl` or `httpdctl`.

TYPE THIS

```
/etc/rc.d/init.d/httpd restart
or
whereis apachectl
returns the path to apachectl
path/apachectl stop
path/apachectl start
```

RESULT

→ Apache restarts and the new Apache and/or PHP configuration goes into effect.

Configure PHP

PHP uses settings in a file named php.ini to control some of its behavior. PHP looks for php.ini when it starts and uses the settings. If PHP cannot find the php.ini file, it starts with a set of default settings.

The php.ini file may be installed by the installation procedure, or you may need to install it manually. On Windows, if you install PHP from the zip file, as shown in this chapter, you must install the php.ini file manually. You copy a default file named php.ini-dist into your Windows directory, renaming it to php.ini. On Windows XP, you copy the file to the WINDOWS folder; on Windows NT/2000, you copy it to the folder winnt. If you use the PHP Windows installer, the installer sets up php.ini.

On Linux and Macintosh, if php.ini is not installed during installation, you need to install it. Copy php.ini-dist into /usr/local/lib, renaming it php.ini.

To communicate with MySQL from PHP scripts, you need to activate MySQL support. Two extensions are available — mysql and mysqli. Which you activate depends on the version of PHP and MySQL that you use, as explained in the section "Introducing Dynamic Web Sites." To activate MySQL support, find the extension section in php.ini and remove the semicolon (;) from the beginning of the line that activates the mysql extension you want to use.

The php.ini file contains many settings. In general, the default settings are satisfactory, but you may need to change some of the settings for specific reasons. The settings are discussed throughout the book, in sections where you may want to change settings.

You must restart Apache after changing PHP settings before the new settings will go into effect.

Configure PHP

① Navigate to the main PHP folder.

  ● The file php.ini-dist is stored here.

② Copy php.ini-dist to your windows folder, renaming it php.ini.

Note: You can use Windows Explorer to copy the file.

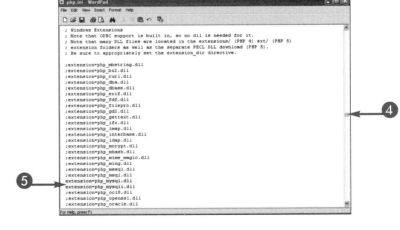

③ Open c:\windows\php.ini in a text editor.

④ Scroll to the Windows Extensions section.

⑤ Find the extension for mysql and/or mysqli and remove the semicolon from the beginning of the line.

Note: If you cannot find an extension line for mysql or mysqli, type the needed line(s).

⑥ Save the file.

⑦ Close the file.

8 Click Start.

9 Click All Programs.

10 Click Apache HTTP Server.

11 Click Control Apache Server.

12 Click Restart.

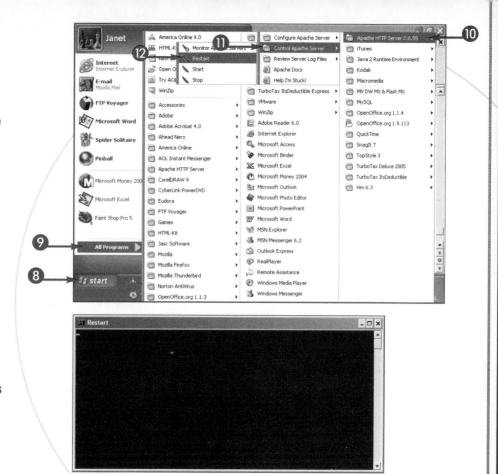

The Restart window opens for a few seconds and quickly closes.

If Apache encounters any errors when restarting, the errors are displayed in the Restart window.

chapter 1: Setting Up Your Development Environment

Extra

PHP consists of a PHP core and PHP extensions. The `mysql` and `mysqli` extensions provide the `mysql` functions used to communicate with MySQL.

PHP offers many extensions, which provide hundreds of functions. Several core extensions are compiled into PHP and are always there by default. Other standard extensions are included in the PHP distribution, but you must activate them, such as the `mysql` and `mysqli` extensions. In addition, many extensions are written and made available by individuals. Many of the best of these are part of PEAR, the PHP Extension and Application Repository.

When you plan your Web site, you may want to look for an extension that offers the functionality that you need, rather than develop the code yourself from scratch. You can browse the standard extensions at the PHP Web site, www.php.net/manual/en/. You can examine the PEAR extensions for helpful functionality at http://pear.php.net.

Test Your Development Environment

After everything is installed, you can test your development environment by running a PHP script. A PHP script is a text file, which you can create in any text editor. The rest of this book explains the statements and functions of PHP that you can include in your PHP script. In this section, the example creates a simple PHP script, with one statement for testing your environment.

Your script must be located in your Web space — the directory and its subdirectories where your Web server expects to find the Web page source files. Apache calls this directory the *document root.* The default Web space for Apache is htdocs in the directory where Apache is installed. For Internet Information Services (IIS), it is

Inetpub\wwwroot. On Linux, it may be /var/www/html. The Web space can be set to a different directory by configuring the Web server. For example, you can change the path for DocumentRoot in httpd.conf to change the Web space for an Apache server. If you are using a Web hosting company, the staff will supply the directory name where you need to locate your Web page source files.

To run a PHP script, you need to access the Web page file through your Web server. You must type the name of the script into your browser address window, such as **www.mywebsite.com/test.php** or **localhost/test.php**. You cannot access the file by clicking File → Open File in your browser menu. If you do, the PHP script will appear as text, rather than run and display its output.

Test Your Development Environment

① Add the opening HTML code.

② Type **<?php**.

③ Type **phpinfo();**.

④ Type **?>**.

⑤ Type the closing HTML code.

⑥ Save the file with a .php extension.

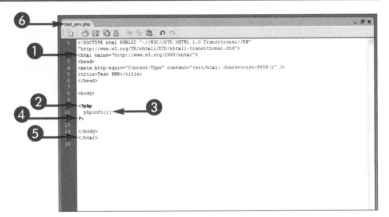

⑦ Open the file in your browser by typing the URL in the browser address field.

A long list of variables and settings is displayed.

● The PHP version is displayed.

● The output shows the path to the php.ini file that PHP is using.

Note: If the path to a directory is shown, rather than a file, PHP is looking for the php.ini file in the specified directory but cannot find the file.

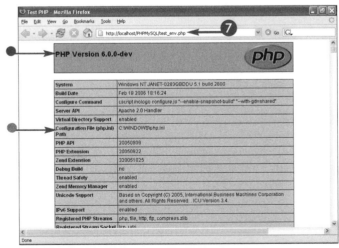

8 Scroll down to find the PHP core section.

PHP settings are displayed.

- `display_errors` is set to On. PHP errors are explained in Chapter 2.

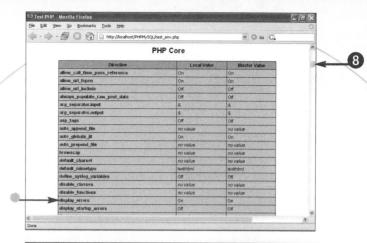

9 Scroll down to the `mysql` or `mysqli` section.

A section is displayed for each extension that is activated.

Note: If no `mysql` section is displayed, then `mysql` support is not activated.

Extra

You can change the location where Apache looks for your Web page source files by editing the `httpd.conf` file. Apache calls the location the `DocumentRoot` and sets it to `htdocs` in the directory where Apache is installed. When you define a new path, use forward slashes in the path, even if you are using Windows. You only need to enclose the path in quotes when it has special characters in it, such as a colon (:).

TYPE THIS	RESULT

Open httpd.conf in a text editor. Find the following line:
 	
`DocumentRoot "C:/Program Files/Apache Group/Apache2/htdocs"`
 	
Change it to the following:
 	
`DocumentRoot "C:/mywebsite"`
	Apache now looks for Web site files in C:\mywebsite. You need to locate your Web page files in that directory before Web visitors can see your Web pages.

How PHP Works

P HP works in partnership with your Web server to enable you to build interactive, dynamic Web pages. The Web server is the software that delivers Web pages to users. Every Web site requires a Web server. The PHP software works in conjunction with the Web server to add functionality to your Web site that is not available using HTML alone.

How the World Wide Web Works

The World Wide Web is a network of computers offering millions of Web sites. Each Web site has an address, called a URL (uniform resource locator), which includes a domain name and a filename, such as www.myfine company.com/welcome.html.

When a user types a URL into a browser address window or clicks a hyperlink, the browser sends a message out onto the Web requesting the specified Web page. The message is sent to the computer at the address specified in the URL, where the Web server on the addressee computer receives the message and searches the Web site for the requested Web page file. The Web server sends the requested file to the Web browser that requested it, or if the file cannot be found, sends a message stating that it cannot find the file. The browser displays the Web page based on the HTML code in the file that it receives.

How the Web Server Processes PHP Files

The Web server begins processing the requested file in HTML mode, meaning that it sends the HTML code directly to the browser. When the Web server encounters a PHP section, it switches into PHP mode, sometimes called *escaping from HTML,* and executes the PHP statements, sending any output to the browser. The Web server continues in PHP mode until it reaches the end of the PHP section, where it returns to HTML mode. The Web server processes the entire file, switching into PHP mode to process any PHP sections that it finds.

The browser renders and displays all the code it receives as HTML code. The PHP code is never sent to the browser; the browser only receives the output from the PHP code. Any formatting instructions sent to the browser must be HTML code. In other words, the output from the PHP code must be HTML code if it is intended to format the Web page display.

Adding PHP Code to a Web Site

PHP code is embedded into HTML files. You create and edit PHP files the same way that you create and edit regular HTML files. Tags mark the beginning and end of the sections containing PHP code. Adding PHP sections to a Web page is described in the next section of this chapter.

The Web server is configured to look for PHP code embedded in files with specified extensions — usually .php or .phtml, but the Web server can be configured to specify any extension or set of extensions that you want to use. When the Web server receives a request for a file with one of the specified extensions, it scans the file for PHP sections.

Add PHP Code to a Web Page File

To use PHP code to add interaction to your Web page, you add PHP sections to your Web page source file. Each PHP section is enclosed by PHP tags, as follows:

```
<?php

    PHP code

?>
```

All PHP code must be enclosed in PHP tags. Any code not in PHP tags is not sent to PHP for processing. Instead, the code is sent directly to the browser, which handles it as HTML code, displaying the code in the Web page.

You can add as many PHP sections as needed. You can start the script with HTML code. You can then include a PHP section, containing PHP code. You can end the section with the closing PHP tag. You can then continue in the file with HTML code. Later in the script, you can include another PHP section, with PHP tags enclosing PHP code. You can include as many PHP sections and HTML sections as you need.

The results from the code execution in one PHP section are available to PHP code in later sections. This means that if you set a variable in one PHP section, the variable will retain its value in later PHP sections. Using variables is discussed later in this chapter in the section "Using PHP Variables."

You cannot nest PHP sections. You must end one PHP section before starting another PHP section.

Add PHP Code to a Web Page File

① Create or open a file containing HTML code only.

In this example, one HTML statement displays a line of text.

② Type the opening tag for a PHP section.

③ Type one or more PHP statements.

In this example, one PHP `echo` statement outputs one line of text.

④ Type the closing tag for a PHP section.

⑤ Add a PHP statement after the closing PHP tag.

⑥ Save the file with a .php extension.

⑦ Open the Web page in a browser.

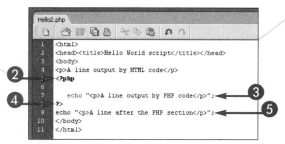

- ● The browser displays the output from the HTML section.

- ● The browser displays the output from the PHP section.

- ◉ The browser displays the line after the PHP section, showing the PHP code.

Note: Because this was outside the PHP tags, it was not processed by PHP.

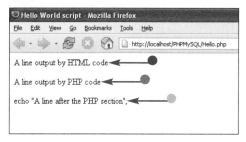

The PHP section that you add to your HTML file consists of a series of PHP statements. Each PHP statement instructs PHP to perform an action. Each statement executes in order, from top to bottom of the source code file.

PHP code consists of simple statements and complex statements. A simple statement is a single PHP instruction, ending with a semicolon (;). When reading simple statements, PHP ignores white space and the ends of lines, continuing to read the simple statement until it encounters a semicolon or a closing tag (?>). A missing semicolon is a common error, resulting in an error message.

Complex statements are statements that contain more than one instruction, usually including more than one simple statement. For example, consider the following complex statement:

```php
if ($x < 1)

    echo 1;

else

    echo 2;
```

This statement echoes 1 if the variable x contains a value less than 1. If the value of x is 1 or greater, the statement echoes 2.

This chapter discusses simple statements. The most frequently used complex statements, such as `if` statements and `while` loops, are discussed in Chapter 4.

Simple statements can be combined into a block, causing the statements to execute together. Blocks of statements are often used in complex statements.

Using PHP Statements

1 Add more than one statement in the PHP section.

- Make sure that each statement ends with a semicolon.

2 Save the file.

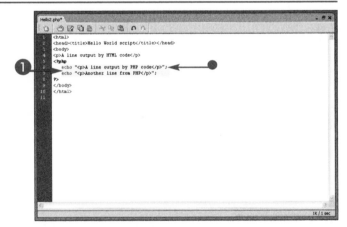

3 Open the file in a browser.

The output from the `echo` statements is displayed in order.

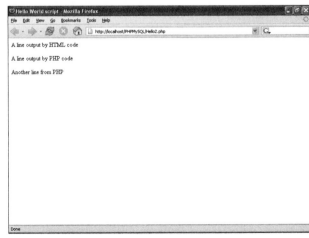

④ Remove the semicolon from one of the PHP statements in the source code.

⑤ Save the edited file.

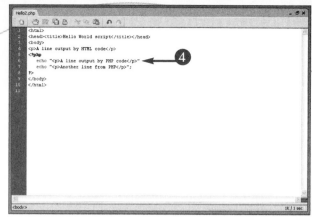

⑥ Open the file in a browser.

The browser displays a PHP parse error.

Note: Error messages are described in the section "Understanding Error Messages."

● The error message shows that it found an ECHO command, where it expected to find a comma or a semicolon.

Note: PHP does not find the error until it tries to execute line 7, even though the error is at the end of line 6 in this example.

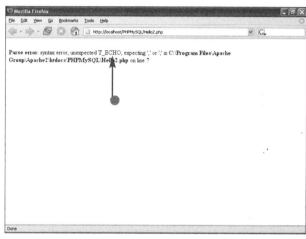

Extra

Because PHP ignores white space and line endings, you can write a script with any format you want. However, future modification and maintenance of the script require a format that is easy for humans to understand. In most cases, each simple statement is on a line by itself. If the statement is too long to fit on one line, it continues to the next line without ending in a semicolon.

TYPE THIS

```
echo "This is a long string that
cannot fit on one line of the script,
    so the string continues to a
second line.";
```

RESULT

```
This is a long string that
cannot fit on one line of
the script, so the string
continues to a second line.
```

Sometimes you want to use PHP to output a small string that is part of a larger string. You can use a small PHP section within an HTML section, instead of using PHP to echo the entire string.

TYPE THIS

```
<p>This string is mostly HTML, with
a  <?php echo "small PHP section;" ?>
within the string</p>
```

RESULT

Only the small PHP section is sent to PHP for processing. The following is displayed in the browser:

```
This string is mostly HTML, with a small
PHP section within the string
```

33

PHP provides two output statements that output a text string: the `echo` statement and the `print` statement. PHP also provides some built-in functions, such as `printf` and `sprintf`, that output formatted text strings. Built-in PHP functions are discussed in Chapter 6.

The general syntax for `echo` and `print` is as follows:

```
echo outputitem1, outputitem2, outputitem3
...;
```

```
$var = print outputitem;
```

As shown, `echo` can output more than one string, whereas `print` can output only one string. The `print` statement, however, behaves more like a function than the `echo` statement; functions are explained in Chapters 5 and 6. The `print` statement always returns the value 1, whereas the `echo` statement does not return a value. In practice, storing a return value in a variable, as shown, is

rarely useful, so the `print` statement is most often used as follows:

```
print outputitem;
```

An `outputitem` can be a number, string, or variable. A string must be enclosed in quotes. A string can include special formatting characters, such as `\n`, which starts a new line. Constructing valid character strings is discussed in this chapter in the section "Work with Character Strings." Variables are explained in the next section of this chapter, "Using PHP Variables."

PHP sends the output string from the output statements to the Web server, which sends it, as is, to the browser. The browser interprets the output string as HTML code and displays it accordingly. If an output string contains HTML tags, the browser interprets the tags when displaying the Web page. If an output string has no HTML tags, the browser just displays the string, ignoring white space and line breaks.

Understanding PHP Output Statements

① Type an `echo` statement with one or more output strings.

- You can include a blank space in the string, as shown in line 5 of this example.

② Type a second `echo` statement with a new line character in the string.

③ Save the file.

④ Open the file in a browser.

- The output is displayed on one line because it contains no HTML tags to format the string in the browser window.

⑤ View the source code in the browser.

- The source starts a new line where the new line special character is inserted.

Note: The browser does not display text as it appears in the source code. The browser fits the text to the browser window, regardless of extra white space and line breaks.

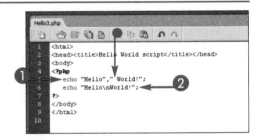

6 Edit the echo statements by inserting HTML tags to format the output for the browser.

7 Save the file.

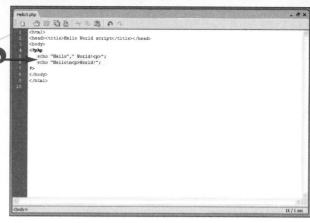

8 Open the file in a browser.

The output displays differently because of the HTML tags in the strings.

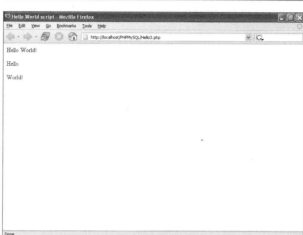

Extra

You can use the echo statement with several different formats. You can echo multiple words by echoing more than one item or by echoing a single string containing words and spaces.

ECHO STATEMENT	OUTPUT
echo "Hello";	Hello
echo 100	100
echo "Hello","World";	HelloWorld
echo Hello World;	Not Valid; results in an error message
echo "Hello"," World";	Hello World
echo "Hello World";	Hello World

You can also echo variables. Using variables is discussed in the next section of this chapter.

Using PHP Variables

Variables are containers that hold information. You can use the information wherever it is needed in the script. A variable has a name and stores a value. Variables are frequently used to store information that a user types into a form or data retrieved from a database.

PHP variable names have a dollar sign ($) in front of them. Names can be any length and can include letters, numbers, or underscores. They cannot begin with a number. PHP distinguishes between upper- and lowercase letters. Consequently, NAME and Name are two different variables. Names should represent the value stored in the variable, so the script is easy to understand. Words connected by underscores or with the second word capitalized, such as $first_name or $firstName are common variable names.

You assign a value to a variable with an assignment statement. If the variable does not already exist, the assignment statement creates it.

You can assign a number or a character string to a variable. A character string is enclosed by single or double quotes. The difference between single and double quotes is discussed later in this chapter in the section "Work with Character Strings." You can also create Boolean variables, which contain TRUE or FALSE, and NULL variables, which contain no value.

You can display the contents of a variable by echoing or printing it. In addition, PHP provides two functions to display the contents of a variable: var_dump and print_r. The print_r function displays the variable contents; the var_dump function displays the variable contents plus the data type and, if the variable value is a string, the length of the string. If you attempt to display a variable that does not exist, an error message is displayed.

Using PHP Variables

① Add an assignment statement to create a variable.

② Repeat step 1 for all the variables that you want to create.

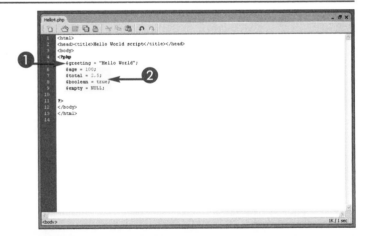

③ Add an echo statement to display the variables.

Note: You need HTML tags to format the output in the browser.

④ Add one or more print_r statements to display the variables displayed in step 3.

Note: You need to echo HTML tags to format the output in the browser.

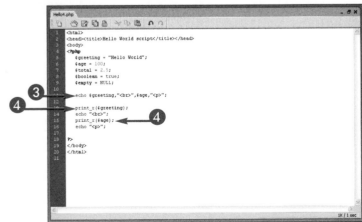

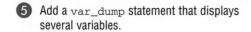

5 Add a `var_dump` statement that displays several variables.

6 View the script in a Web browser.

The values of the variables are displayed from the `echo` statement and the two functions.

● The output of the `var_dump` statement is displayed on one line because no HTML tags were included in the `var_dump` statement.

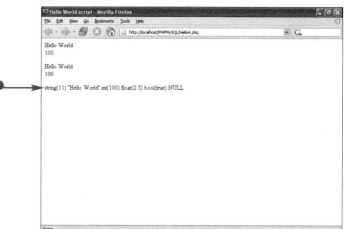

Extra

Although you do not need to specify the data type of a variable, you can if you want to. For example, you may want a number to be stored as a string. To make sure that a value is stored as a specific data type, you can include an instruction to PHP in the assignment statement.

TYPE THIS		RESULT
`$year = (string) 2006;`	→	The number is stored as a string rather than as an integer.

When you use a variable within a string in an `echo` statement, you sometimes need to isolate the variable name within curly braces so that PHP can distinguish the variable name from the string.

TYPE THIS		RESULT
`$str = "bird";` `echo This is a {$str}cage.;`	→	`This is a birdcage.`

If you do not use curly braces in the `echo` statement, PHP looks for a variable named `$strcage`.

onstants are similar to variables, except that you cannot change the value of a constant. You can use a constant anywhere in your script, but you cannot change its value. By storing the value in a constant, instead of a variable, you ensure that the value will not be changed accidentally.

Constants are given a name, and a value is stored in them. Constant names can include letters, numbers, and underscores (_) but cannot begin with a number. PHP distinguishes between upper- and lowercase letters. By convention, constant names are all uppercase letters, although PHP does not require it. Constant names cannot be words used in the PHP language, called *keywords*. A list of keywords is available in the PHP online documentation at www.php.net/manual/en/reserved. php#reserved.keywords.

You create a constant and assign a value to it with a define statement, as follows:

```php
define("CONSTANTNAME",value);
```

If you attempt to define the same constant again in your script, you will see an error message.

The constant value can be a number or a character string. A string is enclosed by quotes.

You can display the contents of a constant with an echo or print statement. If you enclose a constant name in quotes, the echo statement interprets it as part of the string, not as a constant name, and displays the constant name, rather than the constant value. To echo a constant as part of a string, use the following format:

```php
echo "string",constantname,"string";
```

In addition, the PHP functions var_dump and print_r can display the value of a constant. The print_r function displays the constant value; the var_dump function displays the constant value plus the data type and, if the value is a string, the length of the string.

Using PHP Constants

① Add a statement to define a constant.

② Add an echo statement to display the constant.

③ Add a print_r statement to display the constant.

④ Add a var_dump statement to display the constant.

Note: You need HTML tags to format the Web page displayed in the browser.

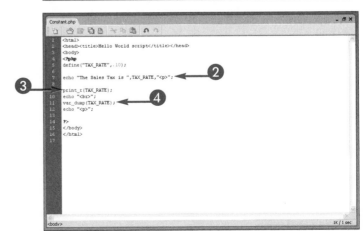

5 Add a statement to define the same constant to a new value.

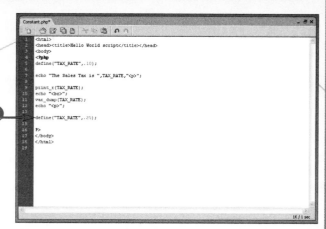

6 View the script in a browser.

The constant is displayed by the `echo`, `print_r`, and `var_dump` statements.

● The second statement that tries to define the same constant results in a notice.

Note: Whether the notice is displayed depends on your PHP settings. Error messages are described in the section "Understanding Error Messages."

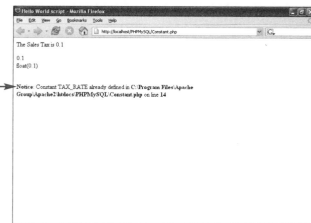

Extra

PHP includes many predefined constants that you can use in your scripts. For example, PHP provides the constant PHP_OS, which contains the name of the current operating system, and the constant PHP_VERSION, which contains the version number of the PHP that you are using. A list of PHP predefined constants is available in the PHP online documentation at www.php.net/manual/en/reserved.constants.php.

TYPE THIS

```
echo PHP_OS,"<br>";
echo PHP_VERSION;
```

→

RESULT

Displays the operating system of the machine running the script and the version number of PHP that is running.

If you attempt to define a constant with the same name as a PHP predefined constant, you will see an error message stating that the constant is already defined.

TYPE THIS

```
define("PHP_OS",3);
```

→

RESULT

Displays an error notice stating that PHP_OS is already defined.

39

Work with Numbers

Numbers can be either integers or floating point numbers — numbers with decimal places. You can do arithmetic operations on numbers. You can add, subtract, multiply, or divide numbers and/or variables that contain numbers. The following are valid expressions:

```
2 + 2.5
```

```
$price - $discount
```

```
$hours * 60
```

```
52 / $weeks
```

PHP provides another operator, %, called *modulus,* which finds the remainder when one number is divided by another number. For example, 9 % 4 evaluates to 1 — the remainder when 9 is divided by 4.

You can combine arithmetic operations, as follows:

```
$result = 1 + 2 * 4 + 1;
```

When you combine operations, the order in which the individual operations are performed can affect the result. PHP performs multiplication and division first, followed by addition and subtraction. If other considerations are equal, PHP goes from left to right. Thus, the preceding statements assigns 10 to $result, as follows: 1) multiplication first, resulting in 1 + 8 + 1; 2) leftmost addition, resulting in 9 + 1; and 3) rightmost addition, resulting in 10.

You can change the order in which the operations are performed by using parentheses. The arithmetic inside the parentheses is performed first. For example, you can write the preceding assignment statement as follows:

```
$result = ( 1 + 2 ) * 4 + 1;
```

This expression evaluates to 13, as follows: 1) addition inside parentheses, resulting in 3*4+1; 2) multiplication, resulting in 12 + 1; and 3) addition, resulting in 13.

Work with Numbers

1 Create some variables that contain numbers.

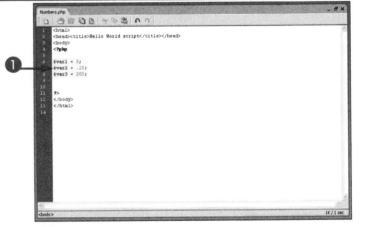

2 Add an assignment statement using two variables.

3 Add an echo statement that displays the results.

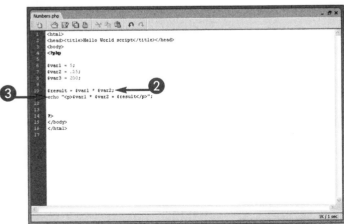

④ Add an assignment statement without parentheses that combines operations.

⑤ Add an `echo` statement that displays the results.

⑥ Repeat the assignment statement from step 4, adding parentheses.

⑦ Add an `echo` statement that displays the results.

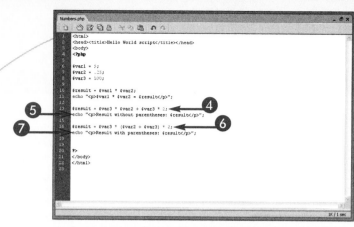

⑧ View the script in a browser.

The results are displayed in the browser window.

Note: In most cases, the results with and without parentheses are different.

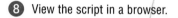

Extra

By default, numbers are displayed in a string, without separation and without displaying any unnecessary zeros. PHP provides several functions that you can use to format the number display. One function is `number_format`, which you can use to separate the number digits into groups of three and to specify the number of decimal places. By default, a dot designates the decimal places, and commas separate the groups, but you can change the default characters with optional parameters 3 and 4, respectively. The decimal places are rounded for display.

TYPE THIS

```
$num = 12345.67;
$num_1 = number_format($num);
$num_2 = number_format($num,1,".","");
echo "$num_1<br>$num_2";
```

RESULT

```
12,346
12345.7
```

PHP provides additional functions that you can use to format numbers, such as `printf` and `sprintf`, described in Chapter 6.

Work with Character Strings

Character strings can include letters, numbers, and punctuation. When you store a character string in a variable, you specify the beginning and end of the string with quotes. A string of numbers enclosed by quotes is stored as a character string, instead of a number. Numbers that you do not plan to use in arithmetical operations, such as phone numbers or zip codes, should be stored as character strings.

When you need to use a quote character inside a string, you must insert a backslash (\) in front of it, called *escaping* the quote, so that PHP handles the embedded quote as part of the string, not as the closing quote.

Character strings can be enclosed in single or double quotes, which are handled differently. Single-quoted strings are stored literally, with the exception of \', which is stored as an apostrophe. In double-quoted strings, variables and some special characters are

evaluated before the string is stored. The quotes that enclose the entire string determine the treatment of variables and special characters, even if there are other sets of quotes inside the string.

The characters \n and \t are the most widely used special characters. The \n special character starts a new line when used in double-quoted strings. The \t inserts a tab when used in a double-quoted string.

You can join two strings together, called *concatenating,* with a dot (.), as in the following statement:

```
$string = "My friend is named "." ".$name;
```

You can append a string to the end of a variable value using the .= operator, as follows:

```
$string = "My friend is named ";

$string .= $name;
```

Work with Character Strings

① Create a variable that contains a string.

② Create a variable that contains a double-quoted string that includes the variable from step 1.

③ Create a variable that contains a single-quoted string that includes the variable from step 1.

④ Create a variable that contains a double-quoted string with single quotes enclosing a variable.

⑤ Add a statement that echoes all three strings.

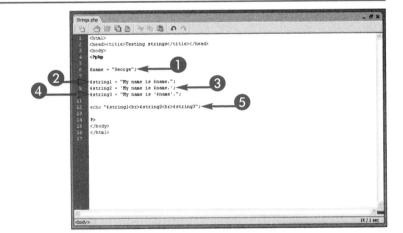

⑥ Create variables containing strings.

⑦ Add an echo statement that concatenates variables and literal strings.

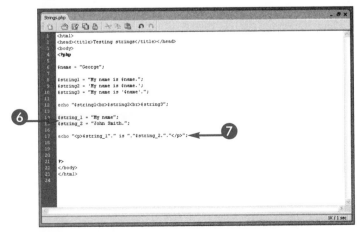

8. Create a variable containing a string.

9. Assign a new string to the same variable with =.

10. Create another variable containing a string.

11. Concatenate a string to the same variable with . =.

12. Add an echo statement that displays both strings.

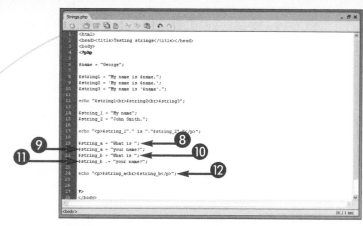

13. View the script in a browser.

- Double-quoted and single-quoted strings are displayed differently.

- The concatenated string appears as one line.

- The first variable contains only the second string, but the second variable contains both strings.

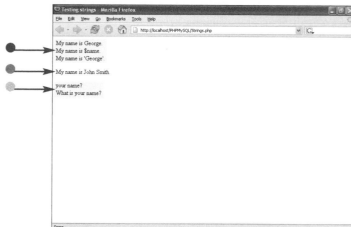

Extra

PHP provides a feature called a heredoc that facilitates entering a long string spanning several lines. With a heredoc, you do not need to enclose the string in quotes or to escape quotes within the string.

You begin the heredoc with any string that you want to use to enclose the heredoc content. You then type the content of the heredoc, including quotes if needed. To signal the end of the heredoc, you repeat the string that begins the heredoc. The syntax requires that the string that begins the heredoc not be followed by any characters on the line. It must end the line. The string that ends the heredoc must start at the beginning of the line, with no character preceding it on the line, and be followed by a semicolon that ends the line, with no characters after the semicolon.

TYPE THIS

```
$dest = "Los Angeles";
$content = <<<ENDOFTEXT
I am driving a long distance.
I am driving to $dest. I plan to
enjoy this "vacation".<br>
ENDOFTEXT;
echo $content;
```

RESULT

The content of the heredoc is displayed, including the double or single quotes. Any variables are evaluated, so their values, not the variable names, are stored in the heredoc.

Work with Dates and Times

PHP can recognize dates and times and handle them differently than plain character strings. You can create a variable that contains a specific date and time or the current date and time. You can display stored dates in your preferred format.

The computer stores a date/time in a format called a *timestamp,* which is the number of seconds from January 1, 1970 00:00:00 GMT to the stored time. This format is convenient for calculating time spans, but is not a desirable format to display on a Web page. PHP can convert dates from a timestamp into conventional date/time format and vice versa.

Beginning with PHP 5.1, you must set a time zone. You can set the date.timezone setting in your php.ini file, or you can set the time zone in your script with the date_default_timezone_set function. A list of valid time zones is available online at www.php.net/manual/en/timezones.php.

You can store a timestamp with the strtotime function, in the following format:

```
$varname = strtotime("keywords");
```

The strtotime function recognizes the following keywords: month names, the days of the week, all numbers, + or -, time units — year, month, week, and so on, and some useful English words — *ago, now, last, next, this, today, tomorrow,* and *yesterday.*

You can convert a timestamp to date/time format with the date function, in the following format:

```
$varname = date("format",$timestamp);
```

If you do not include $timestamp, the current date/time is stored. The *format* is a string that specifies the format to use when storing the date in the variable. For example, the format "yy-m-d" stores 06-8-10, and "M.d.Y" stores Aug.10.2006. A complete list of date format symbols is available in the PHP online documentation at www.php.net/manual/en/function.date.php.

Work with Dates and Times

① Set the default time zone.

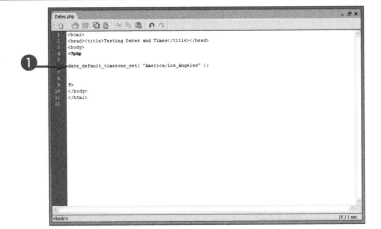

② Create one or more variables containing timestamps.

③ Add an echo statement that outputs the timestamps.

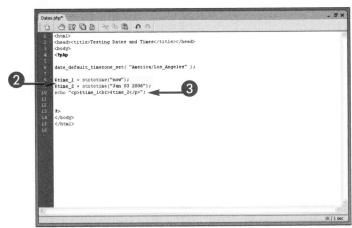

④ Add a statement that formats the timestamp into a date.

⑤ Add a statement that formats the timestamp into a time.

⑥ Add an echo statement that outputs the formatted date and time.

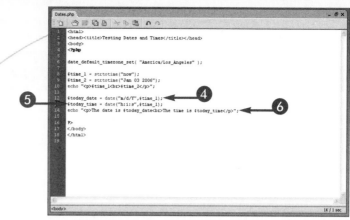

⑦ View the script in a browser.

● The timestamps are displayed.

● The formatted date and time are displayed.

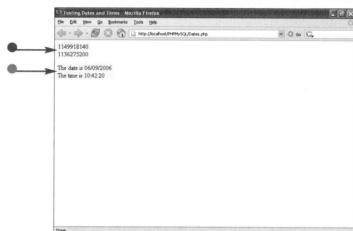

Apply It

Timestamps are convenient for calculating time spans. You can simply subtract one timestamp from another to obtain the time between one date and another. For example, you can use timestamps to determine a person's age when given the birth date. Subtract the current date from the birth date, giving the result in seconds. Then, divide by seconds, minutes, hours, and days to get the exact age in years, with decimal places. Convert the value to an integer to see the person's age in years.

TYPE THIS

```php
$birthdate = strtotime("jan 5 1985");
$today = strtotime("now");
$age_approx = ($today - $birthdate)/60/60/24/365;
$age_exact = $age_approx - (($age_approx / 4) /365);
$age_years = (int) $age_exact;
echo $age_years;
```

RESULTS

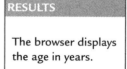

The browser displays the age in years.

Modify or Remove Variables

You can modify a variable value with an assignment statement. The value assigned in the new assignment statement replaces the current value of the variable. You can also use `.=` in an assignment statement to append a value to the end of the current value, rather than replace the current value.

PHP provides some shortcut assignment operators for frequently used mathematical operations. The `++` operator (`$num++`) adds 1 to a variable, and `--` subtracts 1 from a variable.

In addition, you can add, subtract, multiply, or divide by a specified number using the following shortcut assignment operators: `+=n`, `-=n`, `*=n`, and `/=n`. For example, `$num+=2` adds 2 to `$num`, and `$num/=3` divides `$num` by 3.

You can remove the value from a variable by assigning NULL to the variable. You can also assign a string of zero length to a variable, as follows:

```
$string = "";
```

The variable continues to exist but is empty. If you echo the variable, nothing is displayed on the Web page. No error message is displayed because the variable exists, but no value is displayed because the variable contains no value.

You can destroy a variable so that it no longer exists at all with the `unset` statement, as follows:

```
unset($varname);
```

If you echo a variable that has been unset, an `"undefined variable"` notice is displayed because the variable no longer exists.

Modify or Remove Variables

① Create one or more variables with values.

② Add 1 to the number in a variable.

③ Add an `echo` statement to display the variables.

④ Remove the values from the variables.

⑤ Add a second `echo` statement to display the variables.

⑥ Destroy a variable.

⑦ Echo the variable.

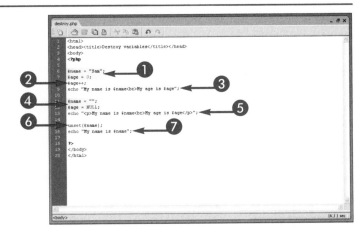

⑧ View the script in a browser.

- The empty variables display nothing on the Web page.
- Echoing the unset variable triggers a notice because the variable no longer exists.

Note: You must have notices turned on to see the notice. Error messages are explained in the section "Understanding Error Messages."

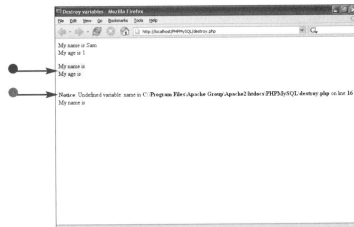

Using Variable Variables

PHP lets you use dynamic variable names, called *variable variables*. You can name a variable with a value stored in another variable. In other words, one variable contains the name of another variable. The format for creating a variable variable is as follows:

```
$nameOfVariable = "age";

$$nameOfVariable = 21;
```

The second statement has two dollar signs ($$) in front of the variable name. The second statement creates a new variable with the name that is the value in $nameOfVariable. The result of the two assignment statements is a variable named $age that contains the value 21.

If you use a variable variable in an echo statement, you need to specify the variable name clearly. You can use one of the following syntaxes:

```
echo $$nameOfVariable;

echo "${$nameOfVariable}";
```

The following statements will not produce the correct output:

```
$nameOfVariable = "age";

$age = 21;

echo "$$nameOfVariable";
```

In this case, the echo statement reads $nameOfVariable as the variable name and reads the first $ as a text character. Consequently, the output is $age, not 21.

Using Variable Variables

1. Create two or more variables that contain values.

2. Create a variable containing the variable name of one of the variables created in step 1.

3. Add an echo statement to display the variable variable.

4. Create a variable that contains a different variable name.

5. Add an echo statement to display the second variable variable.

6. View the script in a browser.

   The echo statements display the variable variable values.

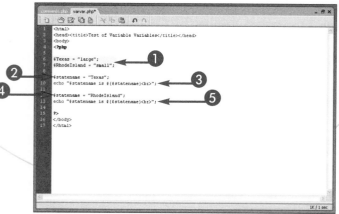

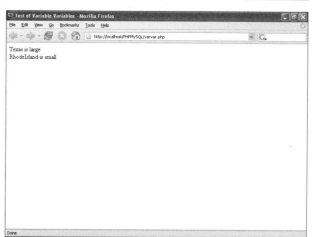

Understanding Error Messages

PHP provides error messages and warning messages. An error message stops the execution of the program; a warning message displays a warning message and then continues executing the program. Messages are displayed in a format similar to the following:

Parse Error: syntax error, *error* in
C:\test.php on line **6**

The message displays the *error*, the name of the script that generates the error, and the line where the error is detected.

A *parse error* is a syntax error that PHP finds when it scans the script before executing it. A parse error is a fatal error, preventing the script from running at all.

Warning messages are displayed as warnings, notices, and strict messages. Warnings are more likely to be serious, needing to be fixed. Notices signal unusual code, often code that is perfectly fine. Strict messages, added in PHP 5, warn about language that is poor coding practice or has been replaced by better code.

You can specify which types of error messages that you want to be displayed on the Web page. In general, when you are developing a script, you want to see all messages, but when the script is published on your Web site, you do not want any messages to appear. You can control the error message level in your php.ini file with the error_reporting setting. Some possible error reporting settings are

```
error_reporting = E_ALL | E_STRICT
error_reporting = 0
error_reporting = E_ERROR
```

The first setting displays E_ALL, which is all errors, warnings, and notices, except strict, and E_STRICT, which displays strict messages. The second setting displays no error messages. The third setting displays all error messages, but not warnings, notices, or stricts.

PHP provides a function that sets the error level for that script only, as follows:

```
error_reporting(E_ALL);
```

Understanding Error Messages

1. Add a statement to set the error reporting level.

2. Add an echo statement to appear at the beginning of the script.

3. Echo a variable that does not exist.

4. Add a statement to connect to MySQL using an invalid password.

5. Add an echo statement to appear at the end of the script.

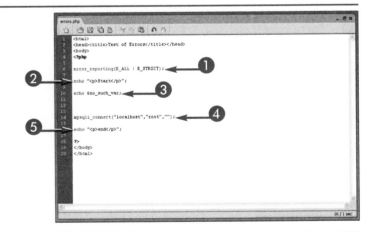

6. View the script in a browser.

- A line is displayed at the beginning of the script.
- Echoing a nonexistent variable triggers a notice.
- The MySQL function with an invalid password triggers a warning.

Note: Neither the notice nor the warning message stops the script, which continues to execute the last echo statement.

7 Open the script for editing.

8 Add a line that calls a function which does not exist.

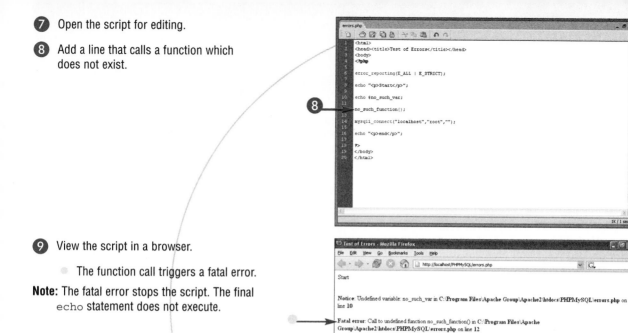

9 View the script in a browser.

● The function call triggers a fatal error.

Note: The fatal error stops the script. The final `echo` statement does not execute.

Extra

In most cases, you want to display all the error messages during development, but you do not want to displays errors when the script is available on your public Web site. You can shut the error messages off in your php.ini file.

TYPE THIS

```
error_reporting = 0
```

RESULT

No error messages are displayed on your Web page.

You can log your error messages in a log file, rather than turn them off entirely. You use two settings in your php.ini file to log error messages.

TYPE THIS

Find and set the following two settings in your php.ini file:

```
log_errors = On
error_log = path/filename
```

RESULT

PHP errors will be logged in the specified filename.

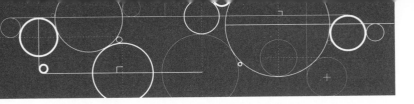

Add Comments to a Script

Comments are notes that are embedded in the script itself. PHP ignores comments. The comments provide information to assist the person — you or someone else — whose job it is to understand and revise the script in the future. Comments are best used to label sections and to explain code that is unusual or complicated, not code that is obvious.

You can embed comments anywhere in your script. Your comments can be as long or short as you need. When PHP encounters code that indicates the start of a comment, it ignores everything until it encounters the code that indicates the end of a comment. PHP comments are not included in the output that is sent to the browser, so the user does not see the comments.

You can designate a comment block. The characters /* signal the start of a comment, and the characters */

signal the end of a comment. The block can span as many lines of text as necessary. The format for a comment block is

```
/*   comment text ... */
```

You can also designate a single line comment. The characters // and # signal the start of a comment line. PHP ignores the text from the // or the # to the end of the line. The line following the line containing // or # is not a comment. You can put line comment characters anywhere in a line, not just at the beginning of the line. The following are valid comments:

```
#This line is a comment.

//This line is a comment. . .

$age = 21;   // The comment starts here
```

Add Comments to a Script

① Add a comment block.

② Add one or more single line comments.

③ Add a PHP statement.

④ Add a comment following the PHP statement, on the same line.

⑤ Add an `echo` statement at the end of the file.

Note: The `echo` statement is needed, or the Web page will be blank.

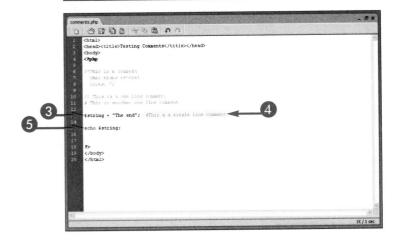

6 View the script in a browser.

The browser does not display the comments.

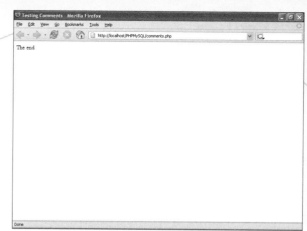

7 View the Web page source in the browser.

The comments do not appear in the source code.

Apply It

There are no rules regarding the formatting of comments. Because PHP ignores comments, you can write any type of comments that you want. However, some formats are commonly used in scripts. Most scripts contain a block of comments at the beginning that provide the name of the script, a description of its functionality, the name of the person who wrote the script, and the dates the script was created and modified.

TYPE THIS

```
/* Name:     Login.php
 * Desc:     Checks the username and password entered
            by the user to

            compare them to entries in the
            user/password database.
 * By:       John Smith
 * Created: 2/9/06
 */
```

RESULT

Only the source code contains the script information. It is not displayed on the Web page.

Sometimes you want to emphasize a comment because you consider it an important comment. A box comment is a common method for making comments very visible.

TYPE THIS

```
#########################

#  Very Important Comment  #

#########################
```

RESULT

Only the source code contains the comment. It is not displayed on the Web page.

Create an Array

Arrays are complex variables that store a group of values under a single variable name. You can use an array to store related values that you want to process as a group. Each value in an array is called an *element*. An array can have as many elements as needed. You do not need to specify the size of an array. PHP will store the array with as many elements as you assign to it.

Each element in an array has a key so that you can access the individual elements. You assign values to an array as follows:

```
$arrayname['key1'] = value1;

$arrayname['key2'] = value2;
```

You can use numbers or strings as keys. String keys should be enclosed in single quotes, such as

$arrayname['cost']. If you do not include a key in the square brackets, PHP assigns a numeric key, starting with 0 as the first element, not 1.

Arrays with string keys are called *associative* arrays. The values can be any data type. You can add another element to the array at any location in the script with a similar assignment statement.

You can create an array with an array statement, with the following format:

```
$arrayname = array("key1" => value, "key2" => value,...);
```

You can leave out the keys in the statement, in which case PHP assigns numeric keys.

You can display array values with an echo statement and with the var_dump and print_r statements, described in Chapter 2.

Create an Array

① Create an array, letting PHP assign the keys.

② Create an array using the array statement.

Keys are specified in the array statement.

Note: The array statement is written with one element on each line. This is not required by PHP. The formatting is used to make the script easier for humans to read.

③ Add a `var_dump` statement to display the contents of an array.

Note: `<pre>` tags enclose the `var_dump` statement to display the output in a more readable format.

④ Add `echo` statements that display one element of an array.

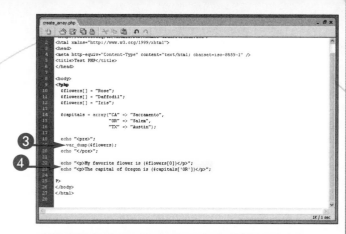

⑤ View the script in a browser.

● The output from the `var_dump` statement is formatted in multiple lines.

The `echo` statements show the value of one array element.

Extra

You can create an array containing a range of values using a `range` statement with two values. An array is created containing all the values between the first and the second values.

TYPE THIS

```
$years = range(1980,2000);
```

RESULT

An array named $years with 21 elements — 1980, 1981, 1982, and so on, up to 2000.

TYPE THIS

```
$letters = range("Z","A");
```

RESULT

An array named $letters that contains 26 elements — all the letters in reverse order, beginning with Z and ending with A.

Modify or Remove an Array

You can modify an array by changing the value in an element or by removing or adding one or more elements. You can change the value in an element with an assignment statement. The value assigned in the new assignment statement replaces the current value of the element.

You can remove the value from an element by assigning NULL to it or by assigning a string of zero length to the element. The element remains, but it contains no value. If you echo the element, nothing is displayed. No error message is displayed because the element exists, but no value appears because the element contains no value.

You can also use the shortcut notations on an element that you can use on a variable, such as ++ to increment the element by one, +=3 to add three to the element, or . = to append a value to the end of the current value.

You can add an element at any point in the script with an assignment statement that assigns a value to an element

with a new key. You can remove an element from an array with the unset statement, as follows:

```
unset($arrayname['key']);
```

If you echo an element that does not exist, either because it was never added to the array or because it was removed from the array, you will see a notice similar to the following:

Notice: Undefined index: *key* in **C:\Program Files\Apache Group\Apache2\htdocs\PHPMySQL\ arrays\test_gen.php** on line **19**

The message displays the key that PHP could not find in the array. You can remove the entire array with the unset statement, as follows:

```
unset($arrayname);
```

The entire array no longer exists after this statement.

Modify or Remove an Array

① Create an array.

② Add a statement to remove one element.

③ Add a statement to remove the value from one element.

④ Add a statement to add an element.

⑤ Display the array.

⑥ Add a statement to remove the array.

⑦ Add a statement that echoes an element.

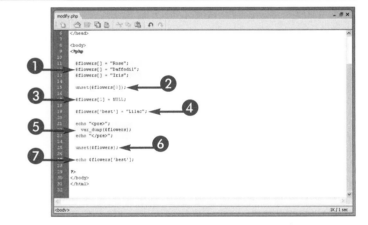

⑧ View the script in a browser.

● The contents of the modified array appear.

● A notice shows that the array no longer exists.

Note: To see the notice, you need to have notices turned on. Error messages are explained in Chapter 2.

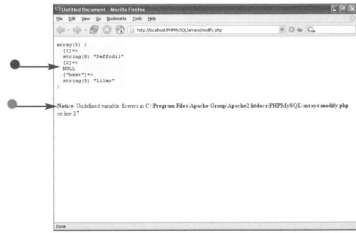

Get Information about an Array

PHP provides features that enable you to get information about an array. You can find out the contents of an array, the values of the elements, and the keys of any elements.

To see the structure and contents of an array, you can use the var_dump() statement described in Chapter 2. When used with an array, the var_dump() statement displays the elements, the keys, the values, and the data types.

You can find out the number of elements in an array using the count() function, as follows:

$n_elements = count($arrayname);

After this statement executes, $n_elements contains an integer that is the number of elements in the array. If the array exists but has no elements, count returns zero (0).

You can find the key of an element using the key() function, as follows:

$key = key($arrayname);

After this statement, $key contains the numeric or string key of the array element where the pointer is currently located. The array pointer is explained in the section "Walk through an Array Manually," later in this chapter.

You can get all the keys in the array using the array_keys() function, as follows:

$array_of_keys = array_keys($arrayname);

After this statement executes, $array_of_keys is an array that contains all the keys from the specified array. The keys are in the array in the same order as in the original array.

Get Information about an Array

1 Create an array with string keys.

2 Display the array contents.

3 Assign the array size to a variable using the count function.

4 Echo the size.

5 Add a statement using array_keys to create an array containing the keys.

6 Display the contents of the key array.

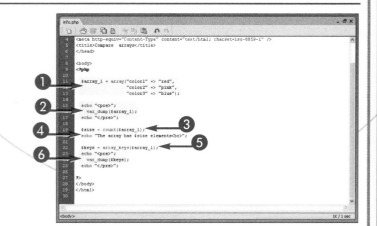

7 View the script in a browser.

The original array is displayed.

The size of the array is displayed.

● The array containing the keys is displayed.

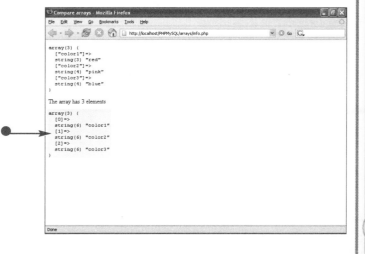

Sort an Array

O ne of the most useful features of arrays is that PHP can sort them for you. PHP originally sorts array elements in the order in which you create them. If you display an entire array without changing the order, the elements are displayed in the order in which they were created. Often, you want to change this order. For example, you may want to display the array elements in alphabetical order.

PHP can sort arrays by value or by key. It can sort the elements in numerical order for numerical values or alphabetically for strings, in forward or reverse order. You can assign new numbers as keys or keep the same keys.

The simplest sort statement is sort($arrayname), used to sort arrays with numerical keys. The sort statement reorders the elements by value and assigns new keys that are the appropriate numbers. The values are sorted

with numbers first, uppercase letters next, and lowercase letters last.

Another widely used sort statement is asort($arrayname), used to sort arrays with string keys. The asort statement reorders the elements by value and keeps the original key for each value, rather than assigning new number keys.

You can sort an array in reverse order using reverse versions of sort() and asort(), called rsort() and arsort().

You can sort an array by its keys using either ksort() — which reorders keys in forward order — or krsort() — which reorders keys in reverse order.

You can simply reverse the existing order of the elements in an array with the following statement:

```
$newarray = array_reverse($arrayname);
```

Sort an Array

NUMERIC VERSUS STRING KEYS

1 Create an array with numeric keys.

2 Add a sort statement and display the array contents.

3 Create an array with string keys.

4 Add an asort statement and display the array contents.

5 Add an arsort statement and display the array contents.

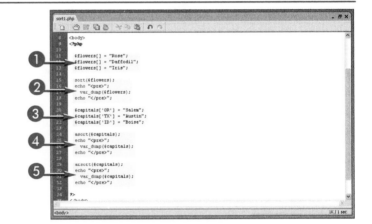

6 View the script in a browser.

- The numeric array is reordered by value, and the keys are reassigned.

- The string array is reordered by value, and keys remain the same.

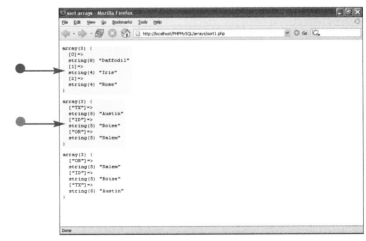

SORTING BY VALUES VERSUS SORTING BY KEYS

1. Create an array with string keys.

2. Add an `asort` statement and display the array contents.

3. Add a `ksort` statement and display the array contents.

4. Add a `krsort` statement and display the array contents.

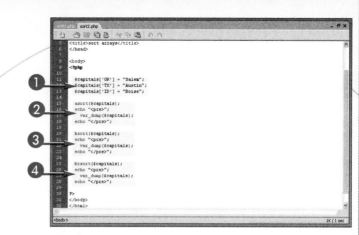

5. View the script in a browser.

- The `asort` statement reorders the array by value, and the keys stay with the same values.

- The `ksort` statement reorders the array by key, and the keys stay with the same values.

The last array is sorted in reverse order.

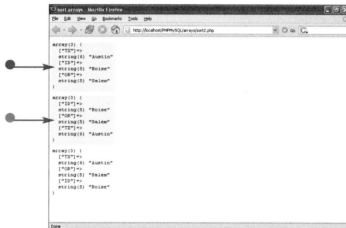

Extra

You can write your own function for sorting an array. Writing functions is discussed in Chapter 5. You can use the following statement to sort an array with a function:

```
usort($arrayname, functionname);
```

Computers sort alphanumeric strings in a different order than human beings would sort them. For example, the sort function would order the following strings into this order: day1, day11, day2, day5. You can use the `natsort()` function to sort into a "natural" order.

TYPE THIS

```
$days =
array("day1","day5","day11","day2");
natsort($days);
```

RESULT

→ $days is in the following order: day1, day2, day5, day11.

Walk through an Array with foreach

You will often want to perform an action on every element in an array, such as echo each value, store each value in a database, or add 5 to each value. Walking through each and every element in an array is called *iteration*, or *traversing* an array.

In most cases, using a `foreach` loop is the easiest and most efficient way to walk through an array. The general format is as follows:

```
foreach ($arrayname as $keyname =>
$valuename)

{

    block of PHP statements

}
```

$arrayname is the array that you want to walk through. In the `foreach` statement, $keyname and $valuename are variable names that the `foreach` loop gives to the key and the value of each element in turn. You can then use the variable names in the block of PHP statements that executes. For example, you may include echo $valuename in your block of statements. PHP does not require you to indent the statements in the block, but indenting makes the script much easier to understand and debug.

You can leave $keyname => out of the `foreach` statement. When $keyname is left out, the `foreach` loop only executes the block of statement on the value of each element.

PHP makes a copy of the array that is traversed in the `foreach` loop. Therefore, changes made in the loop are not changed in the original array unless you specifically save the new values in the original array.

Walk through an Array with foreach

① Create an array with numeric values.

② Type foreach (.

③ Type the array name.

④ Type **as**.

⑤ Type a variable name to contain the values.

⑥ Type).

⑦ Type {.

⑧ Add a statement that increments each value.

⑨ Add a statement that echos each value.

⑩ Type }.

⑪ Display the array contents after the `foreach` loop.

⑫ Create an array with two-letter state codes as keys and the full state names as values.

⑬ Create an array of state capitals with the state code as keys.

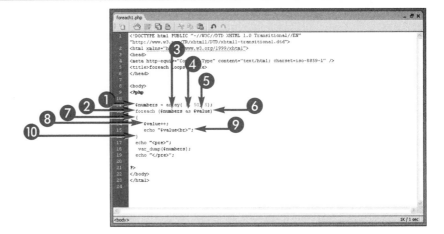

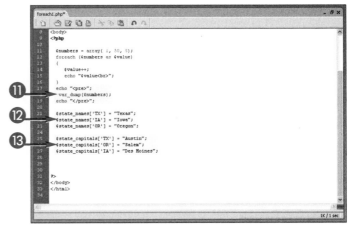

⑭ Add a `foreach` statement that iterates through the state capitals array, setting both the key and the value into variables.

⑮ Add `echo` statements that display the state names and state capitals.

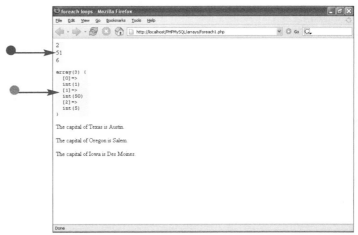

```php
<?php

$numbers = array( 1, 50, 5);
foreach ($numbers as $value)
{
    $value++;
    echo "$value<br>";
}
echo "<pre>";
 var_dump($numbers);
echo "</pre>";

$state_names['TX'] = "Texas";
$state_names['IA'] = "Iowa";
$state_names['OR'] = "Oregon";

$state_capitals['TX'] = "Austin";
$state_capitals['OR'] = "Salem";
$state_capitals['IA'] = "Des Moines";

foreach ($state_capitals as $state_code => $city)
{
    echo "<p>The capital of {$state_names[$state_code]}";
    echo " is $city.</p>";
}
?>
</body>
</html>
```

⑯ View the script in a browser.

- The first `foreach` loop displays the incremented values.

- The original array is displayed after the `foreach` loop.

Note: The values have not changed. The extra information below shows how to change values in the original array.

The second `foreach` loop displays the state capitals.

```
2
51
6

array(3) {
  [0] =>
  int(1)
  [1] =>
  int(50)
  [2] =>
  int(5)
}

The capital of Texas is Austin.

The capital of Oregon is Salem.

The capital of Iowa is Des Moines.
```

Extra

Changes made by statements in a `foreach` block are made in a copy of the original array and therefore do not change the values in the original array. To make changes to the original array, you need to save the changes to the original array using an assignment statement.

TYPE THIS

```php
$numbers = array( 1, 50, 5);
foreach ($numbers as $key => $value)
{
   $value++;
   $numbers[$key] = $value;
}
```

RESULT

→ After the `foreach` loop executes, the array `$numbers` contains the values 2, 51, and 6.

Walk through an Array Manually

You often want to perform an action on several elements in an array. If you want to perform an action on every element in order, you probably want to use a `foreach` loop, described in the previous section. However, you sometimes want to perform an action on every second or third element or each element in reverse order. Traversing the array manually enables you to select elements in the order that you need.

You can select elements in an array manually with a pointer. Think of your array as a list with a pointer pointing to an element in the list. The pointer stays on an element until you move it. After you move it, it points to the destination element until you move it again.

The first time that you access the array, the pointer is located at the first element. If you are unsure where the pointer is located, you can move it to the first element

with the `reset` statement or the last element with the `end` statement, as follows:

```
reset($arrayname);
```

To access values within the array, PHP provides the functions `current()`, which refers to the element currently under the pointer and does not move the pointer; `next()`, which moves the pointer forward one element; and `prev()`, which moves the pointer back one element. The functions move the pointer and return the value of the element that is the pointer's destination, as in the following statement:

```
$value = next($arrayname);
```

After this statement, `$value` contains the value of the next element in the array.

Walk through an Array Manually

① Create an array with several elements.

② Add a statement that gets the value from the last element.

③ Add 20 to the value.

④ Echo the new value.

⑤ Get the previous value.

⑥ Add 20 to the value.

⑦ Echo the new value.

⑧ Add a statement to display the array contents.

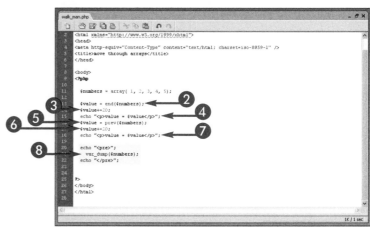

⑨ Get and display the value of the current element.

Note: The pointer still points to the element it was last moved to.

⑩ Move the pointer to the first element and display the value.

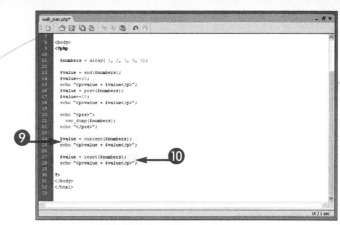

⑪ View the script in a browser.

The values are displayed with 20 added to them.

- The values in the array remain the same.
- The current element is the same as the element displayed previously.
- The first element is displayed.

Apply It

The functions that move the pointer only retrieve the values. The functions cannot change the array. You can change the array with an assignment statement that stores a new value in the array element that you want to change. To do so, you need to retrieve the key, using the `key()` function, as well as the value.

TYPE THIS

```
$testarray = array(1,2,3);
$value = next($testarray);
$value +=20;
$key = key($testarray);
$testarray[$key] = $value;
```

RESULT

The array now contains the values 1, 22, 3.

Find Values in an Array

You may need to know whether an array contains a specified value or which array element(s) contains the value. For example, you may want to modify an array if and only if a certain value is present in the array. Using `if` conditional statements is discussed in Chapter 4.

You can use `in_array` to test whether a value exists in an array, as follows:

```
$bool = in_array("value",$arrayname);
```

The `$bool` variable contains either TRUE or FALSE. If `value` was found in the array, `$bool` contains TRUE; otherwise, it contains FALSE.

You can test whether an element with a specified key exists with the `key_exists` statement, as follows:

```
$bool = key_exists("key",$arrayname);
```

After the `key_exists` statement executes, `$bool` contains either TRUE or FALSE.

If you want to know the key for the element that contains a value, you can use `array_search`, with the following format:

```
$key = array_search(value,$arrayname);
```

If `array_search` finds `value` in the array, it assigns the key of the first element where the value is found to `$key`. If the value does not exist in the array, `$key` contains FALSE.

If you want to find all the elements that contain a specified value, you can use the `array_keys` statement, with the following format:

```
$array_of_keys = array_keys($arrayname,value);
```

`$array_of_keys` is an array that contains the keys of all the elements that contain `value`. If the value does not exist in the array, `$array_of_keys` is an array with zero elements.

Find Values in an Array

① Create an array with some single values and some multiple values.

② Display the array.

③ Use `array_search` to search for a multiple value.

④ Use `array_search` to search for a value not in the array.

⑤ Display the results.

⑥ Use `array_keys` to search for a multiple value.

⑦ Display the results.

⑧ View the script in a browser.

The results are displayed.

● In this case, the first result is the key 4 — the first element where the value was found.

The second result is `false` because the value does not exist in the array.

The last result is an array containing the keys 0 and 1.

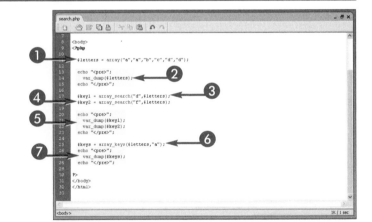

Compare Arrays

Y ou can compare arrays to see whether two or more arrays contain the same values. You can specify that only the values must be found or that the values must have the same keys. You can output the values that are different or the values that are the same.

You can use the functions array_diff() and array_diff_assoc() to find all the values that exist in one array but not in one or more other arrays, as follows:

```
$diff1 = array_diff($array1,$array2,...);

$diff2 = array_diff_assoc($array1, $array2,...);
```

The result stored in $diff1 is an array that contains all the values found in $array1 that are not found in any other array, stored with the keys found in

$array1. If the value is found in two arrays, the value is not in the differences array, even if the keys are different.

The array in $diff2 contains elements for all the key/value pairs found in $array1 but not found in any other array, stored with the keys found in $array1. If any element does not match both key and value, it is considered different and added to the $diff2 array.

PHP provides two similar functions that return an array with matches, instead of differences. The function array_intersect() creates an array that contains all the values in $array1 that are also found in another array, whether or not the elements containing the values have the same key. The function array_intersect_assoc() creates an array that contains all the matching key/value pairs.

Compare Arrays

① Create two arrays with both similar and different elements.

② Display the contents of the two arrays.

③ Create an array of the differences using array_diff.

④ Create an array of the differences using array_diff_assoc.

⑤ Display the contents of the two differences arrays.

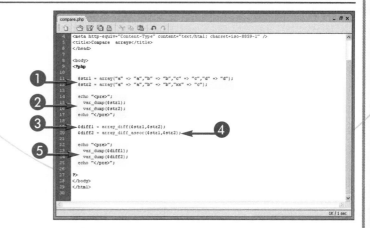

⑥ View the script in a browser.

In this example, the first array has four elements, and the second has three.

● The array produced by array_diff contains 1 element only.

● The array produced by array_diff_assoc contains 2 elements because the labels for the value "c" are different.

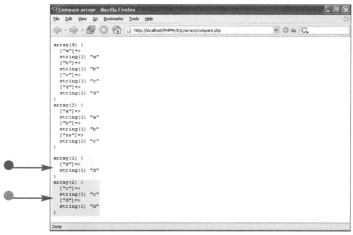

Split and Merge Arrays

You often need to put arrays together or take them apart. For example, you may have lists of names that you need to merge into larger lists or subset into smaller lists. PHP provides functions for splitting and merging arrays.

You can use the `array_slice()` function to create a new array that contains a subset of an existing array. The general format is

```
$array_sub =
array_slice($arrayname,n,length);
```

The `n` in the statement is the sequence number of the array element where the subset should start, such as `0` for the first element or `1` for the second. The `length` is the number of elements to include in the subset. For example, if `n` is `3` and `length` is `2`, the new array contains the 4th and 5th elements from the original array.

You can merge two or more arrays together with the `array_merge()` function, as follows:

```
$array_merged = array_merge($array1,
$array2,...);
```

If you merge arrays that have numeric keys, the elements are assigned new sequential keys. If you merge arrays that have string keys, only one element with a given key is assigned to the merged array. If two or more arrays have an element with the same key, the later element with the key will overwrite the earlier element with the same key.

If you want to merge arrays that have identical keys, you can use `array_merge_recursive()` rather than `array_merge()`. The `array_merge_recursive()` statement creates a multidimensional array when keys are identical, instead of overwriting the value as `array_merge()` does. Multidimensional arrays are explained in the section "Create a Multidimensional Array" later in this chapter.

Split and Merge Arrays

① Create an array with string keys.

② Create two or more subset arrays with an `array_slice` statement.

③ Display the contents of the two subarrays.

④ Create a new array by using `array_merge` to merge the subarrays.

⑤ Display the contents of the merged array.

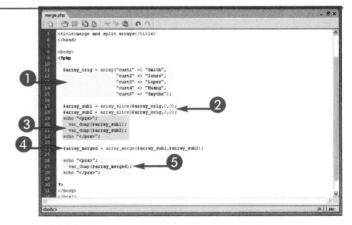

⑥ View the script in a browser.

The subset arrays are displayed.

● The merged array contains the elements from the subarrays.

Note: In this example, one element ended up in both subarrays — `cust3`. The element is included in the merged array only once.

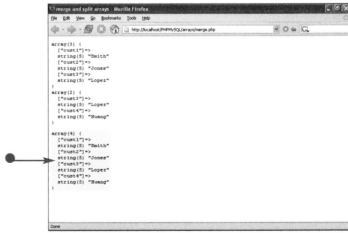

Convert an Array into a String and Vice Versa

You may want to perform an operation on the contents of an array that would be easier to perform if the data were in a string, rather than in an array. Or you may want to perform an operation on a string that would be easier to perform if the data were in an array. For example, you may want to display each word in a sentence on a separate line. To accomplish this, you need a `<br>` tag after each word. In PHP, you can accomplish this task by converting the string to an array with one word in each array element and then converting the array back to a string with a `<br>` tag between each word.

PHP provides functions that you can use to convert arrays to strings and vice versa. You can use the `explode()` function to convert a string into an array, using the following format:

```
$array_from_string =
explode("char",$string);
```

The first parameter, `char`, is one or more characters to use to divide the string. It is common to use a space (" ") as the character that divides the string, but you can use a comma, semicolon, colon, or any other character or combination of characters. The second item is the string itself.

You can use the `implode()` function to convert an array to a string, as shown in the following statement:

```
$string = implode("char",$arrayname);
```

In this statement, `char` is one or more characters to be inserted between each array element in the string. The second item is the name of the array.

Convert an Array into a String and Vice Versa

① Store a sentence in a variable.

② Add a statement that creates an array from the sentence by using the `explode` function.

In this example, the `explode` statement is `explode (" ",$sentence);`.

③ Add a statement that converts the array to a string by using the `implode` function.

In this example, the `implode` statement is `implode("<br>", $array_sentence);`.

④ Echo the final string.

⑤ View the script in a browser.

The final sentence is displayed one word per line.

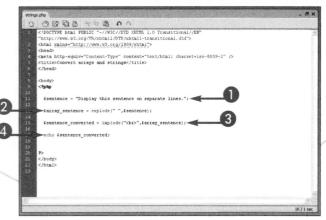

Store a Set of Variables in an Array

Sometimes you want to store the information from a set of variables in an array. If you want to perform an operation on each variable in a set of variables, such as display each value or add a number to each variable value, you can do this more efficiently if you store the variable values in an array. You can use one `foreach` statement to access the variable values one at a time, rather than write several statements to access each variable separately.

You can use the `compact()` statement to store variable values in an array. The variable names become the keys of the array. The format is

```
$array_out = compact("varname1","varname2",
$array_of_names,...);
```

You can provide the variable names as strings, as an array of variable names, or as a combination of both.

After the `compact` statement, the array contains elements for each variable name provided, with the variable name as the key.

The `compact` function adds an element to the array for every variable name passed to it that it can find. If it cannot find one or more of the variables specified by a string, it does not add it to the array, but it does not display an error message. It just ignores the variables it cannot find. If `compact` cannot find any of the variable names passed to it, it creates an array with zero elements. However, if an array of variable names is included in the `compact` statement and the array does not exist, a notice for an `"Undefined variable:"` is displayed, before the array with zero elements is created.

Store a Set of Variables in an Array

1 Add a `compact` statement for variables that do not exist.

2 Display the resulting array.

3 Create one or more variables.

4 Create an array containing one or more variable names.

5 Add another `compact` statement for the variables that you just created.

6 Display the resulting array.

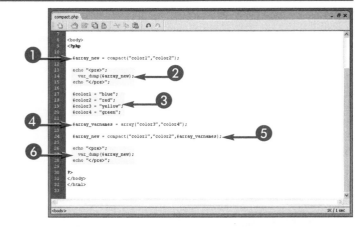

7 View the script in a browser.

● The array created by the first `compact` statement is displayed.

The array contains zero elements.

● The array created by the second `compact` statement is displayed.

The array contains four elements, with the variable names as keys.

Store Array Elements in Separate Variables

S ometimes you want to store the information from array elements in separate variables. For example, if you need to echo different elements on a Web page, it can be more efficient to create separate variables for each element and display the variables where needed. PHP provides a function that creates the set of variables for you.

You can use the extract() statement to store the array information in a set of variables, as follows:

```
extract($arrayname);
```

The extract() function creates a variable for each element in the array. The variable name is the key for the element. The extract() function does not affect the original array; the original array continues to exist as is. The extract() function just creates a new set of variables.

Beginning with PHP 4.0.5, the extract() function returns an integer that is the number of variables created, as follows:

```
$nvars = extract($arrayname);
```

The extract() function can only create variables from an associative array. Because PHP does not allow variable names that begin with a number, no variables can be created from an array with numeric keys. If an array with numeric keys is specified, the extract function does not display an error, but no variables are created.

If you pass an array name to the extract() function that does not exist, extract() displays a notice for an "Undefined variable:". If you pass an array name that is a variable rather than an array, the extract() function displays the following warning:

Warning: extract(): First argument should be an array in **C:\Program Files\Apache Group\Apache2\htdocs\ PHPMySQL\arrays\extract.php** on line **16**

Store Array Elements in Separate Variables

1. Create an array with string keys.

2. Add an extract statement to create a set of variables.

3. Add an echo statement using one or more of the new variables.

4. Display the original array.

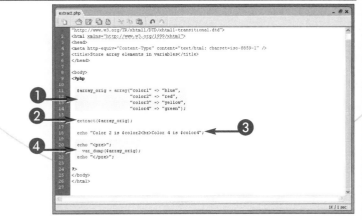

5. View the script in a browser.

   The values from the new variables are displayed.

   - The original array is displayed unchanged.

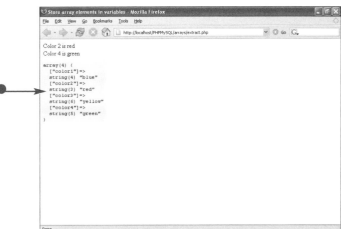

Create a
Multidimensional Array

The value in an array can be any data type, including an array. An array of arrays is called a *multidimensional array.* For example, an array can contain elements with key/array pairs. Then each array in an element contains its own elements that are key/value pairs. This array is a two-dimensional array, with the following structure:

```
$arrayname[level1_key1][level2_key1] = value1
$arrayname[level1_key1][level2_key2] = value2
$arrayname[level1_key2][level2_key1] = value3
$arrayname[level1_key2][level2_key2] = value4
```

PHP allows as many levels as you need, but the more dimensions in an array, the more difficult it is for the programmer to understand and use.

You can create multidimensional arrays in the same ways that you create one-dimensional arrays. You can create

them with assignment statements, using numerical or string keys, or using [] to allow PHP to assign numerical keys. You can also create a multidimensional array by using nested `array()` statements.

You can display multidimensional arrays using the same methods that you use to display one-dimensional arrays, such as using the `var_dump` and `print_r` statements described in Chapter 2 or using a multidimensional array element in an `echo` statement as follows:

```
echo "The price of the table is
{$price['furniture']['table']}.";
```

You can modify and remove multidimensional arrays and array elements using the same methods that you use to modify and remove one-dimensional arrays. Most of the functions described previously in this chapter work on multidimensional arrays as well as one-dimensional arrays. You just need to be specific about which level you want to modify or remove.

Create a Multidimensional Array

CREATE ARRAYS

1 Create a multidimensional array with both string and numeric keys.

2 Display the array.

3 Create a multidimensional array using nested `array` statements.

4 Display the array.

5 View the script in a browser.

● The first array is displayed.

In this example, the array contains two elements that are arrays — the first with two elements and the second with one element.

● The second array is displayed.

In this example, the array contains two elements that are arrays, each of which has two elements — color and price.

MODIFY AND REMOVE ARRAYS

1. Create a multidimensional array.

2. Sort the array.

3. Display the array.

4. Add an echo statement that uses an array element.

5. Remove an array element.

6. Add an assignment statement that changes an existing element.

7. Display the array again.

8. View the script in a browser.

- The sorted array is displayed.
- The echo statement displays the array value.
- The modified array is displayed.

In this example, the array with the key "car" is removed, and the element 0 in the plane array is changed.

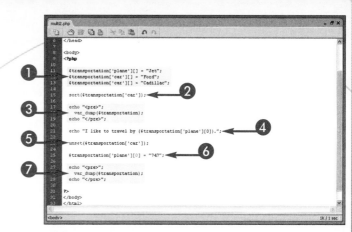

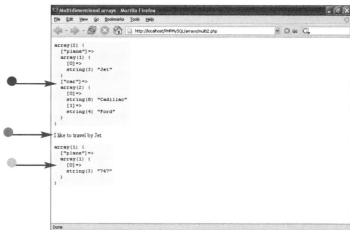

Extra

You can create a multidimensional array containing a range of values using an array statement with range statements inside the array statement. Each element of the higher-level array contains an array created by the range statement.

TYPE THIS

```
$decades = array("1980" =>
              range(1980,1989),
              "1990" => range(1990,
              1999) );
```

RESULT

An array named $decades with 2 elements with the keys 1980 and 1990. The values for each element are an array containing 10 elements — the years in each decade with numeric keys.

Walk through a Multidimensional Array

An earlier section in this chapter, "Walk through an Array with foreach," describes performing an action on every element in a one-dimensional array using a foreach loop. The process is similar when walking through a multidimensional array. Traversing a multidimensional array requires more than one foreach loop — one foreach statement for each level in the array. The foreach loops nest inside the loop for each higher level.

The syntax for walking through a two-dimensional array is

```
foreach($array_level1 as $array_level2)

{

    foreach($array_level2 as $value)

    {
```

block of PHP statements

```
    }

}
```

$array_level1 is the name of the multidimensional array that you want to walk through. In the first foreach statement, the values of the top-level array are accessed one by one. Because the values are arrays, the variable name in the first foreach statement stores an array, named $array_level2.

You can include the parameter $keyname => in either foreach statement, as described earlier. You can then use $keyname in the block of PHP statements.

PHP makes a copy of the array, which is traversed in the foreach loop. Therefore, changes made in the loop are not changed in the original array unless you specifically save the new values in the original array.

Walk through a Multidimensional Array

① Create a multidimensional array.

② Sort the array by keys.

③ Sort all the lower-level arrays by value.

④ Echo a title for your list of values.

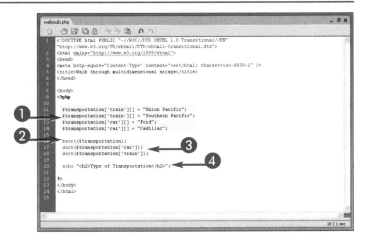

⑤ Type **foreach(**.

⑥ Type the array name.

⑦ Type **as**.

⑧ Type a variable name for the key.

⑨ Type **=>**.

⑩ Type a variable name for the subarray.

⑪ Type **)**.

⑫ On the new line, type **{**.

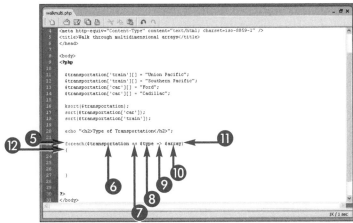

13 Echo the higher-level key.

14 Add a foreach statement to display the values of the subarray, as shown in steps 5 to 12.

15 Echo the key and value for the subarray element.

16 Type } to close the inner loop.

17 Echo </p> to end the paragraph for each key.

18 Type } to close the outer loop.

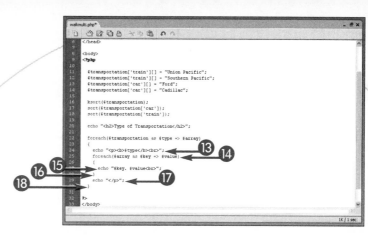

19 View the script in a browser.

All the values from the multidimensional array are displayed.

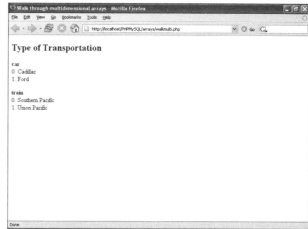

Extra

You can walk through a multidimensional array manually, as described in the section "Walk through an Array Manually," earlier in this chapter. You just need to specify an array that contains string or numbers as values, not arrays.

TYPE THIS

```
$first = current($transportation['car']);
echo $first;
$second = next($transportation['car'];
echo $second;
```

RESULT

→ The first echo statement outputs Cadillac; the second outputs Ford.

In an array of arrays, the values are arrays. The array is returned by the manual functions. When you echo an array, PHP outputs "Array" because it only can output a string.

TYPE THIS

```
$first = current($transportation);
echo $first;
```

RESULT

→ Array

No values are echoed. Only the string Array is displayed.

Using Built-in PHP Arrays

PHP has several built-in arrays that you can use when writing PHP scripts. These arrays, listed in the table below, are called *superglobal arrays* because they have a global scope. *Scope* refers to the context in your program where a variable is available. Superglobal arrays are available anywhere in your program, including in functions.

Different types of information are stored in different arrays. The table below lists the superglobal arrays and the type of information stored in them.

The following built-in arrays are available only if track-vars is enabled. As of PHP 4.0.3, track-vars is always enabled, unless the PHP administrator deliberately turns it off — a rare occurrence.

PHP Arrays

The following table describes the most widely used built-in arrays, called *superglobals* or *automatic global* arrays.

ARRAY	DESCRIPTION
$_POST	Contains all the variables submitted in a form that uses the POST method. See Chapter 10 for further information.
$_GET	Contains all the variables passed in the URL. This includes all variables submitted in a form that uses the GET method and any variables manually added to the URL. See Chapter 10 for further information.
$_COOKIE	Contains all the cookie variables. See Chapter 11 for further information.
$_REQUEST	Contains all the variables that are in $_POST, $_GET, and $_COOKIES. See Chapter 10 for further information.
$_SESSION	Contains all the session variables. See Chapter 11 for further information.
$_FILES	Contains the names of files that have been uploaded. See Chapter 10 for further information.
$_SERVER	Contains information about your server. Because your Web server provides the information, the information that is available depends on which server you are using.
$_ENV	Contains information provided by your operating system, such as the operating system name. This information varies depending on your operating system.
$GLOBALS	Contains all the global variables, including all the variables you create in your script.

Using PHP Arrays

You can use PHP arrays the same way that you use the arrays you create yourself. You can display them with var_dump and print_r. You can use any of the array values in your script, using an array notation, such as $_POST['key']. You can use a PHP built-in array value anywhere you can use a variable, just as you can use a value from your own array anywhere you can use a variable.

The variables that you create yourself are added to the $GLOBALS array. You can then access the variable from the $GLOBALS array anywhere in your script. For example, a variable that you assign a value to in your script can be accessed inside a function as $GLOBALS['varname']. The global statement, discussed in Chapter 5, gets the variable from the $GLOBALS array for you.

Form Variables

PHP makes it simple to process the information that a user submits in a form. When the user clicks the submit button, the information in the form fields is passed to the processing script, where the information is available in the `$_POST` array for forms that use the POST method and in the `$_GET` array for forms that use the GET method. Both POST and GET variables are available in the `$_REQUEST` array. The values from the form are stored in the array with the filenames as the keys. If you want to process every value from the form, you can use a `foreach` statement to loop through the `$_POST` array, as follows:

```
foreach($_POST as $key => $value)

{

    block of PHP statements

}
```

$_SERVER and $_ENV

The `$_SERVER` and `$_ENV` arrays contain different information, depending on the server and operating system you are using. You can see some of the information in the arrays in the output from the `phpinfo()` statement described in Chapter 1. You can see all the values in the arrays for your particular server and operating system with a `var_dump` statement.

One useful value in the `$_SERVER` array is `$_SERVER['DOCUMENT_ROOT']`, which contains the path to your Web space, the location where your Web server expects to find the Web page files. Another useful element in the `$_SERVER` array is `$_SERVER['PHP_SELF']`. This element shows the file that contains the script that is currently running.

Built-in Arrays in Older PHP Versions

The built-in arrays shown in the table were introduced to PHP in version 4.1.0, with the exception of `$GLOBALS`, which has been available since PHP 3.

An older set of built-in arrays is available that PHP has provided since earlier versions. The older PHP arrays are named with a longer format, such as `$HTTP_POST_VARS` and `$HTTP_GET_VARS`. The newer arrays are preferable to the older version. They have a wider scope for use in functions, discussed in Chapter 5. There is no reason to use the older variables unless you are using a version of PHP older than 4.1.

Whether the older variables are automatically created or not is controlled by a setting in your php.ini file. At the current time, this setting is On by default, although it may be Off by default at some point in the future. In most cases, you can turn off the setting. Look for `register_long_arrays` and set it to Off. There is no need for PHP to expend resources to create the long arrays if you do not need to use them. However, a script created on an old version of PHP that uses the long arrays needs the setting turned on in order to run.

Change the Order of Statement Execution

PHP scripts are a series of instructions in a file. PHP begins at the top of the file and executes each instruction in order. Sometimes you want your statements to execute in a different order, such as executing a statement only when certain conditions exist or executing a statement more than once. PHP provides several complex statements that change the order of execution in your script.

Conditional Statements

Conditional statements execute a block of statements only when certain conditions are met. The most common conditional statement is the `if` statement, which tests a condition and executes a block of code when the condition is true. An `if` statement can also have `elseif` and `else` code blocks. The `elseif` sections test different conditions. The `else` block executes if none of the conditions tested by the `if` and `elseif` blocks are true.

Another useful conditional statement is the `switch` statement, which defines a series of conditions. Each block of code executes when a specific condition is true, such as when `$var1` equals 1. PHP executes only the block of code for which the condition is true. For example, PHP may test a variable called `$weather`. If the value in weather is `"raining"`, one block of code executes; if the value in weather is `"sunny"`, a different block of code executes; and if the value in weather is `"snowing"`, a third block of code executes.

Conditions

Conditions are expressions that PHP tests or evaluates to determine whether they are true or false. Conditions are used in both conditional statements and loops to determine whether a block of statements should be executed. To set up conditions, you compare values.

You can compare values using comparison operators that test whether two expressions are equal, one is higher than another, or one is lower than the other. For example, the `==` (two equal signs) operator means that two expressions are equal. A condition such as `$var1 == $var2` is true if the values in the variables are equal and is false if the values are not equal.

You can also set up patterns, called *regular expressions,* and test whether a string matches the pattern. For example, you may want to identify strings that begin with *T* or strings that have numbers in them.

Loops

Loops are statements that execute a block of statements repeatedly. A loop can repeat a specified number of times or only as long as certain conditions exist. The loops discussed in this book are `for` loops, `while` loops, and `do-while` loops.

A `for` loop sets up a counter and repeats a block of statements until the counter reaches a specified number. The `for` loop is very flexible, enabling you to set up complex loops.

The `while` and `do-while` statements repeat a block of statements as long as a certain condition is true. The statement block stops repeating when the condition is no longer true. The `while` and `do-while` statements are very similar, differing only in the location in the loop where the condition is tested.

Infinite Loops

It is possible to set up a loop that repeats endlessly, called an *infinite* loop. An infinite loop is rarely created purposely; it is usually an error. For example, a loop is set up to stop when the counter reaches 10. However, a programming error resets the counter to 1 every time that it reaches 9. This creates an endless loop.

Check the Contents of a Variable

Often a condition tests a variable. The possible conditions for a variable are as follows: The variable does not exist; the variable exists but contains no value; or the variable contains a value that is one of several data types. You may want to execute a block of code only when the variable exists, only if it does not exist, or only when it contains data of a specific type. PHP provides several functions that you can use to test variables.

Two functions test whether the variable exists and/or is set: isset() and empty(). These two functions test related conditions. The function isset() is true if the variable exists and contains a value; the function is false if the variable does not exist or contains NULL. The function empty() is true if the variable does not exist or exists but does not contain a value; the function is false if the variable exists and

contains a value. The isset() function considers an empty string — a string with zero characters — to be a value in a variable; the empty() function does not.

PHP provides several functions that test the type of data contained in a variable. Some useful functions are is_array, is_float, is_int, is_string, and is_numeric. Each returns TRUE when the variable contains the expected type of data and FALSE when the variable contains any other type of data.

Each of these functions can test whether the variable value is not the expected type. Add an exclamation point (!) in front of the function to test the negative. For example, if the variable contains a string, the function is_string() returns TRUE. If you test with !is_string, the function tests whether the variable does not contain a string. Because it does contain a string, is_string() returns FALSE.

Check the Contents of a Variable

① Create variables with various data types.

② Add statements that test the variables with isset and display the results.

③ Add statements that test whether the variables are empty and display the results.

④ Add statements that test whether the variables are not strings and display the results.

⑤ Test whether a variable contains an integer and display the result.

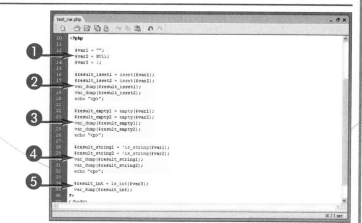

⑥ View the script in a browser.

The Boolean values are displayed by var_dump.

● In this example, both isset and empty return TRUE for the first variable, which contains an empty string.

● In this example, the third set of tests uses ! to test that the variables are not strings, returning FALSE for the variable that is a string.

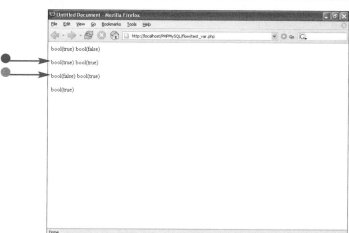

Set up Conditions with Comparison Operators

C onditions are expressions that PHP tests or evaluates to see whether they are true or false. Conditions are used in conditional statements to determine whether to execute a block of statements.

To set up conditions, you often compare values using the following comparison operators: == (2 equal signs), which means equal to; === (3 equal signs), which means equal to and the same data type; != or <>, which means not equal to; !==, which means not equal to or not the same data type; <, which means less than; <=, which means less than or equal to; >, which means greater than; and >=, which means greater than or equal to. The following are valid conditions:

```
$var1 == $var2
```

```
$var1 > 5
```

```
$var1 != $var2+1
```

```
$var2 + $var3 >= 203
```

You can compare both numbers and strings. Strings are compared based on their ASCII code. In the ASCII character set, each character is assigned an ASCII code that corresponds to a decimal number between 0 and 127. Uppercase letters are assigned the codes from 65 to 90; lowercase letters are assigned the codes from 97 to 122. Consequently, all the uppercase characters come before any lowercase characters, making SS less than Sa.

Punctuation characters also have ASCII codes, and therefore an order. For example, a comma, which is coded 44, is smaller than a period, coded 46. However, comparing a comma to a period is rarely useful.

Set Up Conditions with Comparison Operators

1 Create two variables with numbers for values — one a string and one an integer.

2 Compare the two variables using == and display the result.

3 Compare the two variables using === and display the result.

4 Compare one variable to the same number that is stored in the variable using > and display the result.

5 Compare one variable to the same number that is stored in the variable using >= and display the result.

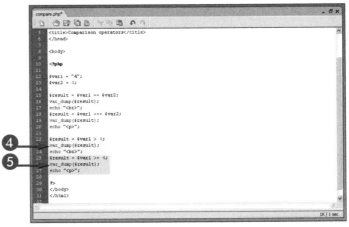

6 Compare one variable to the same number that is stored in the variable using ! = and display the result.

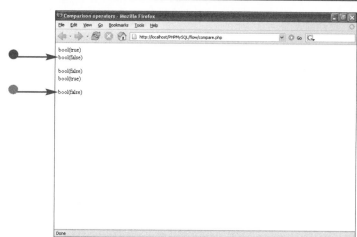

7 View the script in a browser.

The Boolean values are displayed.

- The second comparison is false because the data types are different.

- The last comparison uses the not equal operator; because the variable and value *are* equal, the result is FALSE.

Extra

Confusing one equal sign with two equal signs is one of the most common errors. One equal sign is an assignment statement that stores the value on the right side of the equal sign in the variable on the left side. Two equal signs compare two values to see whether they are equal. It is a very common mistake to use one equal sign when two are needed. A condition that uses one equal sign is always true; it cannot be false.

TYPE THIS	RESULT

`$var1 = 5;`
`$result = $var1 == 5;`
`var_dump($result);`
	The integer 5 is assigned to $var1. $var1 is tested to see whether it is equal to 5. Because it is equal to 5, the Boolean value TRUE is assigned to $result. TRUE is output by the var_dump statement.

If the comparison was accidentally made using one equal sign, as in $var1 = 5, then 5 would have been assigned to result and output by var_dump. Whenever a loop or conditional statement is not working the way you expect it to, check your equals comparisons to be sure that you used two equal signs, not one.

Introducing Regular Expressions

ou sometimes need to test character strings for characteristics, rather than for an exact match to a specific string. For example, you may want to process all strings that contain only letters, with no numbers. In this case, you compare a string to a pattern, called a *regular expression,* sometimes referred to as a *regex.*

A regular expression is a string composed of literal characters and/or special characters. Literal characters are normal characters, with no special meaning. An *A* is just an *A* — one letter of the alphabet. Special characters have special meaning in the regular expression.

Special Characters

Special characters are symbols, or combinations of symbols, that have a special meaning. If you want to use a special character as a literal in a regular expression, you must insert an escape character — the backslash (\) — in front of the special character, which is called *escaping* the character. The escape character is a special character that means to process the next character as a literal.

CHARACTER	MEANING	EXAMPLE
^	Beginning of line	`^The start`
$	End of line	`The end$`
.	Any single character	`.a..`
?	The preceding character is optional	`ger?m`
( )	Groups a section of the regular expression into a subpattern	`g(er)m`
[ ]	Encloses a set of optional literal characters	`g[er]m`
[^]	Encloses a set of optional characters that must not be in the string being matched	`g[^er]m`
–	Represents all the characters between two literals	`[A-Z]`
+	One or more of the preceding items	`bldg[1-3]+`
*	Zero or more of the preceding items	`ger*m`
{n}	Repeat n times	`mo{2}d`
{n1,n2}	Specifies a range of repetitions	`a{2,5}`
\	The following character is literal	`\*`
|	Separates alternate literal strings	`up|down`

Building Regular Expressions

Regular expressions are strings of characters, representing a pattern. Searching for filenames in your directory using wildcards, such as `file*`, which will select all filenames that begin with `file` — `file1`, `file200`, and `file_mine` — is a simple form of pattern matching. Regular expressions can be long and very complex, specifying exactly the strings you want to match.

The following strings are some examples of commonly used patterns.

REGEX	MATCHES
`^[A-Za-z]`	Any line that begins with an upper- or lowercase letter.
`^[A-Za-z '-]+$`	A string that contains only letters, spaces, single quotes, and hyphens, such as customer names or city names.
`^[A-Z]{2}$`	A string of two uppercase letters. State codes match this pattern.
`^Dear (Kim|Rikki)`	`Dear Kim` or `Dear Rikki` at the beginning of a line.
`^[0-9]{5}(\-[0-9]{4})?$`	Any zip code.
`.+@.+\.(com|net)`	An email address that ends in .com or .net.

Using Regular Expressions

Many languages and applications have features that accept regular expressions. In most cases, you enter the regular expression into an application field or use it in a function in a language. PHP provides several functions that make use of regular expressions.

The most common use for regular expressions is testing whether or not a string matches. The `ereg()` function accepts a string and a regular expression. If the string matches the regular expression, `ereg()` returns TRUE; if not, it returns FALSE. Testing for a match is used extensively with conditional statements and loops. One common use for testing with regular expressions is filtering the information submitted by users in HTML forms, discussed in Chapter 10.

Regular expression can also be used to replace subsections of a string or to split a string. A replacement function accepts a string, a regular expression, and a replacement string. The function replaces substrings that match the regular expression with the replacement string. A split function splits the string wherever the string matches the regular expression. Some useful functions that replace and split strings are discussed in Chapter 6.

Types of Regular Expressions

PHP provides functions for two types of regular expressions — POSIX and Perl-compatible. The information in this chapter discusses and provides examples for POSIX expressions. Perl-compatible expressions are more powerful and sometimes faster. However, they are more complex and harder to understand. The more powerful Perl-compatible expressions are sometimes needed, such as when your string contains binary data. For more information on Perl-compatible regular expressions, see www.php.net/manual/en/ref.pcre.php.

The Perl-compatible regular expressions are very similar to Perl regular expressions, but there are a few differences. For example, the `\D`, `\G`, `\L`, `\l`, `\Q`, `\u`, and `\U` options are not available. If you are familiar with Perl regular expressions but find unexpected problems, check the PHP manual.

Match Character Strings to Patterns Using Regular Expressions

You can test whether strings match a pattern using functions that accept a string and a regular expression. If the string matches the pattern, the function returns an integer that is the length of the matched string; if no match is found, the function returns FALSE. Building a regular expression to test a string is discussed in the previous section, "Introducing Regular Expressions."

You can compare the string to the regular expression with the function ereg(). The format is

```
$result = ereg(pattern,string);
```

You can pass the *pattern* and the *string* to the function as a string or in a variable. PHP provides a second function for regular expression matching — eregi(). The eregi() function performs in a similar matter to ereg(), except that it ignores upper/lowercase when matching the string to the pattern.

The ereg() and eregi() functions have an optional third argument — a variable name. After the function is executed, $variablename[0] contains the string that matched. If the regular expression contains any subpatterns, the subpattern matches are added to the array, in order from left to right. That is, $variablename[1] contains the string that matches the first subpattern on the left, $variablename[2] contains the string that matches the second subpattern from the left, and so on.

You can test for a string that does not match the pattern by using an exclamation mark (!) in front of the function, as follows:

```
$result = !ereg(pattern,string);
```

The Boolean TRUE is stored in $result if the string does not match the pattern.

Match Character Strings to Patterns Using Regular Expressions

① Create a string.

② Type **$result = ereg("[a-z]", $string, $regs);**.

Note: This regex tests for any string with at least one lowercase letter.

③ Display the contents of $result and $regs.

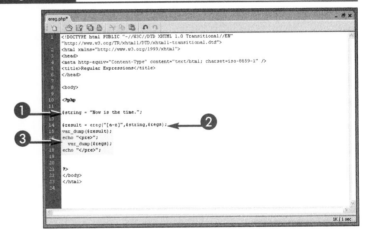

④ Store the regex **[a-z]{4}** in a variable.

Note: This tests for a string of four lowercase letters.

⑤ Add a line that tests for *no* match using !ereg — **$result = !ereg($regex, $string,$regs);**

⑥ Display the contents of $result and $regs.

⑦ Repeat steps 4 to 6, storing the regex **[a-z]+** in the variable $string.

Note: This tests for a string of any length with lowercase letters or spaces.

● Test for a match with ereg, not !ereg.

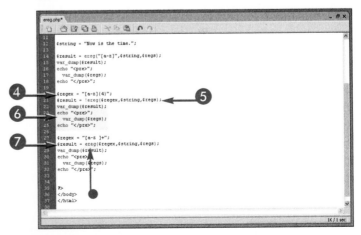

⑧ Store a zip code in a variable.

⑨ Store the regex that tests for a zip code —
^[0-9]{5}(\-[0-9]{4})?$ — in a variable.

⑩ Add a statement that tests for a zip code.

⑪ Display the contents of $result and $regs.

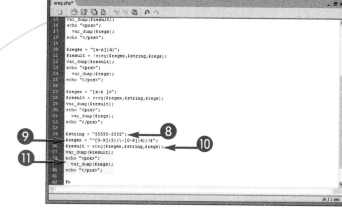

⑫ View the script in a browser.

The first match is one character — the
string o.

● The second test returns FALSE because
it is testing for no match.

The matching string is in the array, even
though !ereg returned FALSE.

● The third test matched almost the entire
string because space was included in the
pattern.

● The last test matched the entire zip code
and stored the subpattern.

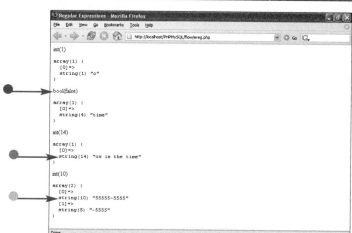

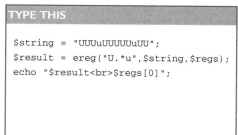

Apply It

Regular expressions will always match the longest string that satisfies the pattern.

TYPE THIS

```
$string = "UUUuUUUUUuUU";
$result = ereg("U.*u",$string,$regs);
echo "$result<br>$regs[0]";
```

RESULT

The echo statement outputs the following:

10

UUUuUUUUUu

The output displays the longest string
that matches the pattern, echoed from
$regs[0]. The string is 10 characters
long, echoed from $result.

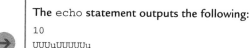

Join Multiple Comparisons with Logical Operators

Often you need to set up more than one comparison in a condition. You can join two comparisons with one of the logical operators — AND, OR, or XOR. The logical operators evaluate each comparison to obtain the Boolean value for each expression and then compare the Boolean values. The AND operator returns TRUE only if both comparisons are true, the OR operator returns TRUE if either comparison is true, and the XOR operator returns TRUE if one, but not both, comparison is true.

For some tests, evaluating the comparison on the left is sufficient. For example, if the first comparison evaluates to FALSE, then AND must evaluate to FALSE. At this point, AND stops, and the second comparison is not evaluated. This process is called *short circuiting*.

You can string together as many comparisons as necessary, with the following format:

```
comparison1 AND|OR|XOR comparison2
AND|OR|XOR comparison3 AND|OR|XOR ...
```

The logical operators, like any other operators, are executed in order of precedence. The order is AND first, XOR second, and OR third. Consequently, all ANDs are executed before all ORs. Within precedence order, the logical operators are executed from left to right.

You can use && as an alternative for AND and || for OR. These alternatives operate in the same manner as AND and OR, except they have a higher precedence. && and || execute before AND, OR, and XOR. && executes before ||.

You can change the order in which logical operators are executed with parentheses. The logical operator inside the parentheses is evaluated first.

Join Multiple Comparisons with Logical Operators

① Create 3 or more variables.

② Type **$result1 = (**.

③ Type one comparison.

④ Type a logical operator.

⑤ Type another comparison.

⑥ Type **);**.

Note: Parentheses enclose the condition so that all comparisons are evaluated before the assignment.

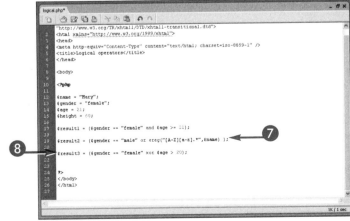

⑦ Add a statement using the `or` logical operator (as shown in steps 2 to 6).

⑧ Add a statement using the `xor` logical operator (as shown in steps 2 to 6).

Note: The `or` statement is true if either comparison is true. The `xor` statement is true if either comparison is true, but not if both comparisons are true.

9 Add a statement with more than two comparisons.

10 Display the contents of $result1, $result2, $result3, and $result4.

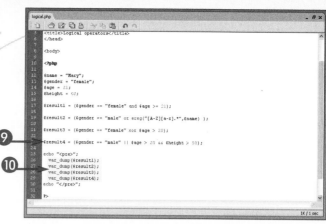

11 View the script in a browser.

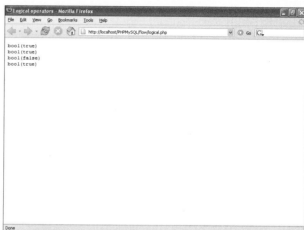

Extra

The not logical operator can be used to test any comparison. The exclamation point (!) tests the negative of the comparison.

TYPE THIS

```
$var1 = "male";
$result = ( ! ( $var1 = "male" ) );
var_dump($result);
```

RESULT

This condition tests whether $var1 is not equal to "male". Because $var1 *is* equal to "male", $result contains FALSE.

The use of the not logical operator can be confusing. In general, a more straightforward condition is better, but occasionally the not construction is the only condition that tests what you need.

Using an if Statement

An if statement tests conditions, executing a block of statements when a condition is true. The general format is

```
if(condition)

{

    block of statements

}

elseif(condition)

{

    block of statements

}

else
```

```
{

    block of statements

}
```

A code block for the if and elseif executes when the *condition* is true. An if statement must contain one, and only one, if section. It can optionally contain one or more elseif sections and one else section.

The script tests the if condition first. If the condition is true, the code block executes, and the script moves to the next statement following the if statement. If the condition is not true, the script does not execute the code block, but moves to test the next condition in the if statement or, if there are no more conditions to test and no else section, to the next statement following the if statement. The script continues to test conditions until it encounters a condition that is true or until it reaches an else section or the end of the if statement.

Using an if Statement

① Create a variable to use in the conditions.

② Create some variables to use in the statement block.

③ Type **if(** to start the if statement.

④ Add a condition.

⑤ Close the condition by typing **)**.

⑥ Add a block of statements, enclosed by curly braces, to be executed if the condition is true.

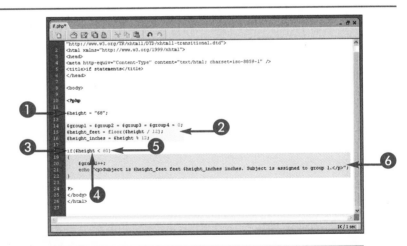

⑦ Add an elseif statement that tests a different condition.

⑧ Add a block of statements to execute if the condition is true.

⑨ Add a second elseif statement that tests a third condition.

⑩ Add a block of statements to execute if the condition is true.

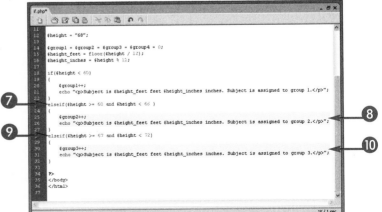

⓫ Add an `else` statement.

⓬ Add a block of statements.

⓭ Add a statement following the `if` statement.

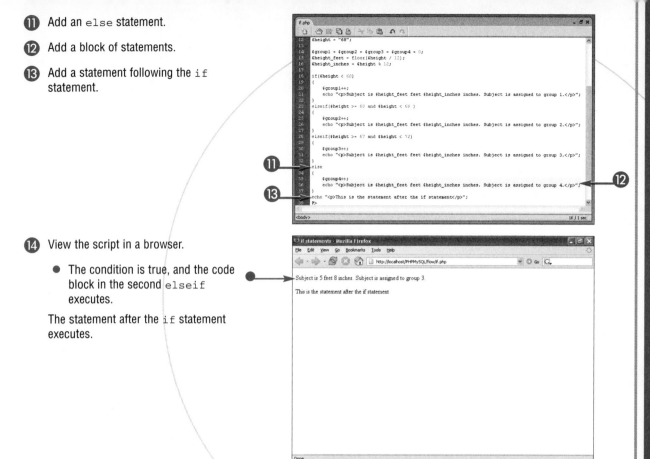

⓮ View the script in a browser.

- The condition is true, and the code block in the second `elseif` executes.

The statement after the `if` statement executes.

Extra

A simple `if/else` statement can be written in shortcut form using a ternary conditional operator. It provides `if` statement functionality in a compact expression format. The ternary conditional operator is `?:`, in the following format:

`(condition) ? expression when true : expression when false;`

PHP evaluates the condition. If it is true, the first expression is evaluated; if it is false, the second condition is evaluated.

TYPE THIS

```
$missing = ($state == NULL) ?
'missing' : 'not missing';
echo $missing;
```

→

RESULT

If `$state` contains NULL, missing is assigned to `$missing`. If `$state` does not contain NULL, not missing is assigned to `$missing`.

Using a switch Statement

Usually, the `if` conditional statement is most appropriate. However, sometimes you want to set up a list of conditions with a block of statements for each condition. You can use the `switch` statement to do so.

The `switch` statement tests the value of one variable and executes the block of statements for the matching value of the variable. The general format is

```
switch ($variablename)
{
  case value :
     block of statements;
     break;
  case value :
```

```
     block of statements;
     break;
  default :
     block of statements;
     break;
}
```

The `switch` statement tests the value of `$variablename` and executes the appropriate block of code. You can use as many `case` blocks as you need.

The `break` statements are essential. If a `case` block does not include a `break` statement, the script does not stop executing at the end of the `case` block.

You can also nest `switch` statements.

Using a switch Statement

1 Create the variables needed for the `case` blocks.

2 Type **switch ( )**.

3 Type the variable name that the `switch` statement is to evaluate.

4 Type **{** to start the `switch` statement.

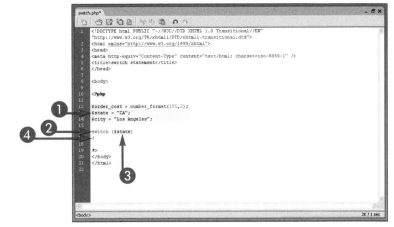

5 Type **case :**.

6 Type the value for this `case` block between `case` and `:`.

7 Add a block of statements for the case.

8 Type **break;**.

9 Repeat steps 5 to 8 for each `case` block and the `default` block.

10 Type **}** to end the `switch` statement.

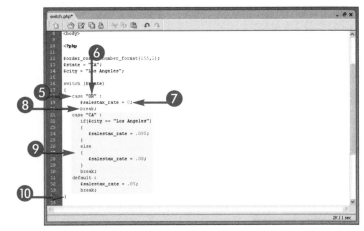

⑪ Create any needed variables using variables created in the `switch` statement.

⑫ Add statements to display the results on a Web page.

In this case, the results are displayed in an HTML table.

⑬ View the script in a browser.

Extra

The `default` section is usually added as the last section of the `switch` statement. The logic is easier to follow to understand the statement. However, PHP does not require the `default` section to be in any particular order. You can add your `default` section in the middle, top, or anywhere in the `switch` statement.

After the `switch` statement starts executing statements, it continues until it encounters a `break` statement or the end of the `switch` statement. In most cases, you want only the statements for one `case` value to execute. However, in some cases, you may want to use the *fall-through* feature of the `switch` statement, which is when you want one value of a case to execute two `case` blocks, but another value of a case to execute only the second block.

Using a for Loop

Loops are used frequently in scripts to set up a block of statements that repeats. The `for` loop uses a counter to determine when the block of statements should stop repeating.

The basic `for` loop, the loop that is most frequently needed, has the following format:

```
for(startvalue;endcondition;increment)

{

    block of statements

}
```

The parameters in the `for` statement can be values or variables or expressions, as follows:

```
for($i=$age;$i<=$age+20;$i++)

for($i=1;$i<count($arrayname);$i++)
```

The first parameter sets up the counter, giving it a variable name and a starting value. The second parameter sets the ending value. As long as this statement is true, the loop repeats; when the statement is not true, the loop stops. The third parameter is an expression that increments the counter.

In the statement block, you can use the counter variable as you use any other variable.

You can nest `for` loops inside of `for` loops. Nesting is useful to process tables and multilevel lists.

You can build more advanced `for` loops by including more than one expression in the parameters of the `for` loop. The expressions are separated by a comma (,):

```
for($i=1,$j=0;$i<=$age+20;$i++,j++)
```

This sets up two counters that you can use in your statement block.

Using a for Loop

CREATE A BASIC LOOP

1. Create a variable that has a value.

2. Type **for( )**.

3. Set up the start value for the counter, followed by a semicolon.

4. Set up the ending condition, followed by a semicolon.

5. Add the expression that increments the counter.

6. Add a block of statements, enclosed by curly braces.

7. View the script in a browser.

   The loop executes once for each value of the counter.

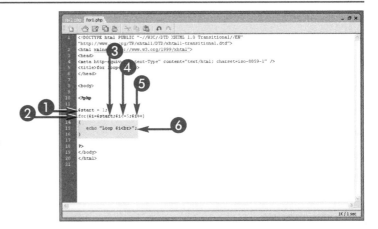

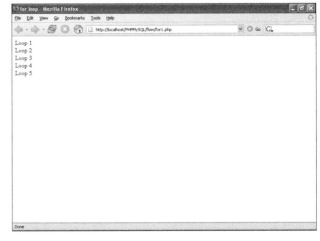

USING MULTIPLE COUNTERS

1 Type **for( )**.

2 Set up start values for two counters, separated by a comma and followed by a semicolon.

3 Set up one ending condition, followed by a semicolon.

4 Add two expressions that increment the counters.

5 Add a block of statements, enclosed by curly braces.

6 View the script in a browser.

The statement block executes once for each value of the counters.

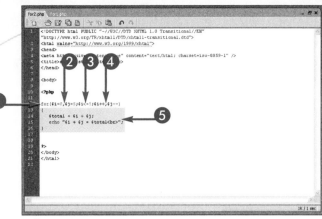

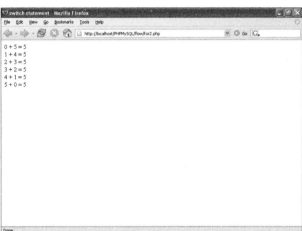

Apply It

Any of the three sections in the `for` loop statement can be empty. You can leave out the starting value, the ending condition, and/or the expression that increments the counter. The most common use for this feature is to leave the ending condition out when you want to end the loop with a conditional `break` statement. The `break` statement is discussed later in this chapter in the section "Break Out of a Loop."

TYPE THIS

```
for($i=1;;$i++)
{
    echo $i;
    if($i > 5)
    {
        break;
    }
}
```

RESULT

When the counter, $i, becomes greater than 5, the loop stops executing, and the script jumps to the statement after the `for` loop.

Using a while Loop

Loops are used frequently in scripts to set up a block of statements that repeats. The `while` loop is a simple loop that continues repeating as long as certain conditions are true. The following is the general format of a `while` loop:

```
while(condition)

{

    block of statements

}
```

At the beginning of the `while` loop, the script checks the condition. If the condition is true, the block of statements executes. At the end of the block of statements, the script returns to the beginning of the loop and checks the condition again. The loop continues repeating until the condition is not true, at which point the script jumps to the statement after the `while` loop.

If the condition at the top of the loop is not true when first tested, the `while` loop can terminate without executing the block of statements even once. Another loop, the `do-while` loop, tests the condition at the bottom of the loop. With a `do-while` loop, the block of statements is always executed at least once. The `do-while` loop is discussed in the next section, "Using a do-while loop."

You can nest `while` loops inside of `while` loops or other conditional statements or loops.

You can break out of the statement block of a `while` loop before reaching the end of the block with a `break` statement or a `continue` statement. See the section "Break Out of a Loop," later in this chapter.

Using a while Loop

① Create the variables needed for the `while` statement.

② Add a statement that echoes a heading for your list.

③ Type **while( )**.

④ Type a condition inside the parentheses.

⑤ Type **{**.

⑥ Add statements that process and echo information in the block.

⑦ Add a statement to increment the counter.

⑧ Type **}** to close the statement block.

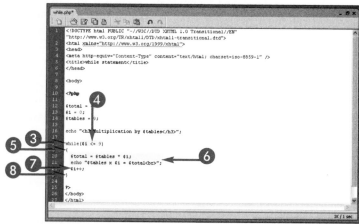

9 Add an echo statement after the end
of the while loop.

10 View the script in a browser.

Apply It

PHP offers an alternate syntax for the while statement. You can begin the statement block with a colon (:)
and end it with endwhile;, instead of enclosing the block in curly braces. This syntax shows the end of the
statement block more clearly, but requires more typing.

TYPE THIS

```
$var1 = 0;
while($var1 < 5) :
    echo $var1;
    $var1++;
endwhile;
```

RESULT

The loop executes five times, echoing
$var1 each time.

Using a do-while Loop

Loops are used frequently in scripts to set up a block of statements that repeats. A do-while statement is a simple loop, similar to a while loop. The loop continues repeating as long as certain conditions are true. The following is the general format of a do-while loop:

```
do
{
    block of statements
} while(condition)
```

The do-while loop checks the condition after the statements are executed. If the condition is true, the loop returns to the beginning and repeats the loop, executing the statements again. The loop continues repeating until the condition is not true, at which point the script does not return to the top of the loop, but instead leaves the loop, dropping to the statement after the do-while loop.

Because the do-while loop tests the condition at the end of the loop, it will execute the statement block at least once, even if the condition is not true when the loop begins. Another loop, the while loop, tests the condition at the top of the loop. With a while loop, the block of statements may not execute at all. The while loop is discussed in the previous section, "Using a while Loop."

You can nest do-while loops inside of do-while loops or other conditional statements or loops.

You can break out of the code block of a do-while loop before reaching the end of the block with a break statement or a continue statement. See the section "Break Out of a Loop," later in this chapter.

Using a do-while Loop

1. Set up the variables needed for the loop.

2. Echo a heading.

3. Type **do**, followed by **{** on the next line.

4. Add statements to perform the loop tasks.

5. Add a statement that increments the counter.

6. Type **}while( );**.

7. Add a condition.

8. Add an echo statement after the end of the do-while loop.

9. View the script in a browser.

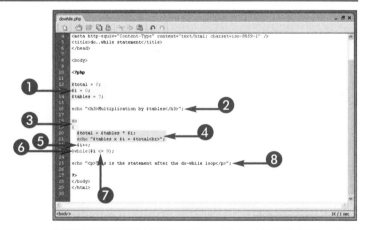

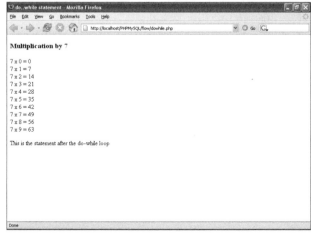

⑩ Change the counter value to a number that is
not true for the condition.

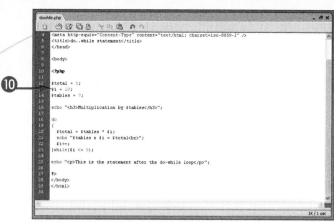

⑪ View the script in a browser.

Even though the condition is false when the
loop starts, the statement block executes once
before the condition is checked.

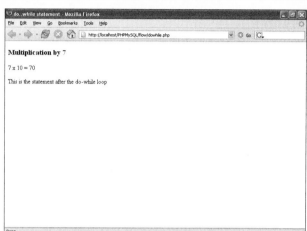

Apply It

When there is only one statement in the statement block, you do not need to enclose the statements in
curly braces.

TYPE THIS

```
$i = 0;
do
  $i++;
while($i <= 3);
echo $i;
```

RESULT

$i is incremented with one in each iteration of
the loop. Because $i starts as 0 and finishes at 3,
the loop executes four times, and $i equals 4
at the end of the execution, which is echoed after
the loop is finished.

Avoid an Infinite Loop

You can easily set up loops so that they never stop. These loops are called *infinite loops.* They repeat forever. Infinite loops are seldom created purposely. They are usually created accidentally, with a mistake in the programming.

Using one equal sign in a condition, instead of two equal signs, is a common cause of an infinite loop. One equal sign is an assignment statement and is always true. The condition never evaluates to false and, consequently, never ends.

Resetting the counter variable inside the loop is also a common error that results in an infinite loop. If you set the counter used in the condition to 0 or 1 inside the loop, the counter never reaches the number at which the loop should terminate, causing the loop to continue to run indefinitely.

Not incrementing the counter inside the code block is another common error. If you do not change the value of the counter used in the condition inside the code block of a loop, the counter never reaches the condition that terminates the loop. That is, if your counter is 1 when you start the loop and you do not change it inside the loop, the counter never reaches the number that changes the condition to false.

If you run your script and an endless loop starts displaying on the Web page, it will stop by itself. PHP stops it after a specified time period determined by the `max_execution_time` setting in your php.ini file. The default time is 30 seconds. The output of `phpinfo()` displays the current time limit in the Core Configuration section. You can change this setting.

Avoid an Infinite Loop

① Create a counter for the loop.

② Create a `while` statement that tests the counter.

③ Echo the counter.

Note: This loop does not increment the counter.

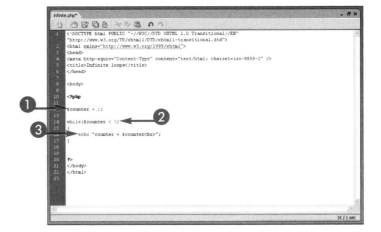

④ Reset the counter.

⑤ Add a `while` statement that tests the counter.

⑥ Set the counter to a value.

⑦ Echo the counter.

⑧ Increment the counter.

Note: The `while` statement resets the counter at the beginning of every loop.

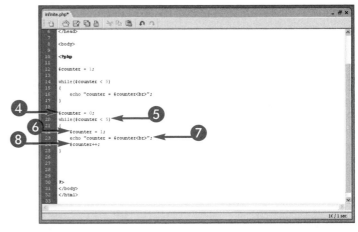

⑨ Reset the counter.

⑩ Create a `while` statement that tests the counter.

Note: The condition uses = where it means to use ==.

⑪ Echo the counter.

⑫ Increment the counter.

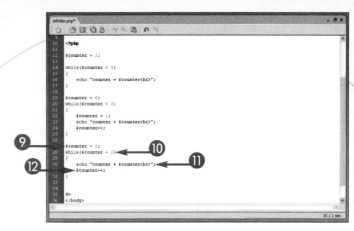

⑬ View the script in a Web site.

The output is an endless loop that echoes the counter.

All three `while` loops in the script produce the same output.

Apply It

Using a single equal sign to test for equality, when you should use a double or triple equal sign, is a common error that results in an infinite loop. You can protect yourself against this error by reversing the order of your comparison, putting the value first.

TYPE THIS

```php
$var1 = "yes"; $i = 0;
while("yes" == $var1)
{
    if($i < 5)
        $i++;
    else
        $var1 = "no";
}
```

→

RESULT

The `while` loop runs correctly. It increments $i until $i equals 5. At that point, the `else` condition is executed, changing $var1 to "no", which causes the `while` loop to terminate. However, if a single equal sign were used in this `while` statement, instead of a double equal sign, the script would display an error, not start an endless loop. The error message would be similar to

Parse error: parse error, unexpected '=' in C:\test_loop.php on line **14**

The error message shows the equal sign as the problem and the line where the problem is.

Break Out of a Loop

Sometimes you want your script to break out of a loop. You can use a `break` statement or a `continue` statement to break out of a `for`, `foreach`, `while`, `do-while`, or `switch` statement before reaching the end of the statement block. You usually want the script to break out of the loop when a specific condition is true, so you use the `break` or `continue` statement in a conditional statement.

The `break` statement breaks completely out of the loop, jumping to the statement after the loop. The `continue` statement jumps to the end of the loop, but still inside the loop, where it continues with the loop.

If the loop is nested, you can break out of the higher-level loops as well as the immediate loop. You can add a number to the `break` or `continue` statement that specifies how many levels you want to break out of.

With no number, the statements break out of only the current loop, continuing to execute the outer-level loop. If you specify 2, the statement breaks out of the current loop and one higher-level loop. You can specify any number of levels.

One common use of the `break` statement is to end a `case` section in a `switch` statement, as discussed in the section "Using a `switch` Statement," earlier in this chapter. Another common use is to break out of an endless loop, such as breaking out when the loop executes a specified number of times. Programmers sometimes add a conditional break to a script during development, as a failsafe, in case the loop has a mistake that results in an infinite loop. The conditional break is removed after the loop is functioning correctly.

Break Out of a Loop

BREAK VERSUS CONTINUE

1. Create a counter.

2. Add a `while` statement that tests the counter.

3. Increment and echo the counter.

4. Add an `if` statement that includes a `continue`.

5. Add an `if` statement that includes a `break`.

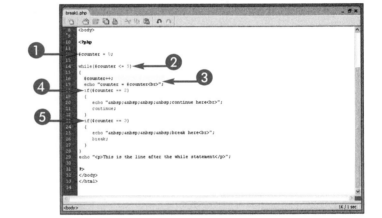

6. View the script in a browser.

- The `continue` statement returns to the top of the loop and repeats it.

- The `break` statement jumps to the line after the loop.

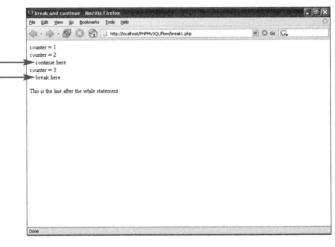

BREAK OUT OF NESTED LOOPS

① Create two counters for nested loops.

② Add a `while` statement that tests the counter.

③ Increment and echo the first-level counter.

④ Add a `while` statement for a nested loop.

⑤ Increment and echo the nested loop counter.

⑥ Add an `if` statement that includes the statement **break 2;**.

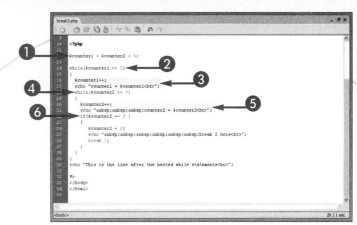

⑦ View the script in a browser.

● The script breaks out of both loops and jumps to the line after the `while` statements.

Apply It

Omitting the semicolon after the `break` or `continue` statement can sometimes cause unexpected results in your script. The `break` and `continue` statements accept a numeric argument after the keyword. If you do not provide a numeric argument and also omit the semicolon at the end of the statement, the next statement sometimes provides a numeric argument, causing an error in script execution that can be difficult to find.

TYPE THIS

```
for($i=0;$i<5;$i++)
{
    continue
    count($arrayname);
}
```

RESULT

Because count returns an integer, the `continue` statement will accept the result of the `count()` function as an argument and break out of the number of loops specified by the `count()` function. No error message may appear, the only consequence of the missing semicolon may be odd behavior in the program that can be difficult to track down.

Include a Code File

Your Web site scripts may need to perform a task repeatedly, such as displaying the company address or storing data in a database. Efficient development dictates that you write PHP code to perform a certain task and use the same code whenever the task is required.

One method for reusing code is PHP include files. You can store as many lines of code as you need in a file, separate from your script, and insert (called *include*) the file into the script wherever you need it.

PHP provides four statements for inserting a file into a script: include, include_once, require, and require_once. You can use the following format for all four, passing a string or a variable:

```
include(path/filename);
```

The include/require statements behave identically except for their behavior when they cannot open the specified file. The include statement issues a warning; the require statement issues a fatal error. The include_once/require_once statements behave identically to the include/require statements, except that a file is included only once. If you use include_once to include a file, PHP will not include the same file again, even if you use another include statement.

The code in the include file is always treated as HTML code, even if the include statement is located in a PHP section of the script. Consequently, if the include file contains PHP code, you must add PHP tags inside the include file.

You can name include files with any name and store them in any directory. However, where you store include files and what you name them can be a security issue. Filenames and locations are discussed further in the section "Store include Files Securely," later in this chapter.

Include a Code File

CREATE AN INCLUDE FILE

1. Add one or more statements.

2. Type **<?php** to start the PHP section.

3. Add one or more statements.

4. Type **?>** to end the PHP section.

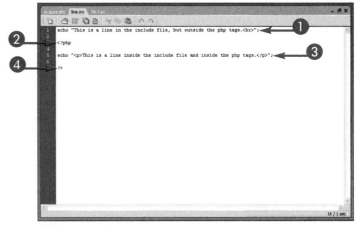

CREATE A SET OF INCLUDE FILES

5. Create two or more files with related filenames.

   In this example, the files file1.inc, file2.inc, and file3.inc are created.

6. Add a statement that echoes some text.

CREATE THE SCRIPT

7. Add one or more statements inside the PHP section before the `include` statement.

8. Add an `include` statement.

9. Add one or more statements after the `include` statement.

10. Add a loop that includes the set of files created in step 5.

Note: See Chapter 4 for more information about loops.

11. View the script in a browser.

- The entire text of the line in the `include` file that is outside the PHP tags is displayed, except for the HTML tag that starts a new line.

- The loop includes three files, each with one `echo` statement.

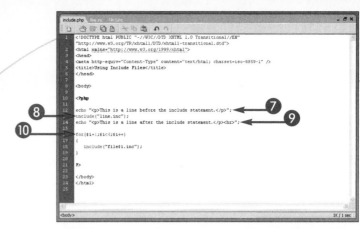

Extra

You can get the names of all the `include` files in a script with the `get_included_files()` function. The function returns an array of filenames with numeric keys. The element with the 0 key returns the name of the script. The array contains one element for each file, even if the file is included more than once. `get_required_files()` is the same function with a different name and returns the same array.

TYPE THIS

```
$array_include = get_included_files();
var_dump($array_include);
```

RESULT

`$array_include` contains an element for each `include` file. The key is numeric, and the value is the complete path to the file. The first element (0) contains the name of the script that includes the files.

Configure the Path to the include Files

PHP looks for `include` files in directories that you specify in your php.ini file with the `include_path` setting. If your `include` files are in a directory in your `include` path, you can access the files without using a path in the `include` statement. PHP searches for `include` files through the path in the order the directories are listed.

You can list more than one directory in your `include` path. The path specification is specific to your operating system. In Windows, your path is set with backward slashes and semicolons (;) between directories, such as `".;c:\php\includes"`. In UNIX, your path is set with forward slashes and colons (:) between directories, such as `".: /php/includes"`.

If you do not specify an `include` path, a default path is set, such as c:\php6\pear. You can see the current `include` path in the PHP Core Configuration section in the output of `phpinfo()`. Running `phpinfo()` is described in Chapter 1.

PHP provides functions that enable you to view and set your `include` path in a script. You can retrieve the current path setting with either of the following statements:

```
$path = get_include_path();

$path = get_ini("include_path");
```

After either statement, `$path` contains the current `include` path. You can echo, print, or otherwise use `$path` in statements.

You can set your `include` path for the current script only, with the following statement:

```
set_include_path("newpath");
```

The specified `include` path is in effect only during the execution of the script. The setting in the php.ini file is not affected. You can restore your `include` path to the path specified in the php.ini file with the `restore_include_path()` function.

Configure the Path to the include Files

① Open php.ini in a text editor.

② Scroll down to the Paths and Directories section.

③ Add a setting for the `include` path.

Note: The format to specify the path is different for Windows and UNIX.

④ Save the changed file.

⑤ Restart the Web server.

⑥ Add a statement that gets the current `include` path.

⑦ Echo the path.

⑧ Add a statement to set a new `include` path.

⑨ Add a statement to get the new path.

⑩ Echo the path.

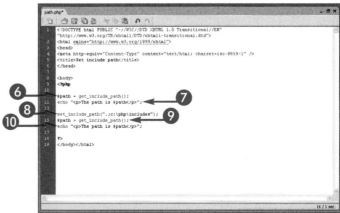

⑪ Add a statement to restore the `include` path to the path in php.ini.

⑫ Add a statement to get the current `include` path.

⑬ Echo the path.

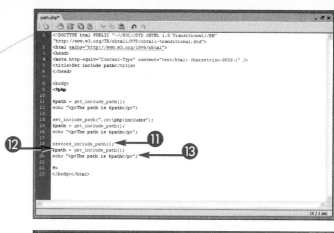

⑭ View the script in a browser.

The current path, changed path, and restored path are displayed.

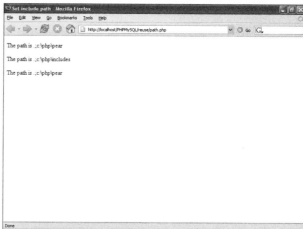

Extra

If you do not have access to the php.ini file, you may not be able to set the `include` path for your site. You can still set the `include` path by directory if you are using Apache. You can create a file named .htaccess that contains Apache directives, which apply to files in the directory where .htaccess is located and its subdirectories. To use the .htaccess file, you must change a setting in the Apache configuration file (httpd.conf) for the directory where you want to use the .htaccess file. The default setting is `AllowOverride None`. You can change it to `AllowOverride All`. For more information on `AllowOverride`, see http://httpd.apache.org/docs/2.0/mod/core.html#allowoverride.

TYPE THIS

```
<IfModule mod_php5.c>
  php_value include_path ".C:\php\includes"
</IfModule>
```

mod_php5 should be mod_php4 or mod_php6, depending on your PHP version.

RESULT

These commands in the .htaccess file set the `include` path for all PHP scripts in the same directory and its subdirectories.

Include Files Automatically

You can tell PHP to process a file at the start of every script and/or at the end of every script. The files are treated as if they were included with an `include` statement. If you have a set of functions or classes that you want to be available to every script, you can store them in an `include` file that you autoprepend to all your scripts.

Settings in php.ini specify which file to process at the beginning or at the end. Open php.ini in a text editor and look for the following settings:

```
auto_prepend_file =

auto_append_file =
```

Add the name of the file following the equal sign. You can add either an `auto_prepend` file or an `auto_append` file, or both.

Because the specified files are processed as if they were included with an `include` statement, the `include` file features all apply to the `auto_prepend` and `auto_append` files. For example, you must include the PHP opening and closing tags in the `include` file if it contains PHP statements, not just HTML code. The `auto_prepend` and `auto_append` files must be located in the `include` path.

You can disable `auto_prepend` or `auto_append` files by adding `"none"` after the equal sign.

If the script ends with an `exit()` statement, instead of continuing to the closing PHP tag, the `auto_append` file is not processed.

Include Files Automatically

① Open php.ini in a text editor.

② Scroll down to the `auto_prepend_file` setting.

③ Insert a filename, enclosed in quotes, after the equals sign.

④ Save the file and restart the Web server.

⑤ Create an `include` file with PHP statements.

Note: See the section "Include a Code File" for information on creating an `include` file.

6 Choose any PHP script to execute to test autoprepend.

In this example, the script chosen is a simple one with just one echo statement.

Note: The script does not have an include command.

7 View the script chosen in step 5 in a browser.

The output from the auto_prepend file is displayed first, even though there is no include statement that includes the file.

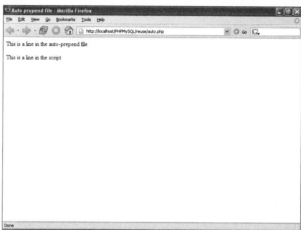

Extra

If you do not have access to the php.ini file, you may not be able to specify an auto_prepend or auto_append file. You can still set auto files by directory if you are using Apache. You can create a file named .htaccess that contains Apache directives, which apply to files in the directory where .htaccess is located and its subdirectories.

TYPE THIS

```
<IfModule mod_php5.c>
  php_value auto_prepend_file
"filename.inc"
</IfModule>
```

RESULT

These directives in the .htaccess file cause filename.inc to execute automatically when any PHP scripts in the same directory are run.

Store include Files Securely

PHP looks for include files in directories that you specify with the include_path setting. A specified directory where you store include files can be located anywhere on your computer hard disk. You do not need to store include files in your Web space. You can store them in a directory that cannot be accessed from the Web. Setting your include path is described in the section "Configure the Path to the include Files," earlier in this chapter.

You can name your include files with any valid filename. Using a filename extension, such as .inc, is useful for organization purposes, enabling you to see immediately whether a file is a PHP script or an include file.

If an include file is accessed directly in the browser, instead of accessed by an include statement in a PHP script, and does not have a .php extension, the code is treated as HTML code — and is usually displayed on the Web page. This could be a security risk. On the other hand, if the file is named with a .php extension, it is processed by PHP when accessed directly, executing the PHP statements in the include file outside their expected context. This could also be a security risk.

The best way to protect the contents of your include files is to store them in a directory outside your Web space. Web site visitors cannot access the files directly when they are stored outside the Web space. If you specify the directory in the include_path, you do not need to specify the path in your PHP code.

Store include Files Securely

SET THE INCLUDE DIRECTORY

1 Open php.ini in a text editor.

2 Scroll down to the include_path setting.

3 Remove the semicolon from the start of the appropriate line.

In this example, remove the ; from the start of the Windows line.

Note: If neither existing line is right for you, add a new include_path setting line, with no semicolon at the start of the line.

4 Save php.ini and restart the Web server.

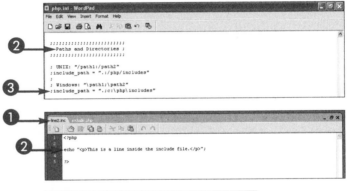

USE AN INCLUDE FILE

1 Create a new file in a text editor.

2 Add some code lines to the include file.

Note: Creating an include file is explained in the section "Include a Code File."

3 Save the include file.

4 Click the down arrow and navigate to the include directory specified in the include_path setting.

5 Type a filename.

6 Click Save.

7 Create a new PHP file.

8 Add an `include` statement that specifies the filename only.

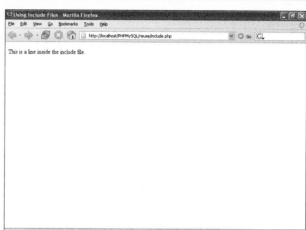

8

```
<!DOCTYPE html PUBLIC "-//W3C//DTD XHTML 1.0 Transitional//EN"
"http://www.w3.org/TR/xhtml1/DTD/xhtml1-transitional.dtd">
<html xmlns="http://www.w3.org/1999/xhtml">
<head>
<meta http-equiv="Content-Type" content="text/html; charset=iso-8859-1" />
<title>Using Include Files</title>
</head>

<body>

<?php

include("line2.inc");


?>

</body>
</html>
```

9 View the script in a browser.

PHP displays the `include` file that resides in the `include` directory, as specified in php.ini.

Using Include Files - Mozilla Firefox

File Edit View Go Bookmarks Tools Help

http://localhost/PHPMySQL/reuse/include.php

This is a line inside the include file.

Done

Extra

When a user types a URL that is a directory name, a default file is displayed — usually index.html. If the Web server cannot find the default file, it displays either a list of the files for the user to select from or an error message, depending on the Web server configuration settings. Displaying the list of files is a security risk. Some files may contain sensitive information in text files, such as `include` files, that the user should not see. Of course, if your `include` files are in a directory outside your Web space, as recommended in this section, the files are protected from the user.

To set Apache to deliver an error message instead of a list of files, open the httpd.conf file in a text editor. Find a Directory section for your main Web site, such as

```
<Directory "C:/Program Files/Apache Group/Apache2/htdocs">
```

Look at the settings for this directory — the settings included before the closing line `</Directory>`. Find a setting similar to `Options Indexes` and insert a minus sign (-) before `Indexes`, so the setting becomes `Options -Indexes`.

Define and Use a Function

When you need to perform the same task at different points in a program or in different programs, you can create a *function* — a block of statements that perform a specific task — and use it wherever you need to perform the task. You can create a function as follows:

```
function
functionname(varname1,varname1,...)

{

    block of statements

    return;

}
```

You can pass values to the function, which it can use in the code block, by listing variable names to contain the values. You can return values from the function to the main script with the `return` statement, which also ends the function. Details of passing values, using variables in functions, and returning values are included in later sections of this chapter.

To use a function, you include its name in a statement, referred to as *calling* the function. A function may be defined anywhere in the script, but the usual practice is to put all the functions together at the beginning or end of the script. Functions that you plan to use in more than one script can be in a separate file that you include in scripts that need the functions.

PHP provides many built-in functions, which are the same as the functions you create, except that PHP does the work for you.

Define and Use a Function

1 Type **function**.

2 Type a name for the function.

3 Type **()**.

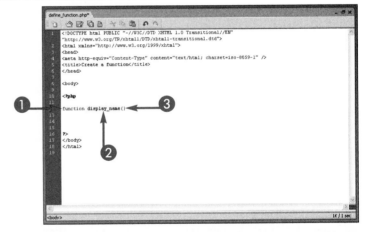

4 Type **{**.

5 Type the statements that perform the function task.

6 Type **}**.

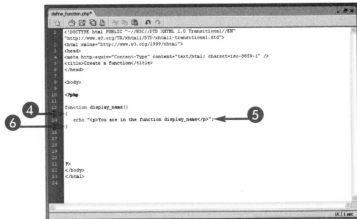

⑦ Add any statements to be executed before the function call.

⑧ Type the function name, followed by ().

⑨ Add any statements to be executed after the function finishes executing.

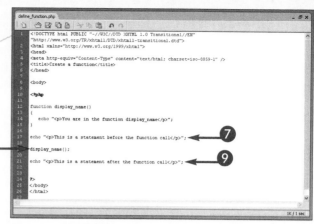

⑩ View the script in a browser.

The statements execute in order.

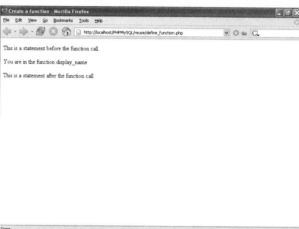

Extra

You can test whether a function exists using a function named function_exists().

TYPE THIS

```
$result = function_exists(display_name);
```

→

RESULT

$result contains TRUE if the function display_name exists or FALSE if the function does not exist.

You can find out what functions are available in a script with the function get_defined_functions(). This function creates an array of all the function names. The array has two elements with the keys "internal" and "user". The "internal" element contains an array of all the PHP functions available, and the "user" key contains an array of all the functions defined in the script.

TYPE THIS

```
$func = get_defined_functions();
echo $func['user'][0];
```

→

RESULT

Displays the name of the first function defined in the current scripts.

Using Variables in a Function

ou can create and use variables inside your functions. Where you can use the variables, called the *scope,* depends on how you define the variables. When you create a variable with an assignment statement inside a function, the variable is *local* to the function. You can use the variable in the function, but it is not available in the main script, outside the function. If you assign a value to a variable inside a function and then echo the variable in the main script, after the function call, the variable does not exist.

You can make a variable *global,* instead of local, using a `global` statement, as follows:

```
global $varname;
```

A global variable can be used anywhere in the script. If you create a variable in a function and define it as global, the variable still exists after the function finishes executing.

Similarly, if a variable is created outside the function, you cannot use it inside the function unless it is global. If you create a variable in the script with an assignment statement before the function call and then assign a value to the variable inside the function, the variable you create in the script and the variable you create in the function are not the same variable. They are two different variables with the same name. You must use the `global` statement before the value assigned to the variable inside the function is also assigned to the variable outside the function.

Using Variables in a Function

① Define a function.

② Create and display a variable in the function.

③ Add a statement that displays a variable created outside the function.

④ Create and display a variable before the function call.

⑤ Call the function.

⑥ Display the two variables after the function call.

⑦ View the script in a browser.

- ● The variable created before the function call does not exist inside the function.

- ● The variable created in the function does not exist after the function call.

Note: Notices are displayed if you have notices turned on. Error messages are discussed in Chapter 2.

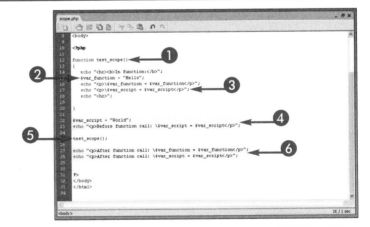

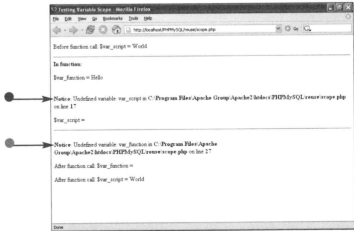

8️⃣ Open the script in a text editor.

9️⃣ Add a `global` statement for the variable created in the function.

🔟 Add a `global` statement for the variable created outside the function.

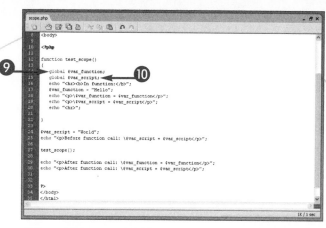

1️⃣1️⃣ View the edited script in a browser.

The two variables are available both inside and outside the function.

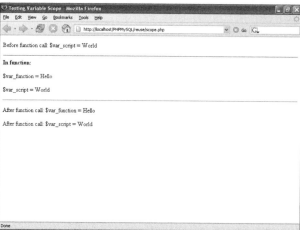

Extra

You can see all the global variables that are available by displaying the built-in PHP array called $GLOBALS. The $GLOBALS array contains the names and values of all the variables in the global scope. The array is large because it contains both the PHP built-in variables and the global variables defined in your script.

TYPE THIS
`var_dump($GLOBALS);`

→

RESULT
Displays an array of all the global variable values with the variable names as keys. The global variables defined in the script are the last elements in the array.

Pass Values to a Function

You can pass values to a function by putting the values between the parentheses when you call the function, as follows:

```
functionname(value1,value2,...)
```

The values can be passed directly or in variables. The values can be any data type.

The function must be defined to expect the values, as follows:

```
function functionname($varname1,
$varname2,...)
```

The values are stored in the variable names in the order in which they are received. If the function call does not send as many values as the function expects, the missing variables do not exist. If the warning level is turned on, a warning message informs you that an argument is missing, but the script continues to execute. If you send too many values, the function ignores the extra values.

If the wrong data type is passed, the function will not work as expected. You can use a conditional statement inside a function to execute the statements if the wrong data type is passed. You can test the data type using functions, such as is_int or is_string.

You can define a default value for an argument by assigning a default value in the function statement, as follows:

```
function
functionname($varname1=1,$varname2=1,...)
```

The function uses the defined default value when a value is not passed. If a value is passed, the function uses the value instead of the default.

Pass Values to a Function

① Add a function statement that passes several values, some with defaults defined and some without defaults.

   In this example, the last value defines a default value.

② Add the statement block, surrounded by curly braces.

③ Add a function call with the correct number of values.

④ Add a function call that does not include the last value.

⑤ Add a function call that does not include the last two values.

Note: This example has no default defined for the second-from-the-last value, although it does have a default for the last value.

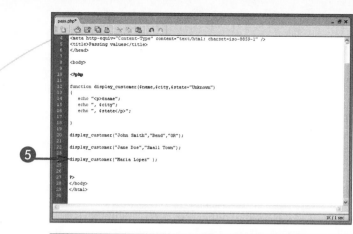

⑥ View the script in a browser.

The first two function calls do not display any error messages.

- A warning is displayed by the third function call because not enough values are passed.

- A notice is displayed when the function echoes a variable that was not passed.

Note: To see the notice, you must have notices turned on, as discussed in Chapter 2.

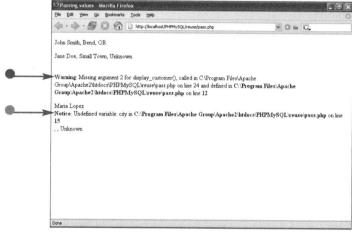

Apply It

When you pass values in variables to a function, you pass a copy of the variable, called *passing by value*. Any changes made to the variable in the function are made only on the copy, leaving the original variable value unchanged. You can change the original value of a variable if you pass the location of the original variable, not a copy, called *passing by reference*. To pass by reference, insert an ampersand (&) in front of the variable name.

TYPE THIS

```
function add_1($num)
{
    $num++;
}
$num = 5;
add_1(&$num);
```

RESULT

→ After this script, $num equals 6. If the & was not included in the function call, $num would equal 6 inside the function, but would still equal 5 outside the function.

Return Values from a Function

You can end the execution of a function with a `return` statement. If you include a value in the `return` statement, the value is sent back to the main script. The general format is

```
return value;
```

value is optional. The `return` statement can return only one value, but the value can be any data type, including an array. The following are valid `return` statements: `return; return "Missing"; return TRUE; return $varname++;` and `return count($arrayname)`.

You can use the `return` statement in a conditional statement to end the function based on the condition, such as executing the `return` statement when a variable equals a specified value. The `return` statement can return a value representing the status of the function, such as `TRUE`, when it completes successfully, or `FALSE`,

when it fails. Or, the function can return a value when it executes successfully or `FALSE` when it fails.

If you want to store the value returned by the function, you need to use the function call in an assignment statement, as follows:

```
$result = functionname(values);
```

When functions return a value, you can use the function in a conditional statement that tests the value returned. For example, you can use one of the following statements:

```
if( functionname(values) > 10)
```

```
if(functionname(values) )
```

The first `if` statement tests whether the function returns a value greater than `10`. The second `if` statement tests whether the function returns `TRUE`.

Return Values from a Function

1. Define a function.

2. Add a statement that returns a value.

3. Define a function that returns a Boolean value.

4. Add a conditional statement that returns `TRUE`.

5. Add a conditional statement that returns `FALSE`.

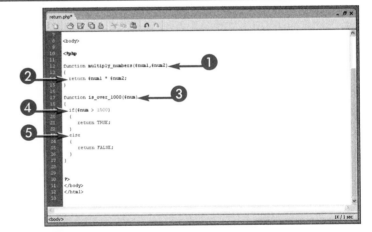

6. Create the variables needed to pass to the functions.

7. Add a call to the function that returns a value, storing the value in a variable.

8. Echo the returned value.

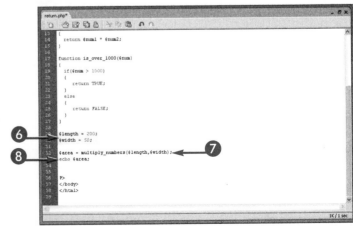

9 Use the value returned in step 4 in a conditional statement that tests the Boolean value returned by the second function.

In this example, the first function returns the value to `$area`, which is passed to the second function in the conditional statement.

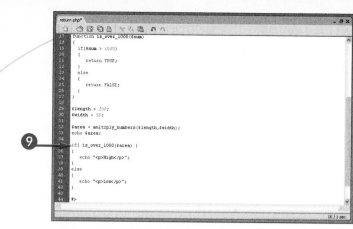

9

10 View the script in a browser.

- The value returned by the first function is displayed.

- The conditional statement executes a block based on the Boolean value returned by the second function.

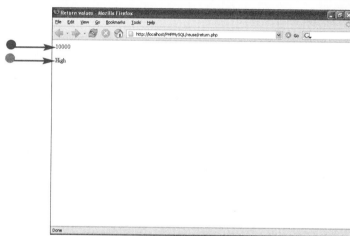

Extra

You can use `return` statements in `include` files, as well as in functions. The `return` statement ends the `include` file and returns immediately to the line in the script that included the file. You can return a value from the `include` file that can be stored in a variable.

TYPE THIS

```
$var1 = include("test.inc");
```

RESULT

If test.inc contains a `return` statement, $var1 contains the value returned by the `return` statement. Without a `return` statement, an `include` statement returns 1 when successful or FALSE when the file cannot be found.

Format a Number

Y ou can specify the number of decimal points that a number displays, a character to separate the number into thousands, and a character to separate the decimal places from the whole number with the number_format() function, as follows:

```
$f_number = number_format($number,
n_dec,"dec_char","thous_char");
```

You can use one, two, or four of the parameters, but not three. The default characters are a decimal point (.) to separate the decimal places and a comma (,) to separate the thousands, such as 1,234.56. If you specify only the first two parameters, the default characters are used.

If you specify a number of decimal places smaller than the number of decimal places in the number, number_format rounds the number to the specified number of decimal places.

You can specify the decimal character and the thousands separator. You specify each by passing the character, enclosed by quotes. If you specify a string as the decimal character or the separator, only the first character of the string will be used.

If you include only the first parameter — the number itself — no decimal places are included in the formatted number. If the original number has decimal places, they are rounded to the nearest whole number.

You can format the number as dollars and cents by specifying two decimal places. If there are no numbers in the decimal places, the number will contain zeros in the decimal places. You can display the number with a dollar sign by escaping the dollar sign in the echo statement, as follows:

```
echo "\$$f_number";
```

Format a Number

① Create a variable containing a number with decimal places.

② Type a variable name for the output.

③ Type **= number_format( );**.

④ Type the name of the variable from step 1.

⑤ Echo the variable name typed in step 2.

⑥ Repeat steps 2 to 5, except pass a number of decimal places.

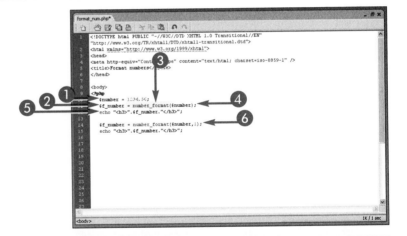

⑦ Repeat steps 2 to 3.

⑧ Type the variable name that contains the number.

⑨ Type a number of decimal places.

⑩ Specify the character that separates the decimal places.

⑪ Specify the character that separates the number into thousands.

⑫ Echo the output.

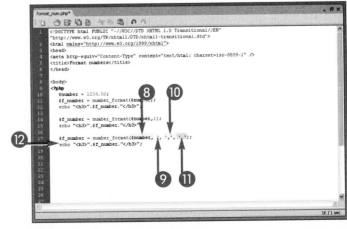

⑬ Repeat steps 2 to 3.

⑭ Type the name of the variable that contains the number.

⑮ Specify two decimal places.

⑯ Echo the output.

⑰ Add an escaped $ in front of the output to echo a dollar sign in front of the number.

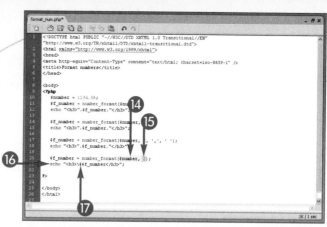

⑱ View the script in a browser.

The number is displayed in four different formats.

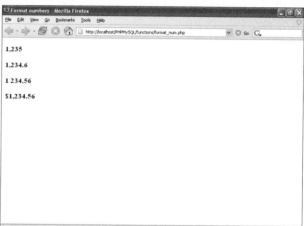

Apply It

If you want to specify characters for the decimal character or the thousands separator, you must specify both. You cannot specify just one. You can, however, specify that no character be used.

TYPE THIS

```
$num1 = number_format($number,2,',','');
$num2 = number_format($number,2,',');
```

RESULT

The first statement specifies four parameters, with empty quotes as the fourth parameter. This statement formats a number with no character separating the thousands, resulting in numbers similar to 12345,00. The second statement specifies only three parameters. This statement results in the following warning message:

Warning: Wrong parameter count for number_format() ...

Round a Number

You can round a number to a specified decimal place with the `round()` function, as follows:

```
$number_rounded = round($number,
dec_places);
```

The number is rounded to the nearest specified place. If the value being rounded is .5 or higher, the number is rounded to the higher value for the specified decimal place. If the value being rounded is .4 or lower, the number is rounded to the lower value for the specified decimal place. That is, 3.5 becomes 4, and 3.4 becomes 3.

If you leave out the second parameter — the number of decimal places — the number is rounded to the nearest integer.

You can round a number with one or more decimal places to the next higher integer. For example, if the number to be rounded is 3.4 or 3.8, the number becomes 4. You can round higher with the `ceil()` function, as follows:

```
$number_higher = ceil($number);
```

You can round a number with one or more decimal places to the next lower integer. For example, if the number to be rounded is 3.4 or 3.8, the number becomes 3. You can round lower with the `floor()` function, as follows:

```
$number_lower = floor($number);
```

Round a Number

1 Create a variable that contains a number with decimal places.

2 Type a variable name.

3 Type = **round( );**.

4 Type the variable name from step 1.

5 Type a number of decimal places.

6 Echo the rounded number.

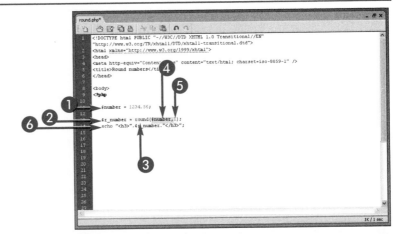

7 Type a variable name.

8 Type = **ceil( );**.

9 Type the variable name from step 1.

Note: `ceil()` and `floor()` round to integers, not decimals.

10 Echo the rounded number.

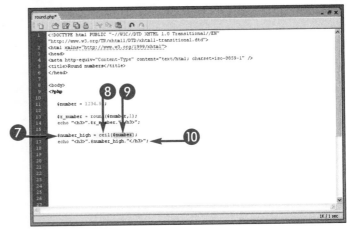

⑪ Type a variable name.

⑫ Type **= floor( );**.

⑬ Type the variable name from step 1.

Note: Again, remember that ceil() and floor() round to integers, not decimals.

⑭ Echo the rounded number.

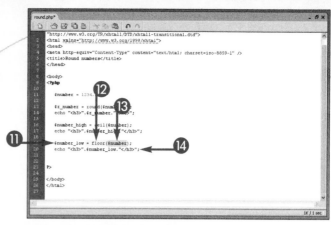

⑮ View the script in a browser.

The numbers are displayed, showing the results of the different rounding functions.

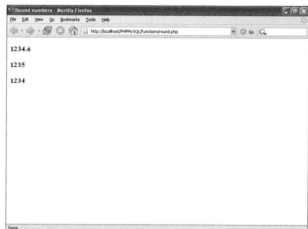

Apply It

If you pass a string to one of the rounding functions, PHP converts the string to zero. The rounding function does not return an error. Instead, it returns the rounded value, zero.

TYPE THIS
| ```
$string = "abc";
$result = round($string);
``` |

→

RESULT
$result **contains a** 0 **(zero).**
```

Find the Largest or Smallest Number

You can find the largest or smallest number in a set of numbers using the `max()` or the `min()` function. You can pass the functions either an array or a set of individual numbers.

To find the largest number in an array, use the `max()` function with an array, as follows:

```
$num_large = max($array);
```

After the function runs, `$num_large` contains the largest value found in an array element. To find the largest number of a set of numbers, pass the numbers to the `max()` function, as follows:

```
$num_large = max($num1,$num2,$num3,...);
```

You can pass either numbers or variable names. You can pass as many numbers as you need to evaluate.

To find the smallest number in an array, pass the array to the `min()` function, as follows:

```
$num_small = min($array);
```

After the function runs, `$num_small` contains the smallest value found in an array element. To find the smallest number of a set of numbers, pass the numbers to the `min()` function. You can pass either numbers or variable names. You can pass as many numbers as you need to evaluate.

If you pass strings to either function, the function will evaluate the first character in the string based on its ASCII value. The relative values are that numbers are lowest, uppercase letters are next, and lowercase letters are highest.

Find the Largest or Smallest Number

① Create two or more arrays with numbers and strings.

② Create two or more variables containing numbers.

③ Type a variable name for the output.

④ Type **= max( );**.

⑤ Type an array name containing numbers.

⑥ Echo the variable named in step 3.

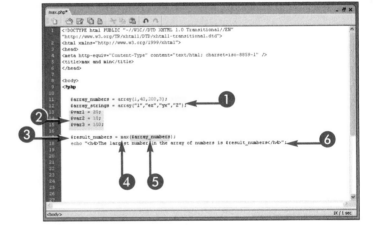

⑦ Repeat steps 3 to 4.

⑧ Type an array name that contains strings.

⑨ Echo the results.

⑩ Repeat steps 7 to 9, substituting `min` for `max`.

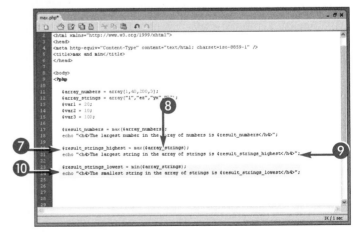

118

⑪ Type a variable name.

⑫ Type **= min( );**.

⑬ Type two or more variable names.

⑭ Echo the results.

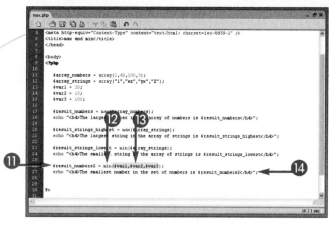

⑮ View the script in a browser.

The results from the `min()` and `max()` functions are displayed.

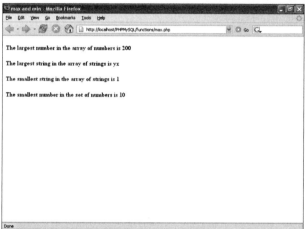

Apply It

If you pass variables, rather than an array, to the `min()` or `max()` function, you must pass at least two variable names.

TYPE THIS

```
$var1 = 10;
$result = min($var1);
```

RESULT

The following error message is displayed:

Warning: Wrong parameter count for min()

Remove Leading and Trailing Blank Spaces

PHP provides several functions that can remove leading and trailing blank spaces from a string. Blank spaces can be undesirable when matching strings, requiring the same number of leading and/or trailing spaces. Removing the blank spaces that users often accidentally type into a form field simplifies form processing.

You can remove the blank spaces from the end of a string with the rtrim() function, as follows:

```
$trimmed = rtrim($string);
```

You can remove the blank spaces from the beginning of a string with the ltrim() function, as follows:

```
$trimmed = ltrim($string);
```

You can remove the blank spaces from both the beginning and the end of a string with the trim() function, as follows:

```
$trimmed = trim($string);
```

The trim() function removes several characters: spaces, tabs, new lines, carriage returns, NULL bytes, and vertical tabs. If you do not want to remove all these characters or if you want to trim additional characters, you can specify the set of characters that trim() should remove with a second parameter, as follows:

```
$trimmed = trim($string, " \t");
```

When this statement is executed, blank spaces and tabs are removed.

Remove Leading and Trailing Blank Spaces

1 Create a variable containing a string with blank spaces and other characters on the end.

2 Type a variable name.

3 Type = **rtrim( );**.

4 Type the variable name from step 1.

5 Type the characters to remove, enclosed in quotes.

6 Echo the trimmed string.

7 View the script in a browser.

The trimmed string is displayed.

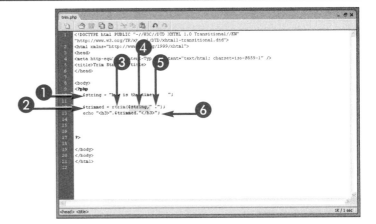

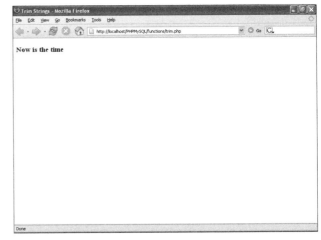

Change the Case of a String

You can change a lowercase string to uppercase or an uppercase string to lowercase. PHP provides two functions to change the case: strtolower() and strtoupper(). To change a string to all uppercase characters, use the following format:

```
$string_upper = stringtoupper($string);
```

To change a string to all lowercase characters, use the following format:

```
$string_lower = stringtolower($string);
```

You can change the first character of a string to uppercase with the ucfirst() function, as follows:

```
$sentence = ucfirst($string);
```

The function does not change the case of any character except the first character of the string.

You can change the first character of every word to uppercase with the ucword() function, as follows:

```
$sentence = ucword($string);
```

The function does not change the case of any character except the first character of each word. A *word* in this case means any string of characters following a blank space, a tab, or a new line character. The first character after each white space character is changed to uppercase.

You can ensure that a string is formatted as a sentence by using two functions, as follows:

```
$sentence = ucfirst(strtolower($string));
```

The strtolower() function changes all the characters to lowercase, and then the ucfirst() function changes the first character of the string to uppercase.

Change the Case of a String

① Create a variable containing a string with mixed-case characters.

② Type a variable name for the output.

③ Type **= strtoupper( );**.

④ Type the name of the variable from step 1.

⑤ Echo the string.

⑥ Add a statement that uses two functions to first change the case to lower and then change the first character to uppercase.

⑦ Echo the string.

⑧ View the script in a browser.

The string converted to uppercase is displayed.

● The string converted to lowercase with the first character changed to uppercase is displayed.

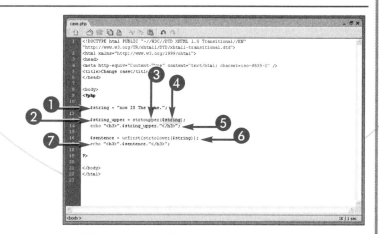

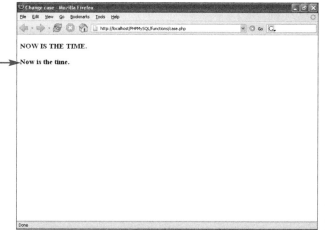

Format a String

The output of an echo or a print statement is always a string, even if the output statement included a variable containing a number. You can format the string for output using the printf() or sprintf() functions. printf() outputs the formatted string; sprintf() stores the formatted string in a variable. You can format strings or numbers, or both together, including variable values. The general format for both functions is

```
$result = printf("format",$varname1,
$varname2,...);
```

After the function executes, $result contains the length of the formatted string. When you use sprintf(), $result contains the formatted string. The *format* parameter specifies the format for the output, including any literal output; the variable name(s) contain the values to be formatted.

The *format* parameter has literal strings and format instructions for outputting the values. A format instruction for a value contains the following components, in the following order:

%pad-width.dectype

The % sign signals the start of the formatting instructions. *pad* is a padding character that is used to fill out the string when the value to be formatted is smaller than the width assigned. A space is used by default, but you can specify a 0 or any character preceded by a single quote. The - character is a symbol meaning to left-justify the characters. If - is not included, the characters are right justified. *width* is the number of characters to use for the value. The .*dec* is a single instruction specifying how many decimal places to use for a number. *type* is a symbol that specifies the type of value. In most cases, use s for string. Use f (float) for numbers that you want to format with decimal places.

Format a String

1. Type **printf( );**.

2. Add a string inside the parentheses.

Note: This statement outputs only a literal, so no format parameter is needed.

3. Create a variable containing a string.

4. Type **printf( );**.

5. Add a literal string.

6. Add a format instruction for the variable.

7. Add the variable name.

8. Create at least one string variable and one numeric variable.

9. Type **printf( );**.

10. Type some literal characters for the output.

11. Insert a format instruction for a number.

12. Insert a format instruction for a string.

13. Add the variable names, separated by commas.

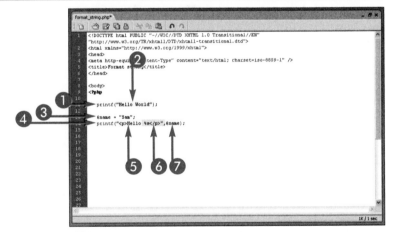

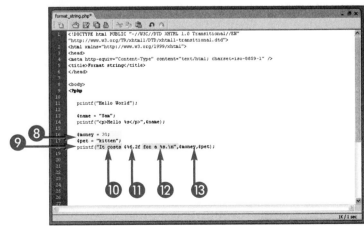

⑭ Type **printf( );**.

⑮ Add literal characters and format instructions.

In this case, %'.-20s is the instruction for the string: '. is the fill character, - means right justified, and 20 is the width.

⑯ Add the variable names, separated by commas.

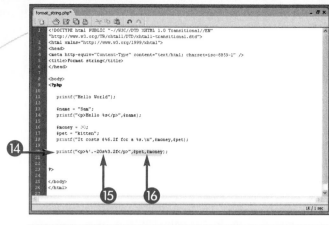

⑰ View the script in a browser.

Each printf() statement displays a line on the Web page.

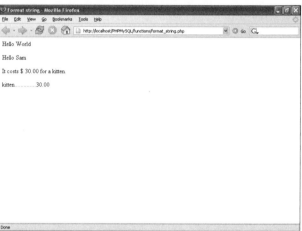

Extra

PHP provides a function that accepts an array of values to format. The function vprintf() operates the same as printf(), except that it accepts an array. Like printf(), it returns the length of the formatted string.

TYPE THIS

```
$array = array("dog","30.00");
vprintf("<p>%'.-20s%3.2f</p>",$array);
```

RESULT

The following string:

```
dog.................30.00
```

Count the Characters or Substrings in a String

You can find the length of the string with the function `strlen($string)`.

You can find out which characters are in a string and how many of each character with the function `count_chars()`, as follows:

```
$array = count_chars($string, mode);
```

If you do not include a mode, the default is 0, which returns an array with an element for every ASCII value from 0 to 255, with the ASCII value as the key and the number of times the character occurs in the string as the value. Mode 1 returns an array that contains only the elements that exist in the string. Mode 2 returns an array containing only the values that do not exist in the string.

Mode 3 returns a string containing one each of the characters that exist in the original string, in the order of their ASCII value. Mode 4 returns a string similar to mode 3, only it contains the characters that do not exist in the original string.

The `count_chars()` function is handy for checking that users have created a password composed of a specified number of unique values.

You can find out how many times a substring appears in a string with the function `substr_count()`, as follows:

```
$count = substr_count($string, 'text');
```

After the function finishes, `$count` contains the number of times that *text* appears in the string. You can search for one character or a string of characters.

Count the Characters or Substrings in a String

① Create a variable that contains a string.

② Type a variable name.

③ Type **= substr_count( );**.

④ Type the variable name that contains the string.

⑤ Type a string of characters.

⑥ Echo the result.

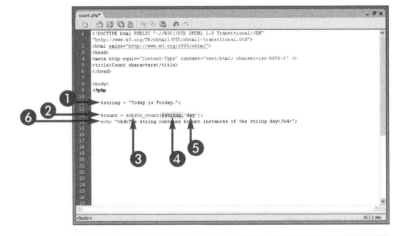

⑦ Type a variable name.

⑧ Type **= count_chars( );**.

⑨ Type the variable name that contains the string.

⑩ Type **3**.

⑪ Echo the results.

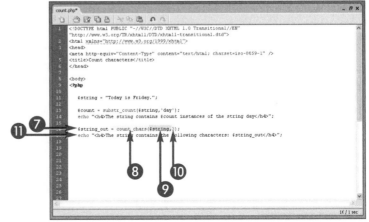

⓬ Type a variable name.

⓭ Type **= count_chars( );**.

⓮ Type the variable name that contains the string.

⓯ Type **1**.

⓰ Echo the results.

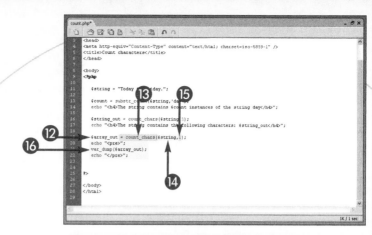

⓱ View the script in a browser.

The output from the three functions is displayed.

Extra

You can find the length of a substring that contains specified characters with the strspn() function. You can specify the character position and length of the string to search for the characters. The first position specified must contain one of the specified characters or the function returns 0. The function strcspn() works similarly, except it finds the length of the string that does not match any of the specified characters.

TYPE THIS

```
$string = "My phone number is 555-5555";
$result = strspn($string,'12345',19,2);
```

→

RESULT

$result contains 2. The search begins at character 19, which is the first 5, and searches two characters. The two characters in character positions 19 and 20 are fives.

Locate a Substring in a String

You can determine whether a substring exists in a string and where it is located using the `strpos()`, `stripos()`, `strrpos()`, and `strirpos()` functions. The functions search a string for a specified substring and return an integer that is the character position where the string begins. If the string is not found, the functions return FALSE.

You can use the `strpos()` function to find the first occurrence of a substring in a string, as follows:

`$location = strpos($string,'text',start);`

The first parameter is the string to be searched. The `text` is the substring that you are searching for. Starting with PHP 5, `text` can be one character or a string; in PHP 4, `text` must be one character. The `start` parameter is an integer that is the character position where the search

should start. If you do not include `start`, the search starts at the first character in the string, which is position zero. If you specify a negative number, the search stops at the specified character location.

You can use the `strrpos()` function to find the last occurrence of a substring in a string. The format is similar to the `strpos()` function, with three parameters. The `start` parameter can be a positive number, as described above, or a negative number. The function returns the position number of the first character of the last occurrence of the substring. If the substring is not found, the function returns false.

The functions `strpos()` and `strrpos()` are case sensitive — a does not match A. You can conduct a case-insensitive search using the functions `stripos()` and `strirpos()`. With these functions, a and A are matching characters.

Locate a Substring in a String

① Create a variable containing a string with mixed case.

② Create a variable containing a substring of the string in step 1.

③ Type a variable name, followed by **= strpos( );**.

④ Type the variable names from steps 1 to 2.

⑤ Type an integer.

In this example, the integer is 1, which means that the function starts searching at the second character in the string.

⑥ Echo the result.

⑦ Type a variable name, followed by **= strrpos( );**.

⑧ Type the variable names from steps 1 to 2.

⑨ Type a negative integer.

Note: A negative integer indicates that the search ends at the specified character position.

⑩ Echo the result.

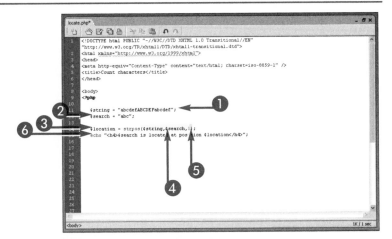

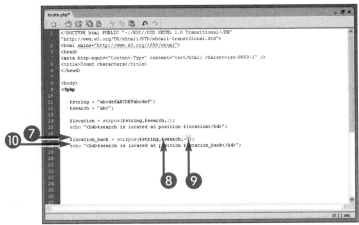

11 Type a variable name, followed by
= stripos( );.

12 Type the variable names from steps
1 to 2.

13 Type an integer.

14 Echo the result.

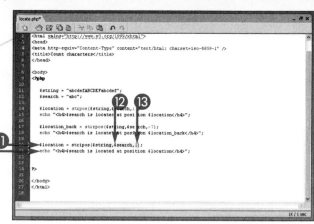

15 View the script in a browser.

The location of the substring as
returned by the three functions is
displayed.

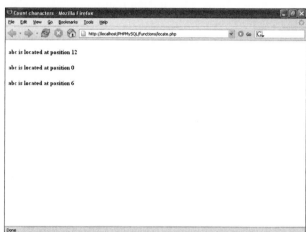

Apply It

The functions return zero when the substring begins at the first character of the string. When using the
function in an `if` statement, a 0 can be interpreted as FALSE. To ensure a correct match when the substring
is not found, use the identity operator (three equal signs).

TYPE THIS

```
if(strpos($string,$substring) === false)
{
    echo "String not found";
}
```

RESULT

The `if` block executes only if FALSE is returned.

Get a Substring

Y ou can get a substring from a string. You can use the functions strstr() and strstri() to get a string beginning with specific characters, as follows:

```
$sub_string = strstr($string,'text');
```

The function searches for *text* and returns all the characters from the beginning of *text* to the end of the string. If *text* is not found, the function returns FALSE. The search is case sensitive, meaning that a is not equal to A. You can use strstri() to perform a search that is not case sensitive — a is equal to A.

You can return a substring based on its position in a string with the substr() function, as follows:

```
$sub_string = substr($string,start,len);
```

The parameter *start* is an integer that specifies the character position where the substring begins. The first character in the string is zero. You must specify at least the first two parameters, or the function displays the following warning:

Warning: substr() expects at least 2 parameters, 1 given

The *len* is an integer that specifies the length of the substring. If you do not specify *len*, the function returns the substring from *start* to the end of the string. If you specify a negative number for *len*, the substring goes from *start* to *len* characters from the end of the string.

Get a Substring

① Create one or more variables containing strings.

② Type a variable name, followed by = strstr( );.

③ Add a variable name from step 1.

④ Add a string to search for.

⑤ Echo the substring.

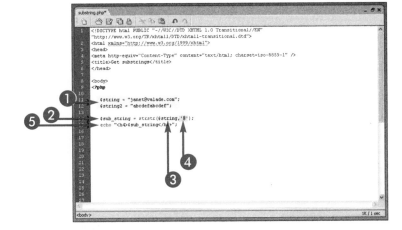

⑥ Type a variable name, followed by = strrchr( );.

Note: See the Extra section for information about strrchr().

⑦ Add a variable name from step 1.

⑧ Add a string to search for.

⑨ Echo the substring.

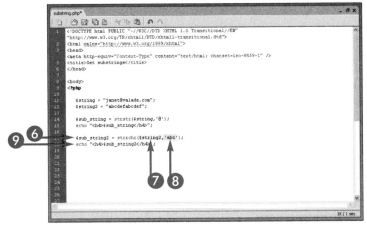

10 Add a call to function `substr()`.

11 Add a variable name from step 1.

12 Type an integer.

13 Type a second integer.

14 Echo the substring.

15 Repeat steps 10 to 12.

16 Type a negative integer.

17 Echo the substring.

18 View the script in a browser.

The substrings are displayed.

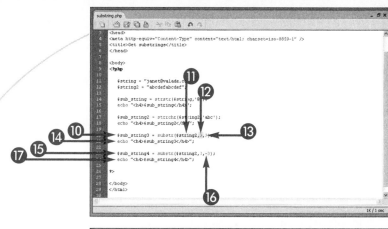

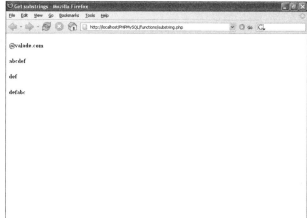

Done

Extra

The function `strchr()` is an alias for `strstr()`.

TYPE THIS		RESULT
`$string = "myabcxxabcqu";` `$sub_string = strchr($string,'abc');`	→	`$sub_string` contains abcxxabcqu, the characters from the beginning of the first occurrence of abc to the end of the string.

You can search for the last occurrence of a substring with the function `strrchr()`.

TYPE THIS		RESULT
`$string = "myabcxxabcqu";` `$sub_string = strrchr($string,'abc');`	→	`$sub_string` contains abcqu, the characters from the beginning of the last occurrence of abc to the end of the string.

Find and Replace Substrings

You can find and replace all the occurrences of a substring in a string with the str_replace() function, as follows:

```php
$newstring = str_replace('substring', 'newtext',$string);
```

The function searches through $string, replaces every occurrence of *substring* with *newtext*, and returns the changed string. Beginning in PHP 5, you can include a fourth parameter — a variable name — in the function call, such as $count. After the function executes, the variable contains an integer that is the number of replacements that were made.

You can replace single characters in a string with the function strtr(), as follows:

```php
$newstring = strtr($string,'chars', 'newchars');
```

Both *chars* and *newchars* are strings of one or more characters that are replaced in order. The first character in *chars* is replaced by the first character in *newchars*, the second character in *chars* is replaced by the second character in *newchars*, and so on. If one string is longer than the other, the extra characters are ignored.

The function strtr also accepts two arguments, as follows:

```php
$newstring = strtr($string,$array);
```

In $array, the text to be changed is the key of each element, and the new text is the value of each element. For example, if the array contains an element, $array['abc']=cba, all occurrences of abc are changed to cba.

Find and Replace Substrings

① Create a variable containing a string.

② Create two variables containing the text to find and the replacement text.

③ Type a variable name for the new string, followed by **= str_replace( );**.

④ Type the variable names from step 2.

⑤ Type the variable name from step 1.

⑥ Type a variable name to contain the count.

⑦ Echo the count and the new string.

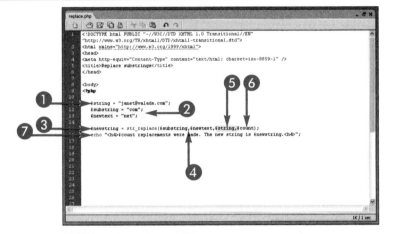

⑧ Type a variable name for the new string, followed by **= strtr( );**.

⑨ Type the variable name from step 1.

⑩ Type a string of characters to be replaced.

⑪ Type a string of characters to replace them.

⑫ Echo the new string.

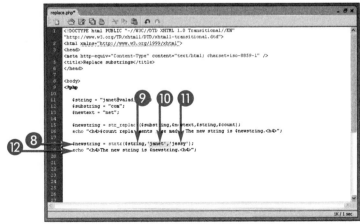

⑬ Create an array.

Note: The keys are strings to be replaced, and the values are the replacement values.

⑭ Add a function call to `strtr`.

⑮ Type the variable name from step 1.

⑯ Type the array name from step 13.

⑰ Echo the new string.

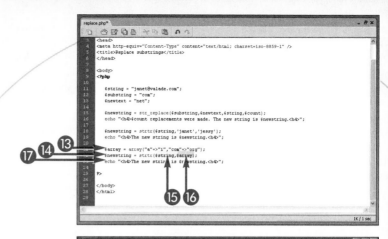

⑱ View the script in a browser.

The changed strings are displayed.

Extra

The function `str_replace()` accepts arrays for the substring and the text to replace the substring. If you pass an array for the substring, the function searches for each element in order and replaces it with the new text if the new text is a string or, if the new text parameter is an array, with each element of the new text array. When both the substring and the new text are arrays, if the new text array has fewer elements than the substring array, an empty string replaces the extra substring elements.

TYPE THIS

```
$string = "Go up the stairs and turn left";
$substring = array("up","left");
$newtext = array("down","right");
$new_string = str_replace($substring,$newtext,$string);
```

RESULT

```
$new_string = Go down the
stairs and turn right
```

Add a Substring to a String

You can add text to a string at a specified position in the string. The text can replace other text in the string or be inserted into the string without replacing any text. The substr_replace() function adds text, as follows:

```
$new_string = substr_replace($string,
'newtext',start,length);
```

The first parameters can be a string, a variable, or an array. The second character can be a string or a variable. The third and fourth parameters must be integers.

The newtext is the text that will replace part of the string or will be inserted into the string. The integer start specifies the first character position where newtext will be added. The integer length specifies the number of characters to be replaced.

You can specify start with a positive or negative number. If the number is positive, the function starts the replacement at the start character position from the beginning of the string, with the first character being zero. If the number is negative, the function starts the replacement at the start character position from the end of the string.

The length parameter is optional. If you do not specify a length, the function replaces the characters from start to the end of the string. You can specify the length with a positive or negative number. If the number is positive, length characters are replaced. If the number is negative, the function stops replacing characters at the specified number of characters from the end of the string.

You can insert text into the string, without replacing any characters, by specifying a length of zero.

Add a Substring to a String

① Create a variable containing a string.

② Create a variable containing new text.

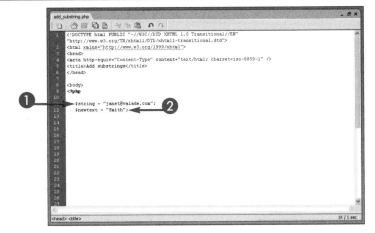

③ Type a variable name for the new string, followed by **= substr_replace( );**.

④ Add the variable name from step 1.

⑤ Type a string to add to the current string.

⑥ Type an integer.

⑦ Type another integer.

⑧ Echo the new string.

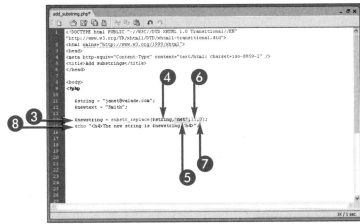

9 Repeat steps 3 to 6.

10 Type 0.

11 Echo the new string.

12 Repeat steps 3 to 4.

13 Type the variable name from step 2.

14 Type an integer to start the replacement.

15 Type a negative integer.

16 Echo the new string.

17 View the script in a browser.

The new strings are displayed.

In this example, the first function call replaced the last three characters, the second call inserted three characters, and the third call ended the replacement three characters from the end of the string.

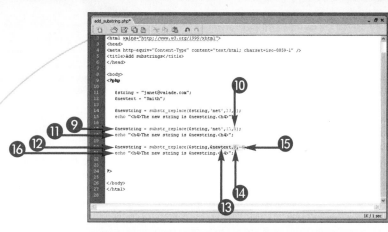

Extra

The function `substr_replace()` accepts an array as the string to be changed. When an array is passed, the function changes each element in the array and returns an array with the changed strings. The return array has numbers for keys, regardless of the keys in the array that was passed to the function.

TYPE THIS

```
$array = array("abcdef","ghijkl");
$new_string = substr_replace($array,'xx',3,0);
```

RESULT

`$new_string` is an array with two elements: `abcxxdef` and `ghixxjkl`.

133

Using Regular Expressions to Replace Text

You can search for patterns, called *regular expressions,* in a string and replace them with new text. Regular expressions, often called *regex,* are described in Chapter 4.

PHP supports two types of regular expressions: POSIX and Perl-compatible. POSIX regular expressions are less powerful than the Perl-compatible functions but are easier to use and read. The functions that support POSIX regular expressions begin with ereg; the functions that support Perl-compatible regular expressions begin with preg.

You can use the function ereg_replace() to find and replace text that matches a regular expression, as follows:

```
$new_string = ereg_replace('regex',
'newtext',$string);
```

The parameters passed can be strings or variables. The function searches the string for matches to regex, which

it replaces with newtext. The function returns the modified string. If no matches are found for regex, the original string is returned, unchanged.

The function ereg_replace() is case sensitive, meaning that it does not consider A to be equal to a. You can modify the string with the function eregi_replace(), which is not case sensitive.

The functions preg_replace() and pregi_replace() operate the same as ereg_replace() and eregi_replace(), except that they support the extra features available with Perl-compatible regular expressions. The functions created to handle POSIX regular expressions do not recognize some of the extra symbols and features used in Perl-compatible regular expressions. For example, POSIX regular expressions are designed for use only with textual data, not binary characters.

Using Regular Expressions to Replace Text

❶ Create a variable containing a string to be modified.

❷ Create a variable containing a regex.

❸ Create a variable containing the string to replace the text that matches the regex.

❹ Type a variable name for the new string, followed by = **ereg_replace( );**.

❺ Type the variable name from step 2.

❻ Type the variable name from step 3.

❼ Type the variable name from step 1.

❽ Echo the new string.

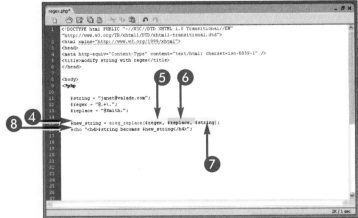

9. Store a new regex in the same variable name.

10. Store a new replacement string in the same variable name.

11. Repeat steps 4 to 8.

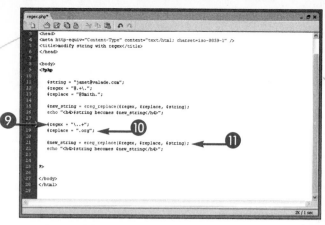

12. View the script in a browser.

The new strings are displayed.

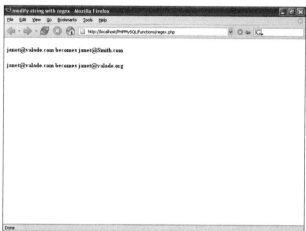

Apply It

The functions `ereg_replace()` and `eregi_replace()` handle an integer as the replacement text in a way you may not expect. If the replacement text is a number rather than a string, the functions treat the number as the ASCII value of a character. Thus, the character that replaces the regex may not be what you thought it would be.

TYPE THIS

```
$replace = 33;
$string = "I am thirty-three years old.";
$new_string = ereg_replace('thirty-three',
$replace, $string);
```

RESULT

`$new_string` contains the string

`I am ! years old.`

because 33 is the numeric code for an exclamation point. For this to work correctly, you need to assign a string to `$replace`, as in `$replace = '33';`

Pad or Repeat a String

You can add one or more strings or characters to a string to increase the length of the string to a specified length, called *padding the string*. You can use the function str_pad() to pad the end or the beginning of the string with a specific character or string of characters, as follows:

```
$new_string = str_pad($string, length,
'pad', position);
```

Only the first two parameters are required. The parameter *length* is an integer that is the length of the string after it is padded. If *length* is negative or less than the length of the original string, no padding is added.

The third parameter, which is optional, is the character or string that you want to use to pad the string. If you do not include a pad character, the function adds blank spaces by default.

The last parameter is an optional constant that determines the location where the padding is to be added. You can specify STR_PAD_RIGHT, STR_PAD_LEFT, or STR_PAD_BOTH. If *position* is not specified, STR_PAD_RIGHT, padding on the end, is the default.

You can create a string that consists of a substring repeated a specified number of times with the function str_repeat(), as follows:

```
$new_string = str_repeat($string, repeat);
```

The *repeat* parameter is an integer specifying the number of times the string should be repeated. After the function executes, $new_string contains $string repeated *repeat* number of times. If *repeat* is zero, the function returns an empty string. If *repeat* is a negative number, a warning message is displayed.

Pad or Repeat a String

① Create a variable containing a string.

② Type a variable name for the new string, followed by **= str_repeat( );**.

③ Add the variable name from step 1.

④ Type an integer for the number of times to repeat the string.

⑤ Echo the new string.

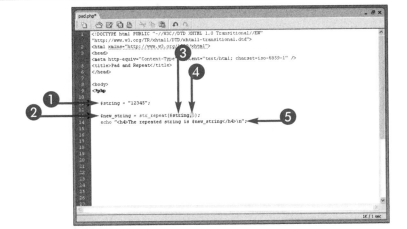

⑥ Type a variable name for the new string, followed by **= str_pad( );**.

⑦ Type the variable name from step 1.

⑧ Type an integer that is the length to pad the string.

⑨ Type a character to pad the string with.

⑩ Echo the new string.

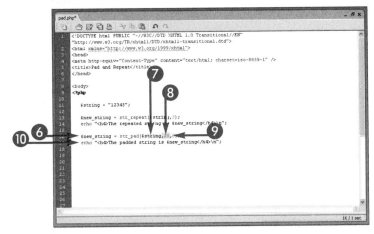

11 Repeat steps 6 to 9.

12 Type a constant that determines the padding location.

In this example, the constant is STR_PAD_BOTH.

13 Echo the new string.

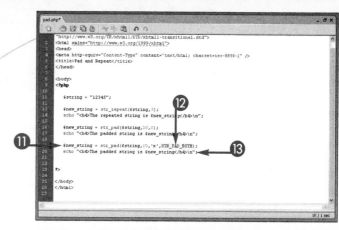

14 View the script in a browser.

The script displays the new string.

● In this example, the second function pads with a zero in the default location.

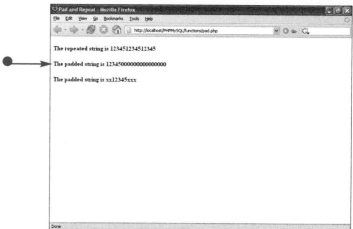

Apply It

The function str_pad() pads the string to a specified length. When you pad with a string, the string is truncated when it reaches the specified length. Sometimes you need to pad with the exact number of characters so that the string is not truncated. You can do this by using the length of the string when specifying the length of the padded string.

TYPE THIS

```
$string = "Indent this line";
$pad = " ";
$new_string = str_pad($string,strlen
($string)+3*strlen($pad),$pad,STR_PAD_LEFT);
```

RESULT

$new_string contains the following string:

   Indent this line

137

Convert a Character to and from an ASCII Value

You can work with ASCII values in a PHP script. ASCII stands for American Standard Code for Information Interchange and is a system that helps standardize the values of characters for portability across computer systems and languages.

Characters stored as ASCII text are mapped to numeric character codes. The ASCII system contains 127 codes for standard characters. An extended ASCII set contains 255 codes. Each character has an associated ASCII value, including special control characters and white space characters, such as the tab character. You can see an ASCII table at www.asciitable.com.

PHP provides the ord() function that returns the ASCII character code when passed a character, as follows:

```
$ascii_code = ord('char');
```

The variable $ascii_code contains an integer that is the ASCII numeric value of char. If you pass a string to the function, it returns the ASCII numeric value of the first character in the string.

You can convert an ASCII numeric code into the character it represents with the chr() function, as follows:

```
$char = chr(code);
```

After the function executes, $char contains the character represented by code. You can pass either an integer or a string to the function.

Convert a Character to and from an ASCII Value

① Create a variable that contains a character.

② Create a variable that contains a number.

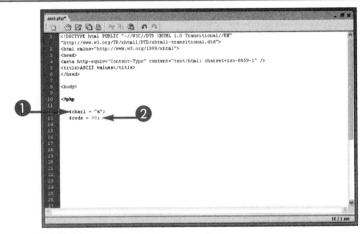

③ Type a variable name for the ASCII value.

④ Type = **ord( );**.

⑤ Type the variable name from step 1.

⑥ Echo the ASCII value.

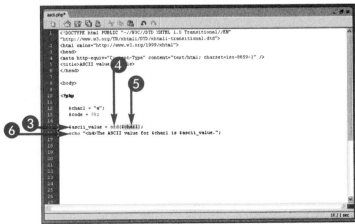

7 Type a variable name for the character.

8 Type = chr( );.

9 Type the variable name from step 2.

10 Echo the character.

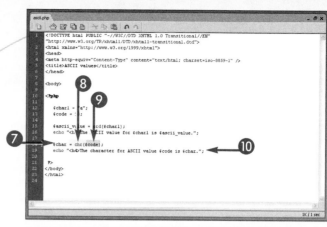

11 View the script in a browser.

The conversion characters are displayed.

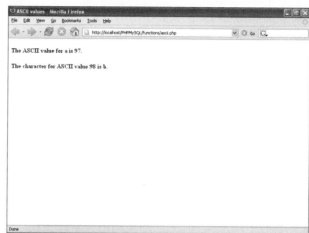

Extra

You can also convert an ASCII numeric code into its character with the sprintf() function by using the c conversion code in the format. The sprintf() function is described earlier in this chapter in the section "Format a String."

TYPE THIS
| ```
$code = 99;
$char = sprintf('%c',$code);
``` |

RESULT
$char contains the character for the ASCII code 99, which is c.
```

Compare Strings

You can compare strings to see whether they are the same using the strcmp() function, as follows:

```
$result = strcmp($string1,$string2);
```

If $string1 is less than $string2, the function returns a number less than zero. If the two strings are equal, the function returns zero. If $string1 is greater than $string2, the function returns a number greater than zero. The strings are compared using their ASCII values, which count uppercase letters as smaller than lowercase letters. Each character position in the string is compared until a difference is found. Thus, aac is smaller than abb. If characters are otherwise equal, the longer string is larger.

You can compare a specified number of characters in the string using the strncmp() function, as follows:

```
$result = strncmp($string1,$string2,n);
```

The function compares the two strings in the same manner as strcmp(), except that it compares only the first n characters of both strings.

The two functions strcmp() and strncmp() compare the strings in a case-sensitive mode — a is not A. You can also compare strings with the functions strcasecmp() and strncasecmp(), which are not case sensitive. strcasecmp() operates like strcmp(), and strncasecmp() behaves like strncmp(), except that the functions are not case sensitive, considering a to be equal to A.

Compare Strings

① Create two string variables, using some lower- and some uppercase letters.

② Create an if statement that tests the two strings using a function.

Note: See Chapter 4 for information about if statements.

③ Type the function call inside the if statement.

In this example, the function call is strcmp($string1,$string2).

④ Type a comparison operator and a value.

In this example, the comparison is < 0.

Note: The output can only be less than 0, 0, or greater than 0.

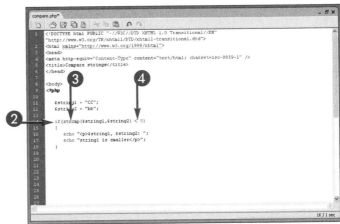

⑤ Add a second `if` statement.

⑥ Type a function call with a different function.

In this example, the function is `strcasecmp`.

⑦ Type a comparison operator and a value.

In this example, the operator and value are `> 0`.

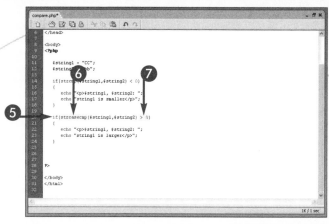

⑧ View the script in a browser.

The output from both functions is displayed.

In this example, the output from the two functions produces different results because the first function is case sensitive and the second function is not.

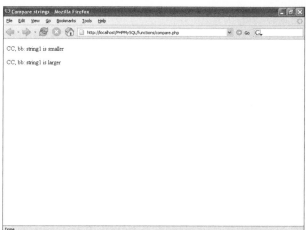

Apply It

The functions that compare strings return 1 when the first string is larger than the second string. You can get misleading results when you use the functions in an `if` statement because, in an `if` statement, 1 is interpreted to mean TRUE.

TYPE THIS

```
if(strcmp('bbb','aaa'))
    echo "The strings are equal";
if(strcmp('bbb','aaa') == 0)
    echo "The strings are equal";
```

RESULT

The first `if` statement evaluates as TRUE and displays `"The strings are equal"`. The second statement compares the two strings correctly and does not evaluate to TRUE.

You can convert a string into an array with each element of the array containing a specified number of characters, as follows:

```
$array = str_split($string,length);
```

The parameter *length* is an integer that specifies the length of the substring stored in each element of the array. If *length* is not included, each character in the string is stored in a separate element of the array. If *length* is less than one, the function returns FALSE. If *length* is greater than the length of the string, the entire string is stored in the only array element. This function was added in PHP 5.

You can convert a string to an array, based on characters specified as the separator, with the explode() function. The string is separated into substrings, and each substring becomes a value in the array. The format is

```
$array = explode('sep',$string);
```

The parameter *sep* specifies a string to use to separate the string into substrings. If *sep* is an empty string, explode() returns FALSE. If *sep* does not exist in the string, the function returns an array with one element with the entire string as its value.

You can convert a string into an array of substrings using a regular expression to define the separator with the function split(), as follows:

```
$array = split('regex',$string);
```

The function operates the same as the explode() function, except that the separator is a regular expression. You can use the spliti() function for a search that is not case sensitive.

Convert a String into an Array

① Create a variable containing a string.

② Type a variable name to contain the array, followed by **= explode( );**.

③ Type a separator.

④ Type the variable name from step 1.

⑤ Display the array.

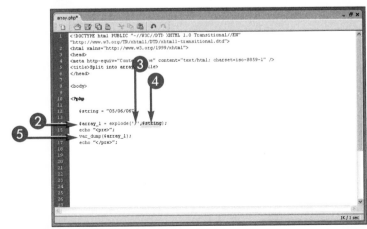

...

⑥ Type a variable name for the array, followed by **= split( );**.

⑦ Type a regex.

⑧ Type the variable name from step 1.

⑨ Display the array.

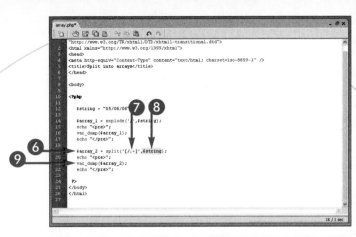

⑩ View the script in a browser.

The arrays are displayed.

In this example, both functions separate a date into its separate components.

Note: In this example, the first function will only separate dates that are formatted with slashes. The second function will separate dates that are formatted with slashes, dots, or hyphens.

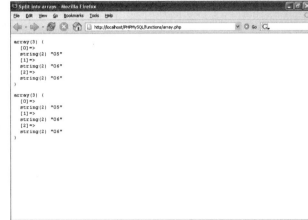

Extra

The explode() and split() functions accept a third parameter that specifies an upper limit on the number of elements in the array. The remainder of the string is then stored in the last element of the array.

TYPE THIS

```
$array = split('[.,]',$string,5);
```

RESULT

Five substrings, separated when a period or a comma is encountered, are stored in the array. The remainder of the string is stored in the sixth element of the array.

Send an Email Message

PHP provides the function `mail()`, which sends email from your PHP script, as follows:

`$result = mail(address,subject,message);`

The parameters can be strings or variables. The `address` is the email address to receive the message, `subject` is the subject line for the email message, and `message` is the content of the email message.

For the `mail()` function to work correctly, you must set up your email configuration in php.ini. The outgoing SMTP server needs to be defined for Windows. The default is `SMTP = localhost`. If you are not running a mail server on your own computer but instead are using the mail server at an ISP (Internet server provider) or your employer's email server, you need to change

`localhost` to the name of the server that you are using. You should be able to find the name in the settings of the mail software, such as Outlook, that you are using, or you can ask your ISP. The name is in a format similar to `mail.ispname.net`. You also need to set up your return address in the `sendmail_from` setting, such as `sendmail_from = Janet@Valade.com`. Beginning with PHP 4.3, a setting for the mail port is available in your php.ini, set to 25 by default.

For Linux and Mac users, the email setting that needs to be correct is `sendmail_path`. During installation, PHP locates the `sendmail` software, if possible, and sets up the default `sendmail_path`. If your `sendmail` software is in your path, PHP is more likely to be able to locate it. In most cases, the default is correct, but you can change the setting if you need to.

Send an Email Message

① Open php.ini in a text editor.

② Scroll down to the `[mail function]` section.

③ Type the name of your SMTP outgoing mail server.

  If you are using Linux, Mac, or UNIX, set `sendmail_path` instead.

④ Type the `from` email address.

  If you are using Linux, Mac, or UNIX, do not set `sendmail_from`.

⑤ Save the file.

⑥ Restart the Web server.

⑦ Create a variable containing the email address to send to.

⑧ Create a variable containing a subject line.

⑨ Create a variable containing the email message.

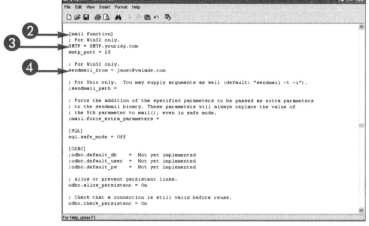

⑩ Type a variable name for the status, followed by **= mail( );**

⑪ Type the variable name from step 7.

⑫ Type the variable name from step 8.

⑬ Type the variable name from step 9.

⑭ Echo the result.

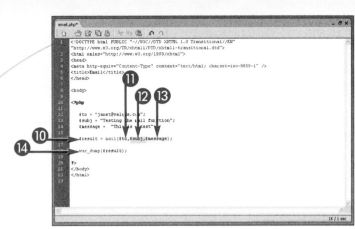

⑮ View the script in a browser.

The output from the mail function shows that the mail was sent successfully.

Note: mail() returns TRUE if the mail was sent successfully and FALSE if it was not.

Extra

A fourth, optional parameter is available in the mail() function that enables you to set the email headers that are sent with your email message, such as From, cc, bcc, and so on. The header parameter is a string of one or more headers, each header ending with \r\n, which is the new line special character.

TYPE THIS

```
$headers = "From:
me@myhome.com\r\nbcc:myboss@mycompany.com\r
\n";
mail('me@myhome.com','Test','This is a
test',$headers);
```

RESULT

→ The email message is sent to me@myhome, which also is the email address in the from line in the email message. A blind copy is sent to my boss's email address.

Send an HTTP Header

Whenever the browser requests a Web page or the Web server sends a Web page to a browser, HTTP messages, called *HTTP headers,* are sent. HTTP is the language that Web servers and browsers use to communicate with one another, sending needed information along with the Web page content, such as date, server, and content length. Most of the communication takes place automatically, behind the scenes. However, in some cases, you may want to send headers manually.

PHP provides the `header()` function that sends a header to the Web server, as follows:

```
header("header");
```

There are many HTTP headers. The Location header, which sends a specified Web page file to the user's browser, is often sent from PHP script. The Location

header is discussed in Chapter 11. Another header sent from a PHP script is the Authentication header, sent when you use the Web server's built-in authentication features, as follows:

```
header('WWW-Authentication: Basic
realm="realmname"')
```

A description of HTTP and all the headers is available at www.w3.org/Protocols/rfc2616/rfc2616-sec14.html.

Headers must be sent before any output is sent. Using a `header()` function in a script after output has been sent is a common mistake. Any HTML code sends a header, so even a single space before the PHP tag (`<?php`) can result in an error message.

You can see the headers that have been sent or are about to be sent using the `header_list()` function. The function returns an array that contains all the headers sent.

Send an HTTP Header

① Type **header( );**.

Note: There is no output before the `header()` function. There is no HTML or blank spaces before the `<?php` tag.

② Type the header to be sent inside the parentheses.

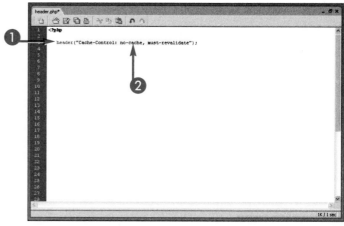

③ Echo the HTML for the Web page.

Note: The HTML cannot be output until after the `header` statement.

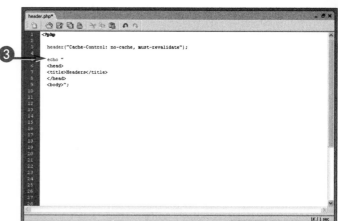

④ Type a variable name for the headers array.

⑤ Type **= headers_list();**.

⑥ Echo the array of headers.

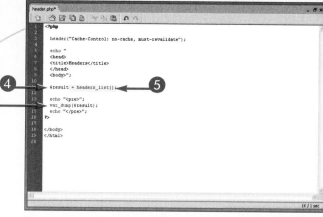

⑦ View the script in a browser.

The array of headers that have been sent is displayed.

● The header sent by the `header()` function in the script is included in the array.

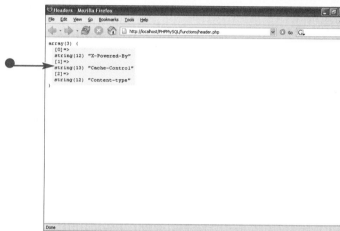

Extra

You can test whether a header has already been sent with the `header_sent()` function.

TYPE THIS

```
if(!header_sent())
{
    header('Location: next_page.php');
}
```

RESULT

If a header has not been sent, the `if` statement executes the `header()` call.

Read Configuration Settings

When your script starts, PHP reads the settings from your php.ini file or uses default settings if it cannot locate the php.ini file, called *global settings*. You can also set *local settings* that apply only to the current script. See the following section, "Set a Local PHP Configuration Option," for information on local settings. You can see the current global and local settings by running a script that contains the statement `phpinfo()`.

You can test the current values of configuration settings with the `ini_get()` function, as follows:

```
$value = ini_get('setting');
```

After the statement runs, `$value` contains the current value for `setting`, where `setting` is the name of a PHP option, such as `include_path` or `log_errors`. If the function fails, `$value` contains FALSE. The PHP online manual provides a list of all the configuration options at www.php.net/manual/en/ini.php#ini.list.

Some configuration options can be set by Apache directives, as well as in the php.ini file. The *access level* indicates where the setting can be changed. The function `ini_get_all()` returns an array containing all elements for all the configuration options. The value for each option is an array containing the global value, the local value, and the access level. The format is

```
$array = ini_get_all();
```

The access levels are returned as integers with the following meaning: 1 — can be set in user scripts or the Windows Registry; 2 — can be set in php.ini or the Apache configuration files .htaccess and httpd.conf; 4 — can be set in php.ini or httpd.conf; or 7 — can be set anywhere.

You can pass an extension name, such as `ini_get_all('mysql')`, and only the configuration options for the extension are returned.

Read Configuration Settings

① Type a variable name for the setting followed by **= ini_get( );**.

② Type the name of a setting that has a string value.

③ Echo the setting value.

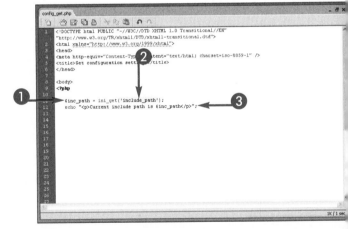

④ Type a variable name, followed by **= ini_get( );**.

⑤ Type the name of a setting that has a Boolean value.

⑥ Echo the setting value.

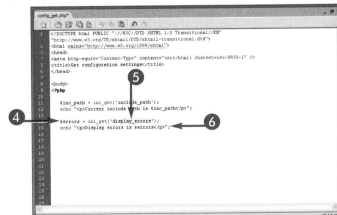

7️⃣ Type a variable name, followed by
= ini_get_all( );.

8️⃣ Type the name of an extension.

In this example, the specified
extension is `mysql`.

9️⃣ Echo the array that is returned by the
function.

🔟 View the script in a browser.

The value of the settings is
displayed.

Note: The value of a Boolean setting is a
string containing 1 or 0.

● The output of `ini_get_all()`
is an array.

Apply It

Some configuration options are Boolean values — on or off. If the setting is off, `ini_get()` returns an empty
string or a string containing zero. If the setting is on, `ini_get()` returns a string containing a 1. When
testing Boolean settings, you can test for both strings.

TYPE THIS

```
if(ini_get('log_errors') == "0" or
ini_get('log_errors') == "")
{
     echo "not set";
}
```

RESULT

If `log_errors` is not set, the `if` block executes.

Set a Local PHP Configuration Option

You can set your PHP configuration options by editing your php.ini file. However, in some cases, you may not have access to the php.ini file, such as when using a Web hosting company. To set configuration options in your script, you can use the `ini_set()` function, as follows:

```
ini_set("setting","value");
```

The function sets the configuration option temporarily, only for the current script. When the script finishes running, the configuration option is returned to the value that is set in the php.ini file.

All the PHP settings are listed in an appendix to the PHP online documentation at www.php.net/manual/en/ini.php#ini.list. The listing includes the default values

for the settings, which are the settings that PHP uses when it cannot find a php.ini file.

Many, but not all, of the PHP options can be set in your script with the `ini_set()` function. The listing of PHP settings shows whether the settings can be changed in your script. If the table column labeled "Changeable" contains PHP_INI_ALL or PHP_INI_USER, the settings can be changed in your script.

The `ini_set()` function returns a value that you can store in a variable, as follows:

```
$result = ini_set('setting','value');
```

If the setting is changed successfully, the old value, which is now changed, is returned. If the setting is not successfully changed, FALSE is returned.

Set a Local PHP Configuration Option

1 Add a statement that gets the value of a configuration setting.

In this example, the value of `include_path` is retrieved.

Note: Functions to get configuration settings are described in the previous section, "Read Configuration Settings."

2 Echo the value of the configuration setting.

3 Type a variable name, followed by = `ini_set( );`.

4 Type the name of the configuration setting.

5 Type the new value.

Note: The new value can be a string or a Boolean value of 0 for off and 1 for on.

6 Echo the value that is returned and stored in the variable in step 3.

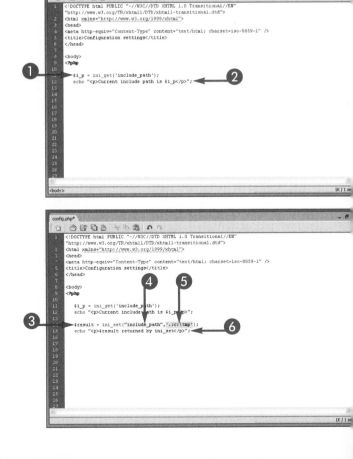

7 Add a statement that gets the value of the same configuration setting.

8 Echo the value of the configuration setting.

The setting should have a new value.

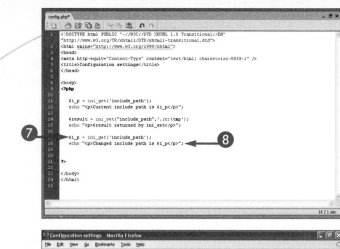

9 View the script in a browser.

The settings are displayed.

● The value returned by `ini_set` is the old value of the setting.

Extra

If you are using the Apache Web server, some configuration options that cannot be set with `ini_set()` can be set locally in a configuration file specific to a directory in your Web site. The file is named .htaccess and is located in the directory containing the scripts that the options should apply to. You use the `php_value` directive for settings with values and the `php_flag` directive for settings that are Boolean — either on or off.

TYPE THIS		RESULT

Add the following to the .htaccess file:
 	
`php_value auto_prepend_file info.inc`
`php_flag log_errors 1`
	→	The settings apply to all scripts in the same directory as the .htaccess file or in its subdirectories.

How a MySQL Database Works

MySQL is a relational database management system (RDBMS) — a system that organizes data into tables that are related to each other. The MySQL software consists of the MySQL server, several utility programs, and some supporting software. The MySQL server is the database manager. It runs all the time, in the background, waiting for instructions. The database is a set of files that contain the data. You can create new databases, add data to databases, and retrieve data from a database by communicating with the server — sending messages that the server executes.

Communicating with the MySQL Server

You can manage your database, retrieve data from it, or add data to it by sending messages to the MySQL server. You communicate using SQL (structured query language), a language developed specifically to interact with databases. You build and send a SQL message, called a *query,* to the MySQL server. The server responds by performing the action defined by the query or, if the server is unable to perform the requested operation, it returns an error message with information about the problem.

The Database Structure

MySQL is an RDBMS, which means that the data is organized into tables. Each database can have many tables. Database tables are organized like other tables that you are familiar with — in rows and columns. Columns are called *fields,* and rows are called *records.*

The focus of each table is an *object,* also called an *entity,* that you want to store information about, such as a customer, a product, or an order. Each entity has *attributes.* In the table, each row represents an entity, and the columns contain the attributes for each entity. For example, in a table of customers, each row contains information for a single customer, such as name, address, and phone number.

You can establish relationships between the tables. Most often, a row in one table is related to several rows in another table. For example, a customer may make more than one order, so the customer row in one table connects to several rows in the order table. A column in one table connects to the related rows in other tables.

The details of setting up a table are explained in the section "Define a MySQL Table," later in this chapter.

The SQL Language

SQL is a simple, English-like language that you can learn quickly. For example, a SQL query that retrieves all the data from a database table is

```
SELECT * FROM Customer
```

The first word of each query is its name, which specifies the action to perform. Some commonly used queries are CREATE, SELECT, DELETE, INSERT, UPDATE, and ALTER. The query name is followed by words and phrases that define the action, such as the table name to be updated or the name of the database to be created.

The SQL words used in this book are capitalized, not because it is required, but to make them easier to recognize. SELECT is the same as select to SQL. However, the parameters, such as table names, must use the correct case if you are on a Linux system. To Linux, Customer is not the same as customer. Windows, however, is not case sensitive.

This chapter and later chapters provide a basic set of SQL queries commonly used with back-end MySQL databases on dynamic Web sites. SQL provides additional SQL queries, which may be needed in other situations. For more information about SQL, see the MySQL online manual section on SQL (http://dev.mysql.com/doc/refman/5.0/en/sql-syntax.html) or search Google for **"SQL tutorial"**.

To interact with your database, you must send a SQL query to the MySQL server. Software that sends messages to a server is called a *client*. When you install MySQL, a text-based `mysql` client is installed with it. You can always use this client to send queries to the server.

MySQL provides the MySQL Query Browser, a graphical shell that you can use to execute SQL queries on your database. The ability to build SQL queries with buttons and drag and drop features, display results, reexecute previous queries, and compare results from various queries makes this program quite useful. Installing the MySQL Query Browser is discussed in Chapter 1. Using the program is discussed in the section "Send a Query with the MySQL Query Browser," later in this chapter.

Some third-party programs are available to administer and manipulate data in MySQL databases. For example, phpMyAdmin is popular, open-source software, which you can download and use without cost from www.phpmyadmin.net.

PHP provides functions that send SQL queries to the MySQL server. You use either the `mysql_query()` or the `mysqli_query()` function, depending on the version of PHP and MySQL, to send your queries to the server. You use additional PHP functions to connect to the server before sending a query and to handle the data/information returned when the query executes.

Currently, three MySQL versions are available: 4.1, 5, and 5.1. Version 5 is the current, stable version that most people should install. MySQL indicates on its Web site which is the current stable version, which may be a later version at the time you are reading this book.

MySQL 4 and 3.23 are stable production-quality versions, but are older, so new features are no longer added to these versions. New releases of these versions are only released to fix extremely critical bugs, such as security issues.

All MySQL releases are classified as *alpha, beta, rc,* or *stable*. An alpha release contains new features that have not been thoroughly tested. Major code changes can occur in an alpha release. A beta release is feature complete. A version changes from alpha to beta when there have been no reported fatal bugs within an alpha release for at least a month, and no new major features are planned. An rc — release candidate — is a beta that seems to be working well for quite a while. Only minor fixes are added. When a release has been run for quite a while with no reports of critical bugs, it is labeled stable — a general availability (GA) release. Only critical bug fixes are applied.

The release classification is added as a suffix to the filename, such as mysql-5.0.12-beta. If a filename has no suffix, it is a stable release.

Database Security

MySQL provides a security system for protecting your data. No one can access the data in your database without a valid MySQL account and password. Someone using an account can only access the database from a specified computer. In addition, each account is specifically allowed or not allowed to perform actions on the data, such as insert data or delete data. Setting up accounts, passwords, and permissions is described in Chapter 8.

Send a Query with the mysql Client

When MySQL is installed, a simple, text-based client program is also installed, called `mysql`. The program accepts and sends SQL queries to the MySQL server for execution. The response is returned to the client and displayed onscreen.

The `mysql` client must be started from the command line. That is, you must be in a command prompt window on Windows or a terminal window on Linux and Mac. To start the program, type `mysql`. If the program is not in your path, you may need to find the program and type the entire path. By default, the `mysql` client program is installed in the subdirectory bin, under the directory where MySQL was installed. In Linux and Mac, that may be /usr/local/mysql/bin or /usr/local/bin. In Windows, the default is C:\Program Files\MySQL\MySQL Server *version*/bin, where *version* may be 5.0.

When you start the client, you may need to use an account and password, unless you have installed an anonymous account. Creating and managing accounts is discussed in Chapter 8. To start the client using an account that has no password, type `mysql -u` *accountname*. To start the client with a password, type `mysql -u` *accountname* `-p`. The client will prompt for the password.

You must tell the client which database you want to use by entering the command `use` *databasename*.

To send a query, type the entire query at the `mysql` client prompt — `mysql>`. End each query with a semicolon (`;`). If you do not end the query with a semicolon, the `mysql` client displays a new prompt and waits for more input. It does not send the query until you type a semicolon.

Type `quit` to exit the `mysql` client program.

Send a Query with the mysql Client

1 Change to the directory where the client is located.

Note: If the client is located in your path, you do not need to perform this step.

2 Start the client by typing **mysql**.

Note: You may need to include an account name (**u accountname**) and/or password (**ppassword**).

● The client starts and displays a prompt.

3 Type **show databases**, followed by **;**, and press **Enter**.

● A list of your existing databases is displayed.

4 Type **use**, followed by the name of a database.

● The client responds that the database is changed.

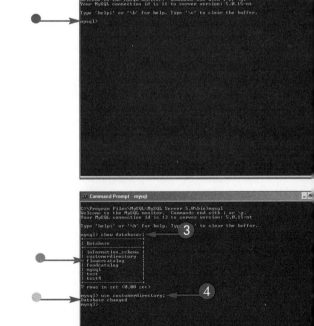

5 Type a query, followed by a semicolon, and press Enter.

In this example, the query is SELECT * FROM tablename;.

tablename is the name of a table in the database.

Note: If you do not know the name of a table in the database, you can type **show tables;** to see the table names.

- The client displays the output from the query.

6 Type **quit** to exit the mysql client program.

- The program displays **Bye**.

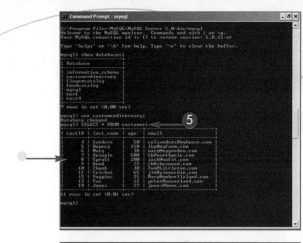

Extra

The MySQL server does not need to be on the same computer as the mysql client program. The client can send the query over a network.

TYPE THIS

```
mysql -h mysqlhost.mycompany.com
-u root -p
```

RESULT

The mysql client connects to the MySQL server on the computer named mysqlhost.mycompany.com using the MySQL account root with a password. The client will prompt for the password.

You can use the mysql client in batch mode. That is, you can create a file that contains SQL queries and send all the queries at once to the MySQL server.

TYPE THIS

```
mysql -u root < queryfile
```

RESULT

If queryfile is a file containing a series of SQL queries, the queries are sent directly to the server and executed. If a problem occurs, the processing of the query file stops, and an error message is displayed. The mysql client never starts in interactive mode.

Send a Query with the MySQL Query Browser

MySQL provides a program called the *MySQL Query Browser* that you can use to send queries to the MySQL server. Downloading and installing the program are described in Chapter 1.

When you start the program, you must select the parameters for the connection, including the host name where the MySQL server is running, a valid MySQL account, a valid password for the account, and the name of the database you want to access. The MySQL default port, 3304, is included. You can change the port number if you need to.

All your databases are listed in the upper-right pane, with the current default database highlighted. You can change the database by right-clicking a name in the schemata panel and clicking Make Default Schema.

You can see the table names for any of your databases by clicking the arrow in front of the database name.

The query bar shows across the top of the window with a query area where you can type any query you want to send. The query area is three lines high by default, but expands and/or scrolls when needed for longer queries. The navigation buttons on the left of the query bar enter the previous or next query into the query area. If you click the History tab in the upper-right panel, a list of your previous queries is displayed. You can double-click any query in your history list to add it to the query area.

To send the query, you can use the Execute command, as described in the steps below, or you can press Ctrl+Enter. The results of the query are displayed in a tabbed window in the main pane.

Send a Query with the MySQL Query Browser

1 Start MySQL Query Browser.

The connection dialog box opens.

2 Type a MySQL account name.

3 Type a password.

4 Type the host name for the MySQL server.

5 Type the name of the database.

6 Click OK.

The program opens.

7 Type a query with an error in it.

8 Click here.

9 Click Execute.

● The Query Browser displays an error message.

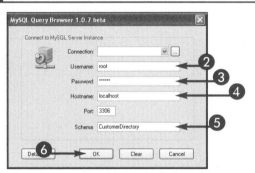

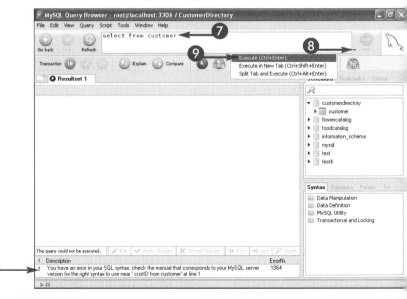

10 Correct the query.

11 Click here.

12 Click Execute.

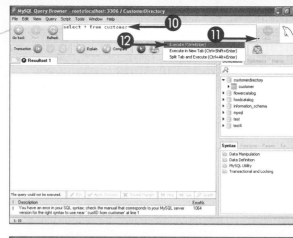

● The results of the query are displayed
   in a tabbed result set.

The error message disappears.

● A summary of the results appears.

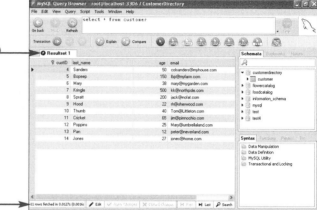

Extra

The Query Browser provides access to several types of help. When you click the Help menu item, a drop-down list of available help is displayed. If you select the first item on the list — Help — a help file, in its familiar format, opens. You can browse or search for information on using the Query Browser. The second item in the Help menu is the Quick Start guide. You can select Online Docs to see the MySQL online documentation or Online Docs - PHP API to see the PHP functions that interact with MySQL. In addition, you can access a list of known bugs or report a bug via Help.

The Query Browser provides documentation of all the query syntax, the functions, and the parameters that you can use in MySQL queries. The lower-right panel contains a list of categories, such as Data Manipulation and Data Definition. If you click a category, a list of items appears under the category. For example, under Data Manipulation, items such as `DELETE`, `SELECT`, and `INSERT` appear. If you double-click an item, documentation for the item opens in a tabbed window in the main pane.

Create, Select, or Remove a MySQL Database

The first step in developing a database for use with your dynamic Web site is to create an empty database. Then, you add one or more empty tables to the database. Finally, you can add data to the tables.

To create an empty database, you can use the following SQL query:

```
CREATE DATABASE databasename
```

The database name must be one word, but can contain underlines. If you uppercase some of the characters in the database name, such as CustomerDirectory, you should use the uppercase letters in SQL queries that include the database name. Linux is case sensitive and will not recognize the name without the uppercase letters. Windows is not case sensitive and does not recognize the difference between Customer and customer, but any scripts that access the database will not work correctly on Linux without the correct uppercase letters.

The MySQL account that you use to create the database must have the necessary privileges, as discussed in Chapter 8. If the account is not allowed to create a database, the following error message is displayed:

```
ERROR 1044 (42000): Access denied for
user 'phpuser'@'localhost' to database
'CustomerDirectory'
```

If you attempt to create a database that already exists, MySQL displays an error message.

Creating a database does not select it. To send queries to a database, you can first send the query USE databasename.

You can remove a database with the following SQL query:

```
DROP DATABASE databasename
```

Create, Select, or Remove a MySQL Database

LIST THE DATABASES

① Send the query show databases.

- The current databases are listed.
- The summary line shows the number of existing databases.

CREATE AN ERROR

② Send the query CREATE DATABASE databasename, where databasename is an existing database.

- An error message is displayed.

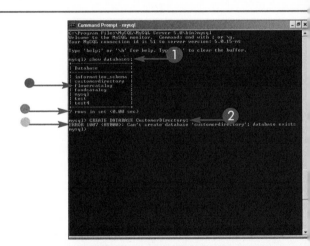

CREATE A DATABASE

③ Send the SQL query CREATE DATABASE databasename, where databasename does not exist.

- A summary line shows that the query was successful.

④ Send the query show databases.

The database list includes the new database created in step 3.

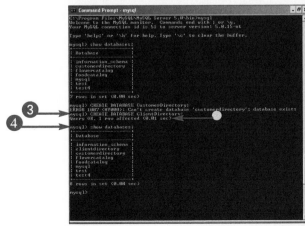

ELECT A DATABASE

5 Type the command **USE *databasename***, where ***databasename*** is the database you just created.

The database is ready to send queries to it, now that it is selected.

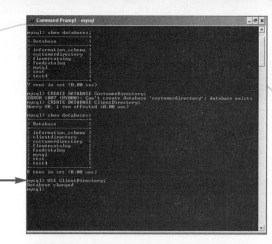

EMOVE A DATABASE

6 Send the query DROP DATABASE *databasename*.

7 Send the query show databases.

The database list does not include the database dropped in step 6.

Extra

As mentioned earlier, creating a database does not select it. Instead of selecting a database as shown in the steps in this task, you can select the database when you start the mysql client by including the database name at the end of the command that starts the client.

TYPE THIS	RESULT
mysql -u user -p CustomerDirectory	The mysql client starts with the database CustomerDirectory already selected. This command will prompt for the password. If you want to include the password in the start command, you insert it after -p with no space before the password, such as -psecret.

Define a MySQL Table

 fter you create an empty database, you need to define its tables. A database can contain as many tables as you need. You use a SQL statement to create an empty table. The SQL defines the table by naming each column and providing a definition for the column.

Table and Column Names

A table or column name can be up to 64 characters long. A column name can include any character that is allowed in a filename for the operating system you are using. A table name can include any characters except a forward slash (/), a backslash (\), or a dot (.).

Reserved words, used in MySQL statements and SQL queries or reserved for future use by MySQL or SQL, cannot be used as column names. A list of reserved words is available online at http://dev.mysql.com/doc/refman/5.0/en/reserved-words.html. If you use a reserved word for a column name, MySQL displays an error, as follows:

```
You have an error in your SQL syntax near 'column name'
at line 1
```

The message tells you which column is causing the problem, but not what the problem is.

Data Types

MySQL can store any type of data. When you create a table, the table definition must specify a data type for each column. The most common types of data are character data, numerical data, and date/time data. Each type can be stored in more than one format. The following are the most common data type formats for MySQL 5:

MYSQL DATA TYPE	DESCRIPTION
CHAR(*length*)	Fixed-length character string.
VARCHAR(*length*)	Variable-length character string, with *length* being the longest possible string.
ENUM ("*val1*","*val2*"...)	Only the listed values can be stored.
BLOB	Variable-length binary string. Its length is limited only by the resources of the computer.
TINYINT	A very small integer with a range from -128 to +127.
SMALLINT	A small integer with a range from -32768 to 32767.
INT(*length*)	A normal-sized integer with a range from -2147483548 to +2147483547. The number is limited by *length*.
MEDIUMINT	A medium-sized integer with a range from -8388608 to +8388607.
BIGINT	A large integer with a range from -9223372036854775808 to +9223372036854775807.
DECIMAL(*length,dec*)	Decimal number where *length* is the number of characters, including decimal points, signs, and exponents, and *dec* is the maximum number of decimal places allowed. For example, 12.34 has a *length* of 5 and a *dec* of 2.
DATE	Date value with year, month, and date, which displays as YYYY-MM-DD.
TIME	Time value with hour, minute, and second, which displays as HH:MM:SS.
DATETIME	The date and time are stored together.
YEAR	Stores a year, which must be within the range 1901 to 2155.

Detailed information regarding MySQL data types is available in the online MySQL manual at http://dev.mysql.com/doc/refman/5.0/en/data-types.html.

The Primary Key

Each row in a table requires a unique identifier. No two rows in a table can contain exactly the same data. The unique identifier for a table is called the *primary key*. The primary key can be one column or more than one column together. When you define your table, you specify which column(s) is the primary key. When you add data to your table, after creating it, MySQL will not allow you to add a new row that has the same primary key as a row already in the table.

Negative Numbers

When you specify an integer format for a column, MySQL sets up the column expecting negative numbers. If you are sure that the number will never be negative, such as a customer ID, you can specify UNSIGNED, and MySQL does not save space for the minus sign. This allows the numbers to get twice as large. For example, if you specify TINYINT, the value can be from -128 to +127. However, if you define the column to be UNSIGNED, the value can be from 0 to 255.

Empty Columns

You can specify that certain columns are not allowed to be empty, or NULL. If you define a column as NOT NULL, MySQL will not create the row if no value is stored in the column. The value can be a blank space or an empty string, but a value must be stored. The primary key must always contain a value, whether you specify NOT NULL or not.

Auto-Increment Columns

You can define a numerical column as an auto-increment column. MySQL populates the column with a sequential number as each row of data is added to the table. You can define a column with the word AUTO_INCREMENT.

MySQL provides a special data type that you can use for an auto-increment column. The type SERIAL defines the column with BIGINT UNSIGNED NOT NULL AUTO_INCREMENT. This data type is often used as a primary key. It assigns sequential numbers handy as ID numbers for orders, customers, and other objects. This data type was added in MySQL 4.1.

Defaults

You can define an optional default value for any column. MySQL will assign the value to a column whenever the column is blank when a row of data is inserted into the table.

Relationships between Tables

Some tables in a database are related to one another. Most often, a row in one table is related to several rows in another table. To connect a row in one table to rows in another table, you create a column in one table to contain data that matches the data in the primary key column of another table. For example, a table containing order information will include a column with an order number. A separate table containing the items in orders will include a column with the order number so that the items can be matched to the order.

Create and Remove a MySQL Table

After you create an empty database, you add one or more empty tables to the database. The data is then stored in a specific table.

When you create a table, you define its structure in a SQL query with the following format:

```
CREATE TABLE tablename (

    columnname1    datatype definitions,

    columnname2    datatype definitions,

...

PRIMARY KEY(columnname1,columnname2,...)    )
```

The definition of each column consists of the column name, followed by the data type and any additional definitions for the column, such as NOT NULL. The previous section, "Define a MySQL Table," describes the data types and column definitions you can use in the SQL query. The column definitions are separated by commas (,). The primary key is specified. All the column definitions are enclosed in parentheses.

The indenting in the format is not required. You can write the query in a single string. However, the indenting makes it easier to decipher the table structure.

You can display a list of the tables that currently exist in your database with the query SHOW TABLES. You can see the structure of an existing table with the query DESCRIBE tablename or EXPLAIN tablename. The columns are listed with their definitions.

You can remove a table with the following query:

```
DROP TABLE tablename
```

DROP is irreversible. After a table is dropped, the table and its data no longer exist.

Create and Remove a MySQL Table

① Create a new database.

Note: See the earlier section "Create, Select, or Remove a MySQL Database."

② Choose the new database.

③ Send the query SHOW TABLES.

  ● The response shows zero tables in the new database.

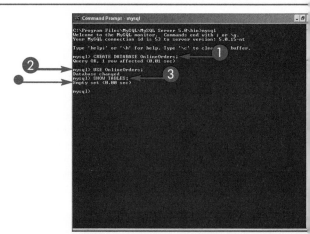

CREATE A TABLE

④ Send a CREATE TABLE query to define a new table.

  ● The response shows that the table was created successfully.

⑤ Send the query EXPLAIN tablename.

The query returns a description of the table structure.

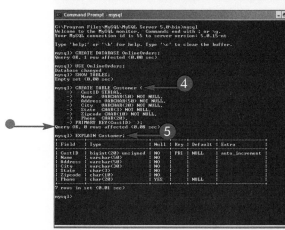

Send a CREATE TABLE query for a second table.

- The second table in this example is connected to the first table by a common column.

Send the query DESCRIBE *tablename*.

The query returns a description of the table structure.

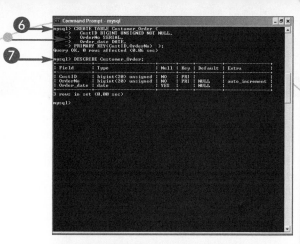

EMOVE A TABLE

Send the query SHOW TABLES.

The two tables just created are listed.

Send the query DROP TABLE *tablename*.

The table is removed from the database.

Send the query SHOW TABLES again.

- The query returns a list of the tables, not showing the table that you just deleted.

Extra

You can create a table with the same structure as another table.

TYPE THIS		RESULT
CREATE TABLE OldCustomer LIKE Customer	→	A new empty table named OldCustomer with the same columns as Customer.

You can create a temporary table. The table exists as long as the current connection to the MySQL server exists. The table ceases to exist when the connection is closed.

TYPE THIS		RESULT
CREATE TEMPORARY TABLE temp1 (Name VARCHAR(20) PRIMARY KEY, City VARCHAR(20))	→	Creates a temporary table, named temp1, with two columns. When the connection closes, such as when you exit the mysql client or the MySQL Query Browser, the temporary table no longer exists.

Modify the MySQL Table Structure

You often need to modify the structure of a MySQL table. You can change the name of the table, add, drop, or rename a column, or change the data type or other definitions of the column. You can use the ALTER query to modify the table, with the following general format:

```
ALTER TABLE tablename changetobemade
```

The changetobemade is one or more SQL words or phrases that specify the change that you want to make. You can change the table name with the following query:

```
ALTER TABLE tablename RENAME newtablename
```

You can add or remove a column with the following queries:

```
ALTER TABLE tablename ADD columnname definition
```

```
ALTER TABLE tablename DROP columnname
```

You can change a column name or definition. Because none of the existing definitions remain when the column is renamed or redefined, you need to redefine the column. You can use one of the following queries:

```
ALTER TABLE tablename CHANGE columnname newcolumnname definition
```

```
ALTER TABLE tablename MODIFY columnname definition
```

The first query changes the column name, defining the new column. If you want to retain the same definition, you need to include the entire definition. The second query changes the definition of a column, applying the new definition. Only the definition specified is applied.

Modify the MySQL Table Structure

① Choose a database.

② Send the query SHOW TABLES.

A list of current table names is displayed.

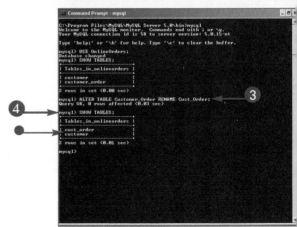

③ Send an ALTER TABLE query to change a table name.

In this example, the query is ALTER TABLE Customer_Order RENAME Cust_Order.

④ Send the query SHOW TABLES.

● The list of current table names shows the changed table name.

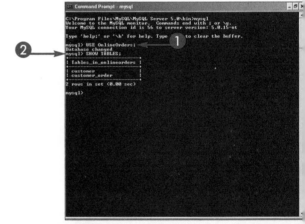

⑤ Send the query DESCRIBE *tablename* to see the current table structure.

A list of column names and definitions is displayed.

⑥ Send an ALTER TABLE query that changes a column definition.

In this example, the query is ALTER TABLE Cust_order MODIFY Order_date DATE NOT NULL, which changes the column to NOT NULL.

⑦ Send the query DESCRIBE *tablename* to see the changed table structure.

The list of columns shows the new definition for the changed column.

Extra

When you send an ALTER TABLE query, or a CREATE TABLE query, you may define columns that MySQL does not allow. In some cases, the definition is silently changed by MySQL. You may change a definition but find that it is not changed when you examine the table structure with DESCRIBE. Some changes that were made silently in MySQL 5.0.2 and earlier versions now produce an error message, beginning with MySQL 5.0.3.

For example, a VARCHAR smaller than four characters is not allowed. Prior to MySQL 5.0.3, it is silently changed to CHAR. As another example, when you have both VARCHAR and CHAR columns in your definition, the CHAR columns longer than three characters are changed to VARCHAR. It does not affect the use of your data; MySQL just stores it differently.

For further details, see http://dev.mysql.com/doc/refman/5.0/en/silent-column-changes.html.

Add a Row of Data to a Database

You can add a row of data to a table with the INSERT query, with the following format:

```
INSERT INTO tablename
(columnname1,columnname2,...) VALUES
(value1,value2,...)
```

The first set of parentheses contains the column names for the data you are adding. The set of parentheses after the word VALUES contains values for the listed columns. MySQL matches the values to the column names in order. That is, MySQL stores the first value in the first column name, the second value in the second column name, and so on. If you do not list the same number of column names and values, the query will fail, and MySQL will return an error. Starting with MySQL 4.1, the word INTO is optional.

If you insert all the columns in order, you can leave out the list of column names, as follows:

```
INSERT INTO tablename VALUES
(value1,value2,value3,...)
```

You need to list column names and provide values for all columns that require values — all columns defined NOT NULL. If you do not provide a value for a NOT NULL column, MySQL will return an error. Columns that do not require a value can be left out of the query, in which case MySQL inserts a default value. If the table definition does not specify a default value for a column, MySQL inserts NULL in any column that accepts NULL, or for columns that do not accept NULL, MySQL inserts zero for numeric columns and an empty string for character columns. For ENUM columns, MySQL inserts the first ENUM value as the default. For date and time data types, MySQL inserts a zero value, such as 0000-00-00.

Add a Row of Data to a Database

1 Select a database.

2 Send the query DESCRIBE *tablename*.

A list of columns with definitions is displayed.

- In this example, only the column Phone allows a NULL value.

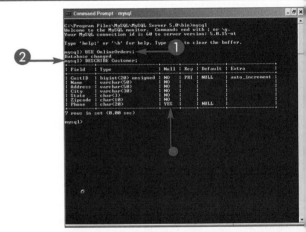

3 Send an INSERT query that does not list a column that is defined NOT NULL.

- MySQL returns an error message and does not add the row of data to the table.

④ Send an INSERT query that does not leave out a
NOT NULL column.

In this example, the query includes the column
names and values for `Name`, `Address`, `City`,
`State`, and `Zipcode`.

In this example, `CustID` is left out because it is
an `AUTO_INCREMENT` column.

● The summary line shows 1 row added.

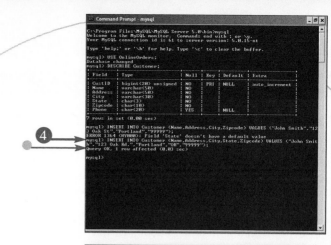

⑤ Send the query `SELECT * FROM tablename`
to see all the data in the table.

Note: See the section "Retrieve Data from a Database"
for information on the `SELECT` query.

● The data in the table is displayed.

Note: `CustID` is an `AUTO_INCREMENT` column.
See the section "Store Incremental Values in
a Column."

Extra

You can insert more than one row at a time by including more than one set of parentheses containing values,
separated by commas.

TYPE THIS		RESULT

`INSERT INTO Customer`
`(Name,State) VALUES`
`("John","OR"),("Joe","TX"),`
`("Bob","NY")`
	→	Three rows of data are added to the table Customer.

You can insert a row of data into a table that you retrieve from a table.

TYPE THIS		RESULT

`INSERT INTO Customer`
`(Name,State) SELECT`
`Name,State FROM`
`OldCustomer`
	→	Two values retrieved from the table OldCustomer by the SELECT query are inserted into a row in the Customer table. SELECT queries are described in the section "Retrieve Data from a Database," later in this chapter.

Add Data from a Text File to a Database

You can add data in a text file to a database table. The data in the text file must be organized in rows and columns. A specific character must separate the columns of data. By default, the query expects a tab character to separate the columns, called a *tab-delimited file.* You can, however, specify a different character as the separator, such as commas for a *comma-delimited file.* Many programs, such as Excel, Access, or Oracle, can output data in delimited files.

The SQL query that reads data from a text file is the LOAD query, with the following format:

```
LOAD DATA INFILE "path/datafilename"
INTO TABLE tablename
```

The query loads data from a text file located on your server. If the filename does not include a path, MySQL

looks for the data file in the directory where your table definition file is located. The file *tablename*.frm is located by default in *mysqlmaindirectory*/data/*databasename*, where *mysqlmaindirectory* is the directory where MySQL is installed and *databasename* is a subdirectory, named with the database name, in the data subdirectory. To use the LOAD query, you must be using a MySQL account that has the FILE privilege, discussed in Chapter 8.

To change the default delimiter, you need to add a clause to the end of the query shown above. The clause is FIELDS TERMINATED BY '*character*'. For example, to read a comma-delimited file, you would add FIELDS TERMINATED BY ',' to the base LOAD query.

Add Data from a Text File to a Database

① Open a file in a text editor.

② Add one or more rows of data.

● In this example, the data in each column is separated by a comma.

③ Save the file.

In this example, the file is saved in the data directory C:\Program Files\MySQL\MySQL Server 5.0\data\OnlineOrders\data1.txt.

④ Select a database.

⑤ Send the query SELECT * FROM *tablename* to see the data currently in the table.

● In this example, the table is empty.

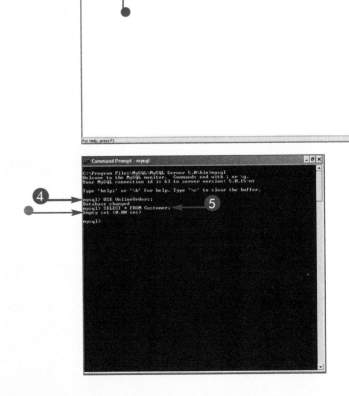

6 Send the LOAD query that loads the data from the file saved in step 3 into a table.

In this example, the data file data1.txt is loaded into the Customer table.

- In this example, the query specifies a comma-delimited file.

- The summary line shows the number of lines added.

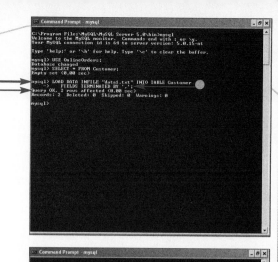

7 Send the query SELECT * FROM `tablename` to see the data now in the table.

- The table now contains the rows from the data file.

Extra

You can also load data from a text file on your local computer by using the word LOCAL. To use LOCAL, both the MySQL server and the client that you are using must be enabled to use it. You need to include a path to the file. Use forward slashes for the path, even on a Windows computer, such as "c:/data/datafile1.txt".

TYPE THIS

```
LOAD DATA LOCAL INFILE
"path/datafilename"
INTO TABLE tablename
```

→

RESULT

The data in `datafilename` is loaded into table `tablename`.

Store Incremental Values in a Column

MySQL provides a column type called AUTO_INCREMENT. When you define an integer column as AUTO_INCREMENT, MySQL adds a sequential number to the column each time a row of data is added to the column. A column of this type is useful when you want a sequential number to identify a row, such as customer IDs or an order number. This column is often used as a primary key.

When you add a row to the table, you can specify a number for the AUTO_INCREMENT column, or you can leave the column name out of the list in the INSERT query, which allows MySQL to add the next number in sequence.

You can specify an integer to begin the sequential series, as follows:

```
AUTO_INCREMENT = 500
```

An AUTO_INCREMENT column does not reuse the sequential numbers. That is, if your table contains the numbers 1, 2, and 3 in the column and you delete the row numbered 1, the column contains 2 and 3. If you then add a row, the new row is numbered 4, not 1.

You can obtain the number that was last added to an AUTO_INCREMENT column by using the LAST_INSERT_ID() function in a SQL query, as follows:

```
SELECT LAST_INSERT_ID()
```

The last number inserted into any AUTO_INCREMENT column in any table in the database is retrieved.

In a PHP script, you can assign the most recent sequential number to a variable with the PHP function mysql_insert_id(), which returns the ID generated for an AUTO_INCREMENT column by the previous INSERT query.

Store Incremental Values in a Column

① Select a database.

② Send a CREATE TABLE query that defines an AUTO_INCREMENT column.

● The summary line shows a successful query.

③ Send the query DESCRIBE tablename.

● The table description shows the AUTO_INCREMENT column.

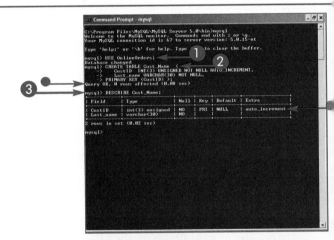

④ Send an INSERT query that adds one or more rows to the table.

⑤ Send the query SELECT * FROM tablename.

The table lists the inserted rows, including the sequential numbers in the AUTO_INCREMENT column.

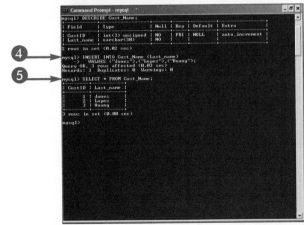

6 Send an INSERT query that adds one row.

7 Send the query SELECT * FROM *tablename*.

The table lists the inserted row.

8 Send the query SELECT LAST_INSERT_ID().

- The sequence number for the last row is displayed.

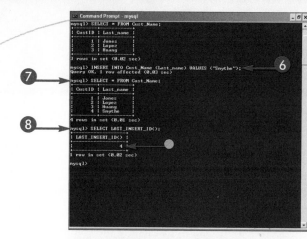

9 Send the query DELETE FROM *tablename* WHERE *columnname* = 2, where *columnname* is the AUTO_INCREMENT column.

10 Send a query to insert a new row.

11 Send the query SELECT * FROM *tablename*.

- Row 2 is gone.
- The new row is assigned a new sequence number, not the deleted number 2.

Extra

MySQL provides a special data type that is often used for an AUTO_INCREMENT column and as a primary key. The type SERIAL defines the column with BIGINT UNSIGNED NOT NULL AUTO_INCREMENT. This data type was added in MySQL 4.1.

TYPE THIS		RESULT
Send the following queries: CREATE TABLE CustomerAge (CustID SERIAL PRIMARY KEY, Age INT(3)) INSERT INTO CustomerAge (Age) VALUES (21)	→	A table with two columns — CustID and Age — that contains one row. In the row, CustID contains 1, and Age contains 21.

Retrieve Data from a Database

You can retrieve information from a database with a SELECT query. The basic query is

```
SELECT colname1,colname2,... FROM tablename
```

This query retrieves the values from all the rows for the specified columns. You can perform mathematical operations on the columns when you retrieve them. You specify the operation, instead of just listing the column, such as colname1 + colname2.

You can change the name of the columns as you retrieve them by adding AS newname after any column name. The data is retrieved and stored as a column named newname. The query has no effect on the data in the database. The new name only applies to the data after it is retrieved.

You can get data from specific rows, such as only rows with customers named Smith, by adding a WHERE clause after the statement shown above. Specifying data with a WHERE clause is described in the next section, "Limit Query Execution to Specific Rows with a WHERE Clause."

You can limit the number of rows that are retrieved by adding LIMIT n at the end of the query, where n is the number of rows to get. You can specify that only one row for each value of a column is retrieved by adding DISTINCT in front of the column name.

You can change the order in which the information is retrieved by adding ORDER BY colname at the end of the query. The data is sorted by colname in ascending order, unless DESC is added to specify descending order.

You can group the rows with GROUP BY colname. The rows with the same value of colname are grouped together.

Retrieve Data from a Database

1. Choose a database.

2. Send the query DESCRIBE tablename.

   The table definition is displayed.

3. Type **SELECT**.

4. Type the columns to select, creating one with a mathematical operation.

   In this case, the columns are Total,Total*.08.

5. Type **AS colname** after the created column.

6. Type **FROM tablename**.

   • The selected and created columns are displayed.

7. Type the same query built in steps 3 to 6.

8. Add **ORDER BY colname** at the end of the query.

   • The columns are sorted by the values in colname.

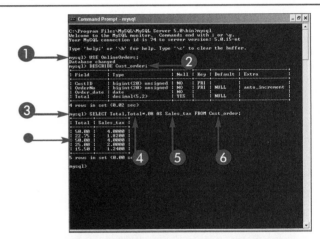

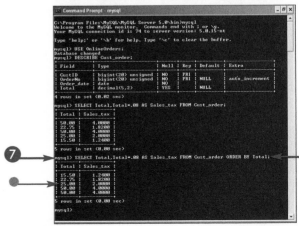

9 Send a SELECT query that selects a column with duplicate values.

In this example, the query is SELECT Order_date FROM Cust_order.

All values are displayed.

10 Send the same query with DISTINCT inserted before the column name.

● Duplicate values are not included in the selected rows.

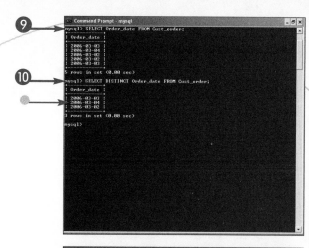

11 Send a SELECT query that selects a column.

All values are displayed.

12 Type the same query and add **ORDER BY colname** to the end.

13 Add **DESC** for descending order.

14 Add **LIMIT value** and send the query.

In this example, value is 3.

● Only the number of rows specified by LIMIT are retrieved.

Extra

You can get information about a column, rather than the actual data that is in the column, using MySQL functions. Some useful numerical functions are AVG(colname) — returns the average of the values in the column; COUNT(colname) — returns the number of column rows that are not blank; and MAX(colname) — returns the highest value in the column. A couple of useful date and time functions are NOW(), which returns the current date and time, and CURR_DATE(), which returns the current date. All MySQL functions are documented in the online manual at http://dev.mysql.com/doc/refman/5.0/en/functions.html.

TYPE THIS

```
SELECT SUM(Price) FROM customer_order
```

RESULT

Gets the sum of all the values in the column named Price.

Limit Query Execution to Specific Rows with a WHERE Clause

You can limit the execution of a query to specific rows using a WHERE clause with the following format:

WHERE *condition* AND|OR *condition* AND|OR *condition* ...

The conditions evaluate to TRUE or FALSE. If you include a single condition, the condition must be TRUE. When you use AND, the conditions on both sides of AND must be TRUE. When you use OR, only one of the conditions connected by OR must be TRUE. Rows that do not match the WHERE condition are ignored. You can use a WHERE clause in a SELECT query, a DELETE query, and an UPDATE query.

Conditions can include the operators =, >, >=, <, <=, and !=. MySQL also provides some words that you can use

in conditions. Some commonly used word conditions are BETWEEN *value1* AND *value2*, IN (*value1*, *value2*,...), and LIKE *value*. You can also specify NOT IN and NOT LIKE.

To specify an exact string, you can use the equal sign (=). To match a simple pattern, you can use the LIKE/NOT LIKE condition, which can include wildcards in its value. You can use % to match a string, such as LIKE "S%" to match any string that begins with *S*, or _ to match any single character, such as LIKE "S_" to match any two-letter string that begins with *S*. The LIKE operator is not case sensitive, so the patterns match either *S* or *s*. A pattern with only wildcards, such as "%", matches any string, including an empty string, but does not match NULL.

Limit Query Execution to Specific Rows with a WHERE Clause

① Choose a database.

② Send the query DESCRIBE *tablename* to see the column names.

③ Send a SELECT query to get data from selected columns from all the rows.

The rows of data are displayed.

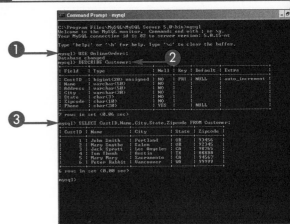

④ Send the same query from step 3 with a WHERE clause after it.

In this example, the WHERE clause is WHERE State="OR" AND City LIKE "p%".

Only the rows that meet all the conditions in the WHERE clause are displayed.

In this example, only one row has the State OR and City beginning with *P*.

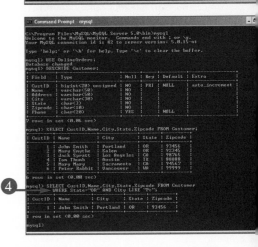

5 Send the same query from step 3 with a WHERE clause at the end that includes NOT LIKE.

In this example, the clause is State NOT LIKE "_A", which selects all state codes that do not end with an *A*.

● Only the rows that match the WHERE clause are displayed.

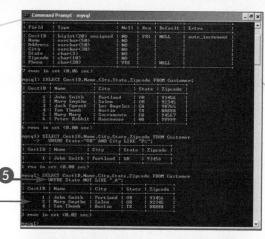

6 Send a SELECT query with a WHERE clause that includes BETWEEN.

In this example, the WHERE clause is WHERE Zipcode BETWEEN 92000 AND 95000.

● Only the rows that match the WHERE clause are selected.

Extra

You can use BETWEEN in a WHERE clause to select strings, as well as numeric data.

TYPE THIS		RESULT
SELECT State FROM Customer WHERE State BETWEEN "OR" AND "TX"	→	This query selects all rows with values in the State column that fall between OR and TX alphabetically, such as PA and RI.

You can select rows that do not have a value stored in the specified column.

TYPE THIS		RESULT
SELECT State FROM Customer WHERE State IS NULL	→	This query selects all rows with no value in the State column.

Retrieve Data from Multiple Tables with UNION

You can combine data from more than one table in a single query. You can use either a *union,* which adds rows to the result set sequentially, or a *join,* which joins data from tables side-by-side in a single row. Joins are discussed in the following section, "Retrieve Data from Multiple Tables by Joining Tables."

In a *union,* two or more SELECT queries are combined in a single query. The data from one query is returned, followed by the data selected in the second query, and so on. Each SELECT query can include any valid SELECT format, including WHERE clauses, LIMIT clauses, ORDER BY clauses, and so on. All the SELECT queries must select the same number of columns, and the selected columns must contain the same type of data. The column names

from the first query are used as the column names for the result set. You build a union by combining SELECT queries with UNION, as follows:

```
SELECT query1 UNION SELECT query2 ...
```

All rows from query1 are added to the result set, followed by all rows from query2, and so on.

You can specify whether you want duplicate rows in your result set. The above query would not add duplicate rows to your result set. You can add the word ALL to specify that duplicate rows are added to the result set, as follows

```
SELECT query1 UNION ALL SELECT query2 ...
```

Retrieve Data from Multiple Tables with UNION

① Choose a database.

② Send a DESCRIBE query to see the structure of a table.

③ Send a DESCRIBE query to see the structure of a second table.

Any two columns with the same data type can be selected to the same record set.

In this example, the columns Name and CustName are VARCHAR.

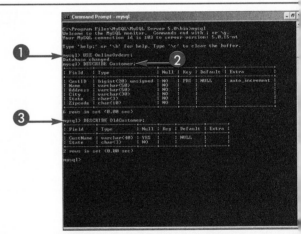

④ Send a SELECT query to see the data in one column in one table.

⑤ Send a SELECT query to see the data in a column with a similar data type in another table.

In this example, the data from Name in Customer and CustName in OldCustomer is displayed.

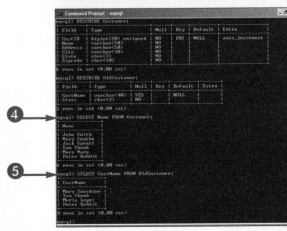

6 Type a SELECT query.

7 Type **UNION ALL**.

8 Type another SELECT query.

9 End the query with ORDER BY
columnname.

The result set uses the column name of the
first query.

- The data selected in both queries is
  sorted together.

- The result set contains duplicate rows.

0 Send the same query built in steps 6 to 9,
except leave out the word ALL.

- The result set contains only one row
  for the duplicate records.

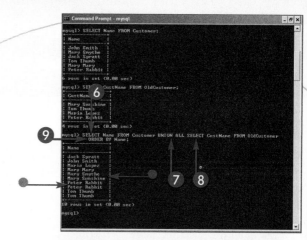

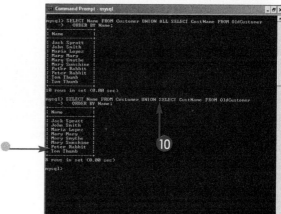

Extra

You can use ORDER BY in a SELECT query with a UNION. If you add an ORDER BY clause at the end of the
query, the entire result set is sorted. If you want the individual SELECT statements sorted but not sorted
together in the final result set, you can add the ORDER BY clause to the individual SELECT query and enclose
the query with parentheses.

TYPE THIS

```
SELECT * FROM Customer1 UNION SELECT
* FROM Customer2 ORDER BY City

(SELECT * FROM Customer1 ORDER BY
City) UNION (SELECT * FROM Customer2
ORDER BY City)
```

RESULT

For the first query, the final result set contains all
the records from Customer1 and Customer2,
all sorted, after the records were combined, by the
name of the city. For the second query, the final
result set contains all the records from Customer1
sorted, followed by all the records from Customer2,
sorted.

Retrieve Data from Multiple Tables by Joining Tables

You can combine data from more than one table in a single query with a *union* or a *join.* In a join, tables are combined side-by-side by matching data in a common column. The SELECT query then retrieves the data from the combined table, which contains all the columns from all the specified tables.

You can use two types of joins: *inner joins* and *outer joins.* The result set from an inner join contains only the rows that exist in all the specified tables. The inner join format is

SELECT *col1,col2,...* FROM *table1,table2,...*

    WHERE *table1.colname = table2.colname*

The WHERE clause specifies the common column on which the tables are matched. You can specify the location of a column by prefixing the table name to the column name, using a dot (.).

The outer join produces a combined table that contains all the rows in one table, with blanks in the row for the columns that do not exist in the other specified tables. Consequently, the results from an outer join will differ, depending on which table is selected to contribute all its rows. You can specify whether the left or right table defines the columns. The format for an outer join is

SELECT *col1,col2,...* FROM *tablename1 direction* JOIN *tablename2*

    ON *table1.colname = table2.colname*

The ON clause specifies the column on which the tables are matched. *direction* can be either RIGHT or LEFT, which specifies the table that contributes all its rows to the combined table — the table on the LEFT side of JOIN or the table on the RIGHT side of JOIN.

Retrieve Data from Multiple Tables by Joining Tables

① Choose a database.

② Send the query DESCRIBE *tablename* for one of the tables to be joined.

③ Repeat step 2 for each table to be joined.

Note: The common column to be used to match the tables must contain the same data type.

In this example, Name and CustName are VARCHAR.

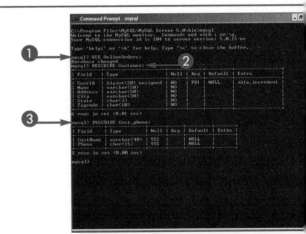

④ Send the query SELECT * FROM *tablename* for one of the tables to be joined.

⑤ Repeat step 4 for each table to be joined.

In this example, one table has 6 rows, and the other has 4 rows.

In this example, the columns Name and CustName have some duplicate names and some different names.

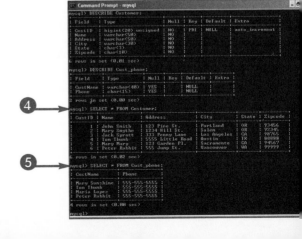

Type **SELECT** *colnames* **FROM**.

 Type two or more table names, separated by commas.

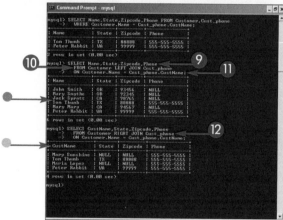 End the query with a WHERE clause that equates one column from each joined table.

- The result set includes only the rows found in both tables.

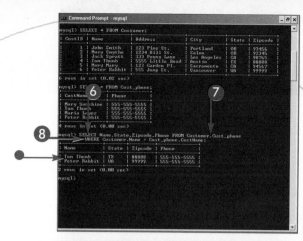

Type **SELECT** *colnames* **FROM**.

Type *tablename* **LEFT JOIN** *tablename*.

End the query with an ON clause that equates one column from each joined table.

- The result set includes all the rows found in the table listed first.

Repeat the query, replacing LEFT with RIGHT.

- The result set includes all the rows in the table specified after JOIN.

Extra

If you have columns in all the joined tables that have the same name, you can use the USING clause instead of an ON clause. The tables are matched on the columns listed in the USING clause.

TYPE THIS

```
SELECT * FROM Customer LEFT JOIN
Cust_order USING (CustID)
```

→

RESULT

The result set contains rows, matched on CustID, which contain all the columns in both tables.

You can create a join that contains all the rows in all the tables, regardless of whether they have matching rows in the other tables, using FULL JOIN.

TYPE THIS

```
SELECT * FROM A FULL JOIN B ON
(A.CustID = B.CustID)
```

→

RESULT

The result set contains rows, matched on CustID, that contain all the columns in both tables, with NULL values for tables that do not have corresponding rows.

Update Data in a Database

Y ou can change information in an existing row in a table with the UPDATE query. The UPDATE query has a straightforward format, as follows:

```
UPDATE tablename1,tablename2,... SET
col1=value1,col2=value2...
```

> WHERE clause

The values in the column(s) are changed to the specified value in the rows that match the WHERE clause. If you do not include a WHERE clause, the column values are changed in all the rows. If you list only one table, you can use LIMIT and ORDER BY.

You can replace an entire row in a table with the REPLACE query. When you insert an entire row, the query fails if the primary key already exists in the database. The REPLACE query works exactly like INSERT, except that if an old row in the table has the same value for a primary key as the new row in the REPLACE query, the

old row is deleted before the new row is inserted. The REPLACE query has the same format as the INSERT query, as shown in the following two examples:

```
REPLACE INTO tablename
(columnname1,columnname2,...)
```

```
        VALUES (value1,value2,...)
```

```
REPLACE INTO tablename
(columnname1,columnname2,...) selectquery
```

If the data for the REPLACE query is obtained by a SELECT query, as shown in the second format above, the query must select the data from a different table, not from the same table specified in the query.

To use REPLACE, you must have both the INSERT and DELETE privileges for the table. Privileges are explained in Chapter 8.

Update Data in a Database

1 Send a SELECT * query to display the data.

2 Type **UPDATE tablename SET**.

3 Add expressions that set a new value in one or more columns.

4 End the query with a WHERE clause to limit the update to a single row.

In this example, the value in Address is updated.

5 Send a SELECT * query to display the data.

The specified column(s) contain new value(s).

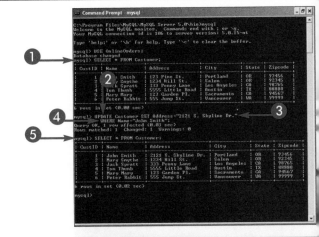

6 Send a query to replace an entire row.

The syntax is similar to INSERT.

- The summary line shows two rows affected because it first deletes the old row and then inserts the new one.

7 Send a SELECT * query to display the data.

- The new row is displayed.

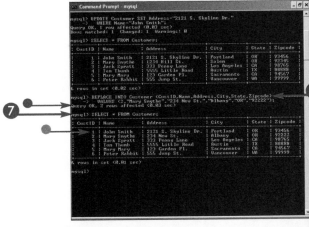

Remove Data from a Database

You can remove rows from a table with the DELETE query, as follows:

DELETE FROM *tablename* WHERE clause

All rows that match the WHERE clause are deleted from the database.

Be careful with the DELETE query. If you do not include a WHERE clause, the DELETE query removes all the rows in the table.

You can remove a column from a table with the ALTER query, as follows:

ALTER TABLE *tablename* DROP *columnname*

This query drops the column, as well as all the data in the column. If you wanted to keep the column but remove all the values in the column, you can use an UPDATE query and change all the values to empty strings or to NULL, as follows:

UPDATE *tablename* SET *columnname* = NULL

You can remove an entire table with the following query:

DROP TABLE *tablename*

You can remove an entire database with the following query:

DROP DATABASE *databasename*

Remove Data from a Database

① Send a SELECT * query to display the data.

② Type **DELETE FROM *tablename***.

③ End the query with a WHERE clause that limits the rows to be deleted.

In this example, the clause is WHERE CustID=3.

④ Send a SELECT * query to display the data.

The specified row is deleted.

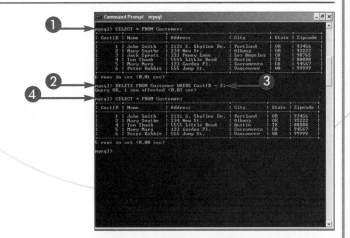

⑤ Send the query DESCRIBE *tablename*.

Note: Any column that allows NULL can be changed to NULL.

⑥ Send a SELECT * query to display the data.

⑦ Send an UPDATE query that sets a row to NULL.

⑧ Send a SELECT * query to display the data.

All values in the updated column are NULL.

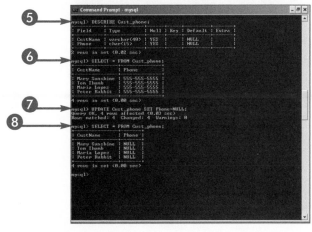

Query a MySQL Database from a PHP Script

To interact with a MySQL database from a PHP script, you use PHP functions developed specifically for use with MySQL — mysql functions for use with MySQL 4 and earlier and, starting with PHP 5, mysqli functions for use with MySQL 4.1 and later. For information on PHP and MySQL versions, see Chapter 1.

In a PHP script, you send a SQL query to MySQL. Before you send the query, you must establish a connection to the MySQL server and choose a database, as follows:

```
$cxn = mysqli_connect(host,account,
password,databasename);
```

The four parameters can be strings or variables. After you establish a connection, you can use it for any mysqli function without needing to reestablish the connection. $cxn contains the information PHP needs to use the connection.

To send a query to the MySQL server after the connection is established, you can use the following statements:

```
$sql = "SELECT * FROM tablename";

$result = mysqli_query($sql,$cxn);
```

If the query does not return any information, such as an INSERT or UPDATE query, $result contains TRUE if the query executed successfully or FALSE if the query failed.

If the query returns information, such as a SELECT that returns data from the database or SHOW TABLES, which returns a list of table names, the data is retrieved and stored in a temporary location. $result contains the information needed to get the data from the temporary location using mysqli functions. Getting the data from the temporary location is discussed in the next section, "Display Database Data on a Web Page in a PHP Script." If the query fails, $result contains FALSE.

Query a MySQL Database from a PHP Script

① Add statements that assign your MySQL account information to variables.

Note: For better security, put these assignments statements into an `include` file that you store in your include directory and include in this script.

② Type **$cxn = mysqli_connect(.);**

③ Insert the variable names inside the parentheses.

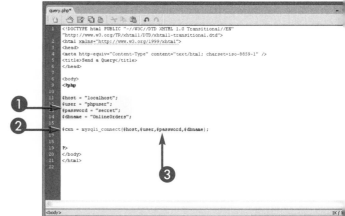

④ Assign a query that returns no data to a variable.

⑤ Type **$varname = mysqli_query(.);.**

⑥ Add the variables that contain the connection and the query.

⑦ Display the result that is returned when mysqli_query executes.

⑧ Add statements to execute a query with an error in it (see steps 4 to 7).

● In this example, the query specifies an invalid table.

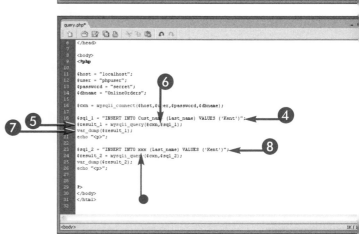

9. Assign a SELECT query to a variable.

10. Send the query (see steps 5 to 6).

11. Display the result returned by `mysqli_query`.

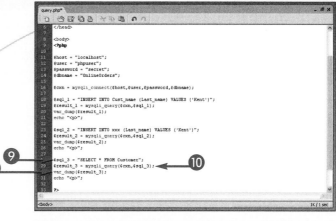

12. View the script in a browser.

The first query executes successfully.

The second query fails because it has an error.

● The result of the third query contains information needed to get the data from its temporary location.

Apply It

You can control the contents of the result set, which can be useful to save resources. You can retrieve only an array with field names as keys with MYSQL_ASSOC or only an array with numeric keys with MYSQL_NUM. The default is both — an array with two elements for each field, one with the field name for a key and one with a number for a key.

TYPE THIS
| ```
$result =
mysqli_query($cxn,$sql,MYSQL_ASSOC);
``` |

RESULT
An array with field names as keys.

If you are using the `mysql` functions, the syntax is slightly different.

TYPE THIS
| ```
$cxn =
mysql_connect($host,$user,$password);
mysql_select($dbname);
$sql = "SELECT * FROM Customer";
$result = mysql_query($sql);
``` |

RESULT
A result set stored in a temporary location that contains all the rows from Customer.

183

Display Database Data on a Web Page in a PHP Script

To display data, you first must retrieve the data from the database by sending a MySQL query. After the query is executed, the data is stored in a temporary location. To display the data, you get it from the temporary location with a `mysqli` function and then echo the data along with the appropriate HTML code to format the data as needed.

You can retrieve the selected data from its temporary location, in rows and columns, with one of several `mysqli` functions provided by PHP. Two useful functions are `mysql_fetch_assoc`, which returns a row of data as an array with the column names as keys, and `mysql_fetch_row`, which returns a row of data as an array with numeric keys. The format is

```
$row = mysql_fetch_assoc($result);
```

`$result` contains the information PHP needs to find the data retrieved by the query. After this function executes, `$row` is an array that contains the columns. You can use the data as `$row['columnname']`.

Often you select more than one row of data, and you need to process all the rows. You can do this using a `while` statement, such as the following:

```
while( $row = mysql_fetch_row($result) )

{

    PHP statements;

}
```

The `while` loop repeats until it runs out of rows. When the function attempts to fetch a row after the last row, it returns `FALSE`, and the `while` loop ends.

Display Database Data on a Web Page in a PHP Script

1 Create variables that contain database access information.

2 Add a statement that connects to the database.

3 Assign a query to a variable.

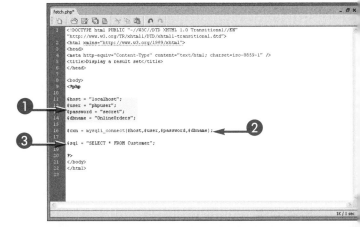

4 Add a statement that executes the query and stores the result in a temporary location.

5 Type **while( )**.

6 Type the function call `$row=mysqli_fetch_row($result)` between the parentheses.

7 Add a block of statements.

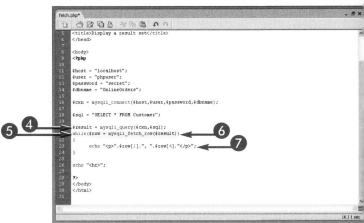

Type **mysqli_data_seek($result,0);**.

The pointer moves to the beginning of the result set.

Type **while( )**.

Type the function call `$row=mysqli_fetch_assoc($result)` between the parentheses.

Add a block of statements.

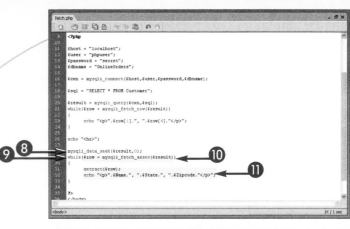

View the script in a browser.

Fields from the database are displayed on the Web page.

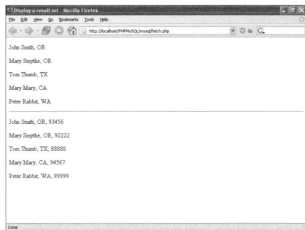

Extra

PHP offers many `mysqli` functions for interacting with the database. Some useful functions are `mysql_affected_rows()`, which returns the number of rows affected by the last query; `mysql_num_rows()`, which returns the number of rows in the result set; `mysqli_fields()`, which returns an array containing all the field names; `mysqli_num_fields()`, which returns the number of columns in the result set; `mysqli_select_db()`, which changes to the specified database; and many more. See www.php.net/manual/en/ref.mysqli.php for information on all the functions.

TYPE THIS

```
$sql = "SELECT * FROM Customer';
$result = mysqli_query($cxn,$sql);
$n = mysqli_num_rows($result);
```

RESULT

$n contains the number of rows selected by the query.

Handle MySQL Errors

When you send a query to the MySQL server from a PHP script, the query can fail. In most cases, if the query fails, the remainder of the script will not execute correctly, so you want the program to stop. The query returns an error message containing information about why the query failed. You want to see that information. The program does not stop when a query fails, and the error message is not automatically sent to the browser. You need to provide explicit error-handling in your script.

To stop the script when the function fails, you can use
```
$result = mysqli_query($cxn,$sql)
or die("message");
```

In this case, a failed query causes the statement after or to execute, which displays *message* and stops the script. This statement, however, does not display the MySQL error message, only the message that you provide.

You can see the error message using the functions `mysqli_connect_error()`, which returns a string error message for connect functions, and `mysqli_error()`, which returns a string error message for all other functions. You can display the error with the following:
```
$result = mysqli_query($cxn,$sql) or
die("message".mysqli_error($cxn));
```

The function returns the message for the last error encountered on the specified connection.

PHP provides another function, `mysql_errno (connection)`, which returns the error number rather than the string description. In some cases, if you cannot fix a problem with the information in the string description, you can find additional information about the error by referencing the error number in the MySQL online documentation at http://dev.mysql.com/doc/ or through Google.

Handle MySQL Errors

1. Create variables that contain database values.

2. Type **if(!)**.

3. Add the connection function call inside the parentheses.

4. Add the block of statements to execute if the connection function fails.

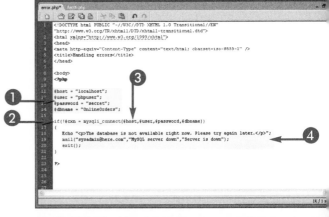

5. Shut down the MySQL server.

Note: Stopping the server is discussed in Chapter 8.

6. View the script in a browser.

The `if` block executes.

Note: On a production server with warnings turned off, the warning would not be displayed. Handling errors is discussed in Chapter 2.

Restart the server.

Assign a query with an error in it to a variable.

In this example, the table name is incorrect.

Add a statement that executes the query.

Add an `or` statement that executes if the query fails.

Add a `while` loop to process the result set.

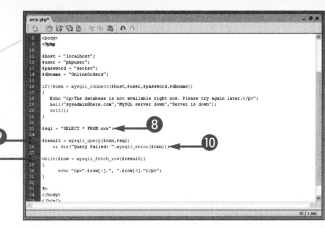

View the script in a browser.

The message in the `die()` statement is displayed because the query failed.

The script stopped when the `die` statement executed.

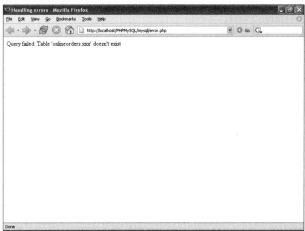

Extra

You can use more elaborate error-handling. If the function does not execute correctly, it returns `FALSE`. You can use an `if` statement to execute any statements that you want when a function fails.

TYPE THIS	RESULT
```if(!$cxn = mysqli_connect($host,$acct,$passwd,$dbname)) { $message = mysqli_connect_error(); echo $message." "; exit(); }```	Displays the error message from MySQL and then stops the script.

MySQL provides a security system to protect access to the information in your database. No one can access your database without a MySQL account. The attributes of each MySQL account include its name, the computer(s) from which the account can access the MySQL server, a password, and a set of privileges that define what the account can and cannot (in the database. Account information is stored in a database named `mysql`, which is created by default whe you install MySQL.

The Account Name and Host

A MySQL account name is defined in terms of its name and the host from which the account can connect to the MySQL server. A MySQL server recognizes a MySQL account as *acctname@hostname*. The account can only access the MySQL server when connecting from the specified host. You can have two accounts with the same account name if the host name is different. MySQL accounts are unrelated to the operating system username that you use to log on to the computer.

MySQL account names can be up to 16 characters long and can include special characters, such as a space or a hyphen.

You can set up an account with a blank name, which means any account name is valid for that account.

The host name can be a domain name or an IP address. You can also use `localhost` as a host name, which allows the account to connect from the machine where the MySQL server is running. The host name can also be blank, which allows the account to connect from any computer.

You can use wildcards in the host name, but not in the account name. The percent sign (%) matches any host name. For example, the account `phpuser@%` can access the server from any computer.

Passwords

Every account has a password field. If no password is provided for the account, the password field is blank, which means that no password is required.

MySQL encrypts passwords. If you look at the password field in the `mysql` database, you see a long string of characters, not the actual password. In MySQL 4.1, MySQL changed to a more secure encryption method. If you update an older version of MySQL to MySQL 4.1 or later, you may encounter problems because later versions of MySQL create a longer string when

encrypting the password. If you encounter the problem, MySQL displays the following error message:

```
Client does not support authentication
protocol requested by server; consider
upgrading MySQL client
```

The online manual explains the issues and solutions for this situation at http://dev.mysql.com/doc/refman/5.0/en/password-hashing.html.

Account Privileges

Each account has a set of privileges that define what the account can do. Any valid account can connect to the MySQL server, but can only perform the actions allowed by the specified privileges. Many of the privileges granted to an account refer to the SQL query that the account can execute. An account with a SELECT privilege can execute a SELECT query, an account with a DELETE privilege can execute a DELETE query, and so on. An account that has a GRANT privilege can change the privileges of accounts.

Other privileges can be granted to an account. The ALL privilege gives all privileges to an account. The USAGE privilege gives no privileges at all to an account; the account can connect to the database, but cannot execute any queries. The

SHUTDOWN privilege allows an account to shut down the MySQL server, a privilege that should be given rarely.

Privileges can be granted for particular databases, tables, or columns. An account may have an UPDATE privilege on one database but only a SELECT privilege on another database — or the ALL privilege on one table but only an INSERT privilege on another table.

New privileges are often added with new versions of MySQL, to accommodate new features. You can check the manual for a complete, up-to-date list of privileges, such as the list for MySQL 5 at http://dev.mysql.com/doc/refman/5.0/en/privileges-provided.html.

The Account Information Database

When MySQL is installed, it creates a database called `mysql`. All the information used to protect your data is stored in this database in *grant tables,* including account names, host names, passwords, and privileges. Privileges are stored in columns. Each column has the privilege name, and the value is `Y` or `N`, for yes or no.

The `user` table stores privileges that apply to all the databases and tables. It contains a row for each valid account with a username, host name, and password. The `db` table stores privileges that apply only to a specific database. It contains a row for the database, which gives privileges to an account name and host name. The account must exist in the `user` table, and the privileges in the `user` table overrule the privileges in the `db` table. Privileges for specific tables are stored in the `tables_priv` table, and privileges for specific columns are stored in the `columns_priv` table.

Default Accounts

When MySQL is installed, some default accounts are set up during installation, depending on your operating system and on choices you make during installation. A MySQL account named `root` is installed. This account is just for MySQL access, unrelated to any `root` account that exists for logging in to your operating system.

The `root` account may be installed with a blank password. The installation wizard on Windows provides an opportunity for you to set a password for the `root` account. If your root password is blank, it is insecure; you should set a password right after installation. The installation wizard also provides an option to install an anonymous account — an account with a blank name and a blank password. This can be useful for development, but should only be installed on your local, development computer, never on a computer that allows access from the Web.

Managing Databases

You can add accounts, change passwords, or add or remove privileges using SQL queries provided for these purposes — `GRANT`, `REVOKE`, and `SET PASSWORD`. When you make changes using these queries, MySQL immediately rereads the grant tables, and the changes go into effect.

You can make changes to the grant tables directly, using the SQL queries described in Chapter 7. For example, you can insert a line for a new account directly into the `user` table, providing the information in the `INSERT` query. When you make changes directly, MySQL is not aware of the changes. You must manually reread the grant tables by sending `FLUSH PRIVILEGES` to the MySQL server. If you do not reread the grant tables manually, the changes will not go into effect until the server restarts.

MySQL automatically includes some administration programs when installed. One program, `mysqladmin`, can be used to create and drop databases and to change passwords. It also provides other features for `mysql` administration, such as reloading the grant tables, shutting down the MySQL server, or displaying the status of the server.

You can download a program called *MySQL Administrator,* for administering MySQL, from the MySQL Web site. You can use this program to manage accounts and privileges, as well as to configure MySQL. Downloading and installing MySQL Administrator is discussed in Chapter 1.

The Access Process

Accessing the database is a two-step process. First, the server checks whether you are accessing with a valid account. It checks the username, the host name from which you are connecting, and the password. If all three are correct, you are connected to the server. Then, the query is passed to the server. The server checks the query against the grant tables that it currently retains in memory to see whether you have the necessary privileges to execute the query you sent.

View Existing Accounts

You can view your existing accounts by sending a SELECT query to the MySQL server. You can check your installed accounts as soon as you install MySQL. You can see the account name and the host name. You can also view all the privileges that are set for the account. You can see the password field, but you cannot see that actual password. It is encrypted and appears as a nonsense string of characters.

The database management information is in a database named mysql. The account information is stored in a table named User, which has one row for each account. You can also view the privileges for the account. The account row in the User table contains a column for each privilege with a value of Y or N, for yes or no.

You can display the privileges for the account that you are currently using to connect to the server with the following query:

SHOW GRANTS

The query returns the GRANT query that would create the account with its existing privileges. The query lists the privileges set for the account.

You can also view your existing accounts in MySQL Administrator. When you choose the User Administration window, a list of accounts is displayed in the lower-right corner. MySQL Administrator manages privileges by the database. You can see the privileges assigned to any account for any database by selecting an account, choosing the privileges window, and clicking a database.

View Existing Accounts

USING SQL QUERIES

① Choose the mysql database.

② Send the query SELECT Host,User,Password FROM User.

- The shorter password means that the account was created with MySQL 4 or earlier.

- Two anonymous accounts exist, one for localhost and one for any host.

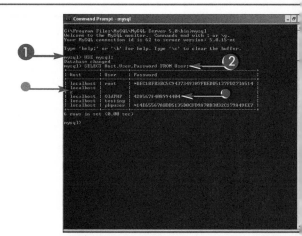

③ Exit and start again, specifying the root account.

④ Send the query SHOW GRANTS.

- The account has all privileges on all tables in all databases, shown by *.*.

⑤ Exit and start again, specifying a different account.

⑥ Send the query SHOW GRANTS.

- In this example, the phpuser account has only SELECT privileges.

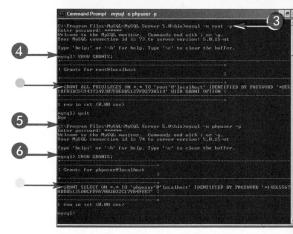

USING MYSQL ADMINISTRATOR

Start MySQL Administrator.

Click User Administration.

A list of accounts is displayed.

Click an account.

Click the Schema Privileges tab.

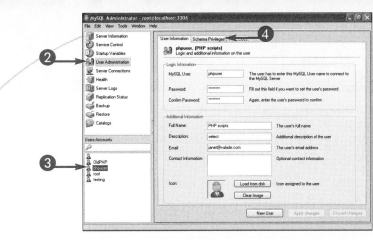

The privileges tab appears.

Click a database name.

● The privileges for the account on the specified database appear in the Assigned Privileges list box.

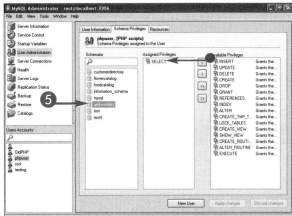

Extra

If the account you are using has the GRANT privilege, you can use SHOW GRANTS for a different account.

TYPE THIS

```
SHOW GRANTS FOR phpuser@localhost
```

→

RESULT

The privileges for the account phpuser@localhost are displayed, even if you are currently accessing the MySQL server from another account, such as root.

If you have two accounts with the same name but different hosts, you need to specify the host to identify the correct account. If you do not specify the host, the mysql client assumes localhost.

TYPE THIS

```
mysql -u sam
mysql -u sam@'%'
```

→

RESULT

The first statement connects to the MySQL server with the account sam@localhost. The second statement connects to the server from the account sam@%.

Create a MySQL Account

Beginning with MySQL 5.0.2, you can create new accounts with the CREATE USER query. You must use an account with the global CREATE USER privilege or the INSERT privilege for the mysql database. The format is

```
CREATE USER username1@host1 IDENTIFIED BY
"password1", username2@host2 IDENTIFIED BY
"password2", ...
```

The IDENTIFIED BY clauses are not required. Without IDENTIFIED BY, a blank password is installed. If you do not include @host for an account, the host value is %. CREATE USER adds accounts to the User table with no privileges. You can add privileges to accounts using the GRANT query as described in the section "Add and Remove Privileges."

You can also create accounts using the GRANT query, as follows:

```
GRANT priv1,priv2,... ON
databasename.tablename TO
accountname@hostname IDENTIFIED BY
'password'
```

You must specify at least one privilege, which can be ALL or USAGE — meaning no privileges. See the section "Understanding MySQL Accounts" for an explanation of privileges. The ON clause specifies the database(s) and table(s) the privileges apply to. The TO phrase specifies the account that you want to create. Beginning with MySQL 5.0.2, you must include an IDENTIFIED BY clause to create an account.

You must use an account that has the GRANT privilege and the privileges that you intend to grant to the account you are creating. For example, if you want to create a new account with SELECT privileges, the account you use to create the new account must have at least the GRANT privilege and the SELECT privilege.

Create a MySQL Account

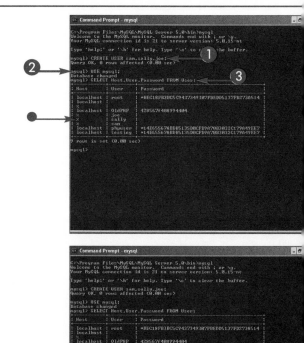

① Send the query CREATE USER
usernames.

   In this example, *usernames* is
   sam,sally,joe.

② Send the query USE mysql.

③ Send the query SELECT
   Host,User,Password FROM
   User.

   ● The new accounts appear in the
   User table.

   In this example, the value % is in the
   Host column because no host was
   specified.

④ Send the query SHOW GRANTS
   FOR *accountname*, where
   accountname is a new account.

   A GRANT query that would create
   this account is displayed.

Note: The USAGE privilege means no
   privileges.

5 Type **GRANT** *privilegelist*.

In this example, *privilegelist* is SELECT.

6 Type **ON *.***.

. applies the privileges to all databases and tables.

7 Type **TO** *accountname*@*host* **IDENTIFIED BY** *password*.

Note: You can leave out @host to use the default host %, which is a wildcard for any string.

8 Send the query SELECT Host,User,Password FROM User.

● The new account appears in the User table.

9 Send the query SELECT * FROM User WHERE User="*accountname*".

All columns in the row for *accountname* are displayed.

In this example, the value in the Select_priv column is Y.

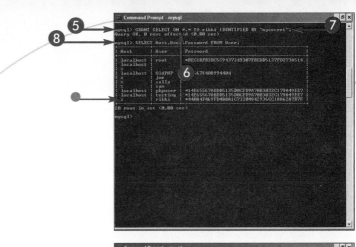

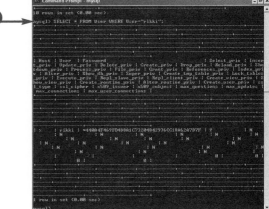

Extra

You can use MySQL Administrator to create new accounts. Administrator applies privileges on a database level, so the account is created with no privileges in the User table. You can specify privileges for a database, which are then stored in the Db table. In the User Administration window, click the New User button and fill in the information. To specify privileges for a database, click the Schema Privileges tab.

You can create a new account directly in the mysql database with an INSERT query that adds a row for the account, specifying the account information and privileges. Any privilege not specified in the INSERT query is added with its default, usually N.

TYPE THIS

```
INSERT INTO User (Host,User,Select_priv)
VALUES ("localhost","test6","Y")
```

RESULT

→ A new account with the name test6, the host localhost, and no password is created. The account has only the SELECT privilege. Because this privilege is inserted into the User table, the account has the SELECT privilege for all databases.

Change the Password of a MySQL Account

You can change the password for an account using the SET PASSWORD query, with the following general format:

```
SET PASSWORD FOR 'username'@'host' =
PASSWORD("newpassword");
```

The query replaces the current password for the account with *newpassword*. The PASSWORD() function encrypts the password using the MySQL encryption procedure. If you do not include the FOR clause, the password is set for the account that you are currently using to send the query.

The SET PASSWORD query is equivalent to the following two queries:

```
UPDATE User SET Password=PASSWORD
('newpassword')

  WHERE User='username' AND Host='host';
```

```
FLUSH PRIVILEGES;
```

You can also change the password using the GRANT query, as follows:

```
GRANT priv1,priv2,... ON
databasename.tablename TO
accountname@hostname IDENTIFIED BY
'newpassword'
```

The GRANT query replaces the current password for the account with the new password. It also grants the listed privileges. If you only want to change the password, without changing any privileges, you can use the SET PASSWORD query. If you use the GRANT query to change only the password, you need to carefully list the privileges and the ON clause to define the privileges so that they are the same as the existing privileges.

Change the Password of a MySQL Account

① Send USE mysql.

② Send SELECT Host,User,Password FROM User WHERE User="*accountname*".

The host, account name, and password for the account are displayed.

● The password is displayed in an encrypted format.

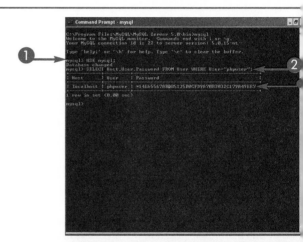

③ Type **SET PASSWORD FOR**.

④ Type ***accountname@hostname*** for the account to be changed.

⑤ Type **= PASSWORD("** .

⑥ Type the password.

In this example, the password is secrets.

⑦ Type **")** and send the query.

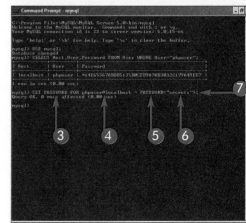

Repeat step 2.

The host, account name, and password for the account are displayed.

● The password is changed.

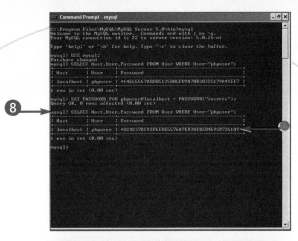

Send SHOW GRANTS FOR *accountname*.

GRANT queries that show the current privileges and password are displayed.

Send a GRANT query that sets the same privileges but changes the password.

Repeat step 2.

The password is changed.

Repeat step 9.

The privileges are the same.

Extra

You can change the password with the `mysqladmin` script that was installed when MySQL was installed.

TYPE THIS		RESULT
`mysqladmin -u test6 -psecret password "secret2"`	→	The password for the `test6` account is changed from `secret` to `secret2`. `mysqladmin` displays no response to show that the command was successful. You can assume success based on the lack of an error message. You can look at the `mysql` database directly to ensure that the command executed successfully. The password is encrypted when you use `mysqladmin`.

Add and Remove Privileges

You can add privileges to any MySQL account using the GRANT query in the following format:

```
GRANT priv1 (col1,col2,...), priv2
(col1,col2,...),... ON
databasename.tablename TO
accntname1@host,accntname2@host,...
```

You must include at least one privilege. If a specified privilege already exists on the account, it remains. If it does not exist, it is added. If no columns are listed, the privileges are applied to all the columns in the specified database table(s).

The ON clause applies the privileges to databases and tables. You can use the wildcards for all (*), for a character (_), and for a string of any length (%). Specifying *.* applies the privileges to all databases and all tables. You can specify databasename.* to represent all tables in databasename. Administrative privileges,

such as SHOW DATABASES and SHUTDOWN, can only be applied when you use *.*, not to specific databases.

The TO clause specifies which account to grant the privileges to. You can use the wildcards % and _ in the host name, but not in the account name. If you do not include @host, the value % is stored in the Host column.

You can remove privileges from a MySQL account with the REVOKE query, as follows:

```
REVOKE priv1 (columnlist1), priv2
(columnlist2),... ON databasename.tablename
FROM accntname1@host,accntname2@host,...
```

The REVOKE query has the same syntax as the GRANT query, except it uses FROM, instead of TO, when specifying the account. If the privilege exists for the specified account(s), it is removed. If it does not exist, it is ignored.

To use a GRANT or REVOKE query, you must be using a MySQL account that has both the GRANT privilege and the privilege that is being granted or revoked.

Add and Remove Privileges

ADD PRIVILEGES

① Send the query CREATE USER *accountname* to create a new account with no privileges.

② Send SHOW GRANTS for *accountname* for the new account.

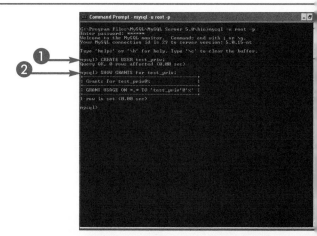

③ Type **GRANT *privileges***.

In this example, *privileges* is SELECT, INSERT.

④ Type **ON *.* TO *accountname***, where *accountname* is the new account, and send the query.

⑤ Repeat step 2.

The privileges added in steps 3 to 4 are shown.

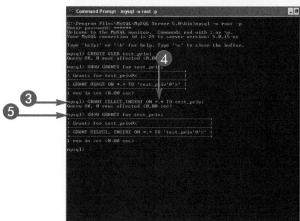

REMOVE PRIVILEGES

6 Send a REVOKE query to remove a privilege that the account does not have.

In this case, the REVOKE query specifies the DELETE privilege.

The summary line shows Query OK.

7 Repeat step 2.

● The privileges are unchanged.

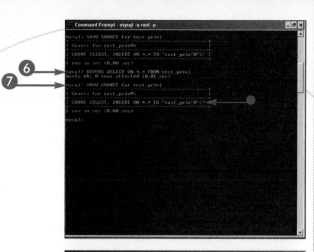

8 Send the query REVOKE ALL ON *.* FROM *accountname*.

9 Repeat step 2.

The privileges show USAGE, which means no privileges.

Extra

You can add or remove privileges directly in the `mysql` database.

TYPE THIS

```
UPDATE User SET
Select_priv="Y",Delete_priv="N" WHERE
User="phpuser"
```

RESULT

The SELECT privilege is added to the User table, and the DELETE privilege is removed for the account phpuser.

You can add or remove privileges from specific databases or tables directly in the `mysql` database as well.

TYPE THIS

```
UPDATE Db SET
Select_priv="Y",Delete_priv="N" WHERE
User="phpuser" AND Db="OnlineOrders"
```

RESULT

The SELECT privilege is added for the account phpuser on the database OnlineOrders, and the DELETE privilege is removed for the account phpuser on the database OnlineOrders.

Change the Name of a MySQL Account

You can change the name of a MySQL account. Starting with MySQL 5.0.2, MySQL provides a RENAME USER query, with the following format:

```
RENAME USER accountname1@host TO
newaccountname1@host, accountname2@host TO
newaccountname2@host, ...
```

You specify both the account name and the host name. If the host name is not included, the default host name (%) is assumed.

To use the RENAME USER query, you must use an account that has the global CREATE USER privilege or the UPDATE privilege for the mysql database.

If you send a query to rename an account that does not exist or to rename an existing account to a name that already exists, MySQL returns an error similar to the following:

```
Error 1396 (HY00): Operation RENAME USER
failed for accountname@host
```

You can change the account name and/or the host name directly in the User table with the UPDATE query, as follows:

```
UPDATE User SET User="newaccountname" WHERE
User="accountname"
```

You can change only the account name, only the host name, or both. If you have more than one account with the same name, all accounts with the name are changed. If you only want to change one of the accounts with the specified name, you must include the host in the WHERE clause.

Change the Name of a MySQL Account

① Send SELECT Host,User,Password FROM User.

All accounts are displayed.

② Type **RENAME USER**.

③ Add accountname@host TO newname@host and send the query.

④ Repeat step 1.

The list of accounts shows the new name.

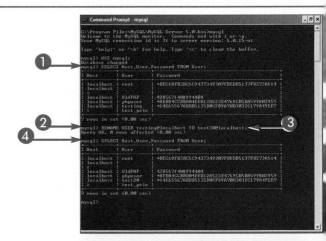

⑤ Type **UPDATE User SET**.

⑥ Type **User="newaccountname"**.

⑦ Add WHERE User="accountname" with the accountname you want to change and send the query.

⑧ Repeat step 1.

The list of accounts shows the new name.

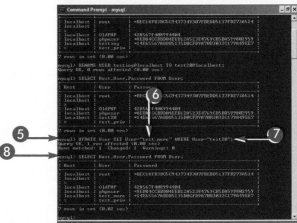

Remove a MySQL Account

Beginning with MySQL 5, you can remove one or more MySQL accounts with the DROP USER query, as follows:

```
DROP USER accountname1@host,
accountname2@host, ...
```

If you do not include @host, the host % is assumed. To use DROP USER, you must use an account that has the global CREATE USER privilege or the DELETE privilege for the mysql database.

With MySQL 5.0.0 and 5.0.1, the query only removes accounts that have no privileges. You must remove all the privileges before using DROP USER. Beginning with MySQL 5.0.2, DROP USER drops the account and all its privileges. It removes the row for the account from the table User. It also removes any rows for the account from the other grant tables, such as a row in the table Db giving the account privileges on a

specific database. You do not need to remove any privileges separately before using DROP USER.

If an account is connected to the MySQL server at the time it is dropped, the account is not dropped immediately. The account remains until the connection is closed. When it is no longer connected, the account is dropped, and the next attempt to connect using the account fails.

You can remove an account directly by deleting the account record from the User table in the mysql database with a DELETE query, with the following format:

```
DELETE FROM User WHERE
User="accountname"
```

Use DELETE carefully. If you mistakenly use the DELETE query without a WHERE clause, it will remove all the account rows.

Remove a MySQL Account

① Send SELECT Host,User,Password FROM User.

All accounts are displayed.

② Send the query DROP USER accountname@host.

③ Repeat step 1.

The list of accounts no longer includes the account specified in step 2.

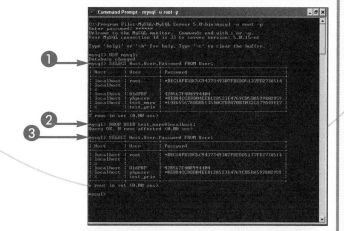

④ Type **DELETE FROM User WHERE**.

⑤ Add User="accountname" and send the query.

⑥ Repeat step 1.

The list of accounts no longer shows accountname.

Stop and Start the MySQL Server

In most cases, the MySQL server is set up to start when the computer starts and run all the time the computer is running, as discussed in Chapter 1. However, sometimes you need to stop the server and/or restart it. For example, when you upgrade MySQL, you need to shut down the server during the upgrade and start the upgraded server.

On Windows, the MySQL server runs as a service. If you open the Services window, you can scroll down the alphabetical list of services and click the MySQL entry. If the service is running, the status shows started, and three options are available: Stop, Pause, and Restart. If the service is currently not running, the Start option is displayed.

You can have more than one MySQL server installed as a service. However, in most cases, you only want one MySQL server running at a time. If needed, you can remove or install MySQL as a service. Change to the bin

directory where MySQL is installed, such as C:\Program Files\MySQL\MySQL Server 5.0\bin. Type one of the following commands:

```
mysqld --remove servicename
mysqld --install servicename
```

servicename is the name that appears in the list of services. If you do not include a name, the server will be added using the MySQL default name. When you remove the service, you must specify the *servicename* if the service is not installed with the default name.

On Linux or Mac, you can start and stop the MySQL server with one of the following commands at the command line:

```
mysql.server start
mysql.server stop
```

You may need to find the script and change to the directory where it is located.

Stop and Start the MySQL Server

① Click Start.

② Click Control Panel.

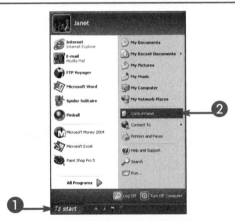

The Control Panel opens.

③ Double-click Administrative Tools.

The Administrative Tools window opens.

④ Double-click Services.

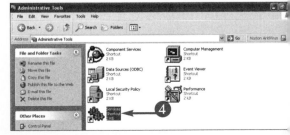

The Services window opens.

⑤ Scroll down to MySQL.

⑥ Click the MySQL entry.

The options are displayed.

⑦ Click Stop.

The Service Control dialog box opens, showing the process of the action.

When the action is complete, the Service Control dialog box closes.

The service is stopped.

Different options are available.

⑧ Click Start.

The service starts.

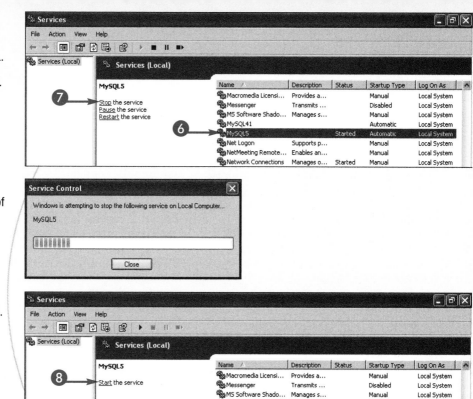

Extra

You can shut down the MySQL server on any operating system with the `mysqladmin` program. If the program is not in your path, you may need to change to the bin subdirectory in the directory where MySQL is installed, such as \user\local\bin or \user\local\mysql\bin.

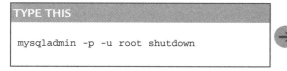

TYPE THIS		RESULT
`mysqladmin -p -u root shutdown`	→	The MySQL server is shut down. It is no longer listening for queries. You cannot access your database until you restart the server.

Using MySQL Logs

MySQL provides diagnostic and error information by default. The information can be stored in an error log or displayed on the console screen. In Windows, by default, the information is written to an error log file stored in the data directory. For Linux or Mac, if you start the MySQL server with the `mysql.server` or `mysqld_safe` scripts, the information is written to an error log file. If you start the server directly on Linux, by typing **mysqld**, the information is sent to the console, but this is not the usual way the server is started.

If your MySQL server refuses to start, the error log is the first place to look for a cause. Server startups, shutdowns, crashes, and other error conditions are recorded in the log file, including information that can be helpful in determining the cause of problems.

The error file is stored in the data directory. By default, the data directory is a subdirectory named data in the directory where MySQL is installed, such as C:\Program Files\MySQL\MySQL Server 5.0\data or /usr/local/mysql/data. The log file is named hostname.err

MySQL can write messages to other types of log files as well, when directed to by startup options. You can add the startup option to your `mysql` configuration file so that MySQL will start with the option every time it starts. The configuration file is my.ini or my.cnf. Add the startup directory to the `[mysqld]` section.

One useful log file is the general query log file, which records each statement that is sent to the MySQL server. To start and send messages to a general query log, use the `log` or `log=path/filename` startup option. If you do not specify a filename, the log is stored in the data directory in hostname.log.

Using MySQL Logs

1 Open the MySQL configuration file in a text editor.

Note: On Windows, the configuration file is usually called my.ini and located in the main MySQL directory. On Linux, it may be called my.cnf and located in /etc.

2 Scroll to Server Section.

3 Add a line: **log**.

4 Save the file.

5 Restart the MySQL server.

6 Change to the MySQL data directory.

In this case, the directory is C:\Program Files\MySQL\MySQL Server 5.0\data.

7 Type **dir**.

● The error log has the file extension .err.

● The file ending .log is the file generated by the log line added in step 3.

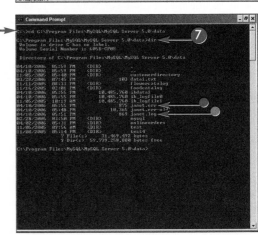

8 Type the command **type**
   logname.log.

Note: You can also open the file in a text
editor to see it.

The file contains records for all
server activity.

● Lines show the server startups.

● Lines show the queries sent.

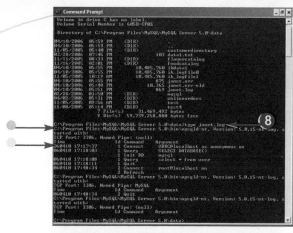

9 Type the command **type**
   logname.err.

The file contains records of all
startups, shutdowns, and errors.

Extra

Log files can get very large, especially the general query log file. You need to start the log file over again
periodically. The usual practice is to rename the current log file, leaving MySQL to start writing into an empty
log file. You cannot rename the log files that the MySQL server is running. You must shut down the server,
rename the files, and restart the server.

The `mysqladmin` program has an option that empties the error file for you. You can use this program while
the MySQL server is running.

TYPE THIS
| ```
cd c:\Program Files\MySQL\MySQL Server
5.0\bin
mysqladmin -p -u root flush-logs
``` |

RESULT
Two files now exist — a file with the extension .err-old, containing the error messages, and a log file with the extension .err, which is now empty.
```

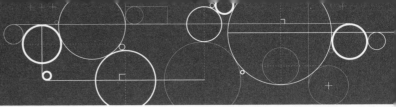

Back Up Data

MySQL provides the program `mysqldump` for making backup copies of databases. This program outputs a set of SQL queries that can re-create your database. It contains the queries that create the structure of the database and its tables and the `INSERT` queries that add the existing data. The backup file is independent of the computer that creates it; you can restore this database on any computer. The `mysqldump` program is useful for transferring the database from one computer to another, as well as for backing up the data.

You can use the `mysqldump` program to back up specific databases and/or tables or all databases, as follows:

```
mysqldump -u accnt -p -r path/filename
database table1,table2,...
```

The program writes the table information into the specified file at the specified path. If you do not list any

tables, information for all the tables in the database is written to the file. You can back up more than one database by specifying `--database database1 database2 ...`, instead of `database table1, table2`, and so on. You can also specify `--all-databases`. If you do, you back up all the databases, including the `mysql` database.

The `mysqldump` program has many options. You can dump only the structure information or only the data using the `--no-data` or `--no-create-info` option. You can specify tables that you do not want to include, rather than list all the tables to include, with the option `--ignore-table=databasename.tablename`. To see a list of all the options available for the version of `mysqldump` you are using, use the `--help` option.

By default, `mysqldump` locks the tables so that no one can write to them in the middle of your backup procedure.

Back Up Data

① Change to the bin directory.

② Type **mysqldump -p -u root -r path/filename**.

③ Type a database name and one or more table names to back up.

④ Type your password when prompted.

⑤ Repeat step 2.

⑥ Type **--databases**, followed by the names of one or more databases.

⑦ Change to the directory specified in step 2.

⑧ Type **dir**.

The backup files are in the directory.

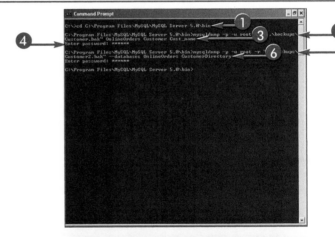

9 Display the first backup file with tables from one database with a system command (`type` or `cat`) or by opening the file in a text editor.

The file contains the SQL queries for each table specified.

- The queries for the structure are first.

- The INSERT query that adds the data is second.

10 Display the second backup file that backs up all the tables for one or more specified databases.

- A query that creates the database appears first.

The queries for all the tables are included one by one.

Extra

You can back up the data only into a tab-delimited file. You can then read the data into any program that can read a tab-delimited file. You can read a tab-delimited file into MySQL with the LOAD query described in Chapter 7.

TYPE THIS

```
SELECT * FROM Customer INTO OUTFILE
c:\backups\Customer.bak
```

Note: The directory must already exist. The `outfile` option does not create a directory, only the file.

RESULT

All the data is written into `Customer.bak`, with a tab between each column field.

Restore Data

I f you use the procedures suggested in the previous section, your backup file is a text file containing SQL queries that re-create your database, both its structure and its data, created by the `mysqldump` program. You can restore your database(s) directly from the backup file, using the following format:

```
mysql -p -u root < path\filename
```

This command executes all the SQL queries in `path\filename`.

You can edit the SQL queries in the dump file. You can remove queries if you only want to restore part of the database. You can comment out any lines in the file by putting `--` at the beginning of a line, which causes MySQL to ignore the line. You can change the queries, such as changing the name of a database or table.

MySQL does not include a query that copies or renames an entire database. You can copy a database, however, by using `mysqldump` to save a file containing the structure and data and then restoring the database under a new name. Just edit the dump file to change the database name in the `CREATE DATABASE` and `USE` queries. If you then `DROP` the first database, you have effectively renamed the database.

Copying a database with `mysqldump` allows you to move a database from one computer to another. You can restore the database on a different computer, regardless of its operating system. The `mysql` client can read the text file using the format shown in this section.

If you back up your data into a tab-delimited file containing the data for a table, you can restore the data by using the `LOAD` query explained in Chapter 7.

Restore Data

① Open the backup file in a text editor.

② Change the name of the database in the `CREATE DATABASE` query.

③ Change the name of the database in the `USE` query.

④ Save the file.

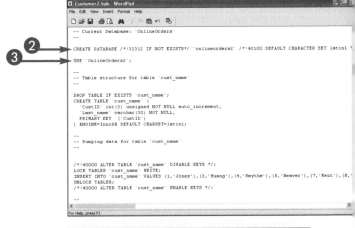

⑤ Send the query `SHOW DATABASES`.

⑥ In the bin directory, type **mysql -p -u root < backupfilename**.

⑦ Enter your password when prompted.

The procedure completes without displaying a message.

⑧ Repeat step 5.

● The database is restored with the changed name.

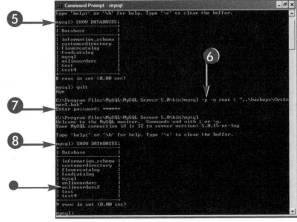

Upgrade MySQL

New versions of MySQL are released periodically. You can upgrade from one version of MySQL to a newer version. However, there are special considerations when upgrading. Upgrading information is provided in the MySQL online manual at http://dev.mysql.com/doc/refman/5.0/en/upgrade.html.

As a precaution, it is wise to back up your current databases before upgrading, including the grant tables in the `mysql` database.

Skipping Versions

MySQL recommends that you do not skip versions. If you want to upgrade from one version to a version more than one version newer, such as from MySQL 4.0 to MySQL 5.0, you should upgrade to the next newest version first. After that version is working correctly, you can upgrade to the next version. And so on. In other words, upgrade from 4.0 to 4.1 first and then from 4.1 to 5.0.

Previous Versions

You can have more than one version of MySQL installed, but, in most cases, you only run one version at a time. You shut down one server version before starting another. Consequently, you must shut down the current MySQL server before upgrading.

On Windows, you can just stop the service, or you can remove the service. If you just shut down the service, be sure to install the upgrade with a different service name, as described in Chapter 1.

Changes to Tables

Occasionally, incompatible changes are introduced in new versions of MySQL. Some releases introduce changes to the structure of the grant tables. For example, MySQL 4.1 changed the method of encrypting passwords, requiring a longer password field in the grant tables. Whenever you upgrade, you should check your tables and update your grant tables.

MySQL Version 5.0.19 and later

After upgrading to the newer version, you should run the `mysql_upgrade` program. It checks your files, repairing them if needed, and upgrades the system tables if needed.

MySQL Version 5.0.18 and earlier

Prior to version 5.0.19, the `mysql_upgrade` program does not run on Windows. You can use this program on UNIX, but not on Windows. On Windows, you can run a program called `mysql_fix_privileges_tables`. The program will upgrade the system tables but does not perform the complete table check and repair that `mysql_upgrade` performs.

Types of Tables

MySQL currently supports two types of tables — MyISAM and InnoDB. The binary files provided for download on the MySQL Web site set InnoDB as the default.

Prior to these table types, MySQL stored data in ISAM tables. Beginning with MySQL 5, the ISAM tables are no longer supported. If your data is stored in ISAM tables, you must convert them before upgrading to MySQL 5. To convert the tables, send the following query for each table to be converted:

```
ALTER TABLE tablename ENGINE = InnoDB
```

You can find out the table type with the command `SHOW TABLE STATUS`.

Change Documentation

The changes from one version to the next are documented on the MySQL Web site. Each manual contains a change history for the versions. For example, you can see the change history for MySQL 5 at http://dev.mysql.com/doc/refman/5.0/en/news.html.

Incompatible changes are emphasized in the upgrading section of the manual. For instance, important changes when upgrading from version 4.1 to version 5.0 are documented at http://dev.mysql.com/doc/refman/5.0/en/upgrading-from-4-1.html.

Display an HTML Form

HTML forms are very important for dynamic Web sites. Users type or select information in the form and submit the form by clicking a button, and the user information is passed to a program that processes it. The program can store the information in a database or use it in conditional statements to deliver individualized Web pages to the user.

To display a form on a Web page, the HTML code is included in the program in an HTML section of the script or echoed in a PHP section. A form has the following general format:

```
<form action="programname.php" method =
"POST">

    form fields

    submit button

</form>
```

The form fields can be text fields, check boxes, radio buttons, drop-down lists, or hidden fields. You can create a form with no fields or with only hidden fields. The HTML code for form fields contains a parameter `name=` that stores the information from the form.

All forms must have one or more submit buttons. When the user clicks the submit button, the information from the form fields is stored in an array with the value of `name` as the keys. The array of information is passed to the program named in the form tag action parameter.

The method can be either `POST`, which passes the information in the body of the message sent to the Web server, or `GET`, which passes the information in the URL of the message sent to the Web server. The advantages and disadvantages of each method are discussed in the section "Choose the `POST` or `GET` Method for a Form."

Display an HTML Form

1 Echo the `form` tag.

2 Add tags for the form fields.

3 Add a tag that displays a submit button.

4 Add the closing `form` tag.

Note: In this example, the entire form is displayed in one `echo` statement. You can use several `echo` statements if you want.

5 View the script in a browser.

The form fields and submit button are displayed on the Web page.

Note: In this example, the form is not very useful or attractive. It has no labels for the fields and is not nicely formatted.

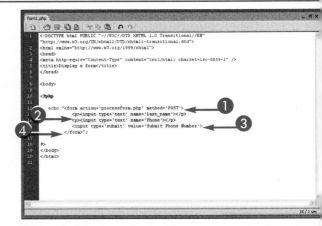

6 Reopen the script in the editor.

7 Add a `table` tag.

8 Add `<tr>` and `<td>` tags to format the form in a table.

9 Add a close `table` tag.

Note: Tables are often used to format forms. You can also use CSS code to format your Web page.

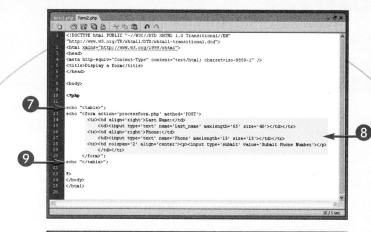

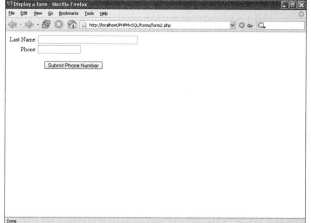

0 View the script in a browser.

The form is formatted and has labels for the fields.

Extra

The action parameter of the `<form>` tag must specify an existing file. If the Web server cannot find the specified file, an error message is displayed.

You can specify the current file using a PHP built-in array rather than name a file. This allows you to process the form information in the same script that displays the form, as discussed in Chapter 10.

TYPE THIS

```
echo "<form
action='$_SERVER[PHP_SELF]'
method='POST'>";
```

RESULT

→ When the user clicks the submit button for this form, the form data is passed to the current script, which is run again.

Add a
Text Field

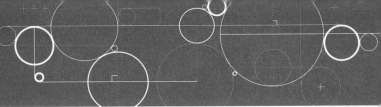

You can display text fields in your form that are blank or that contain information. You may want to display information that users can change or update, such as address or phone number changes, or you may want to redisplay a form, prompting the user to correct fields that are incorrect.

HTML code for text fields includes a parameter called `value`. When information is provided for this value, the information is displayed in the field, as follows:

```
<input type='text' name='First_name'
value='John' maxlength='25'>
```

When the form is displayed on the Web page, the value John is displayed in the field.

The parameter `value` can be assigned a string from a variable. The value in the variable can come from the database, can be passed from another form, or can be

assigned to the variable in the script. You use a variable as follows:

```
$first_name = "John";

echo "<input type='text' name='first_name'
value='$first_name'>";
```

When the field is displayed, the value John is displayed in it. When the user clicks the submit button, the array form information passed to the next script contains an element with the key first_name and the value John. The variable name containing the value is not required to have the same name as the field name, but the form is clearer and programming easier if it does.

Be sure to include the quotes around the variable name assigned to `value` in the input tag, so there are quotes around the value in the HTML code that is sent to the browser.

Add a Text Field

① Create a blank form.

Note: Creating blank forms is described in the section "Display an HTML Form."

② Add the `value` attribute with a variable name to a text field.

③ Repeat step 2 for each text field.

④ Assign a value to some, but not all, of the variables used in steps 2 to 3.

In this example, $lastName is set, but $phone is not.

⑤ View the script in a browser.

A notice is displayed for each variable that is not set.

Note: You could turn off notices so that the notices do not appear, but it is better to change the program to make it run without undefined variables.

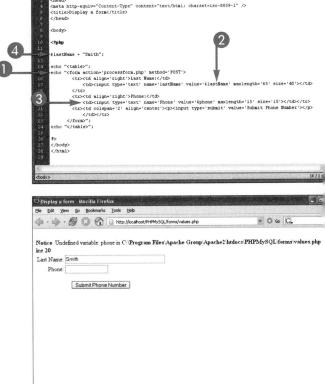

6 Reopen the script in the editor.

7 Type **if(empty( ))**.

8 Type the variable name inside the parentheses.

9 Add a statement to assign an empty string to the variable.

10 Repeat steps 7 to 9 for each variable name used in the form.

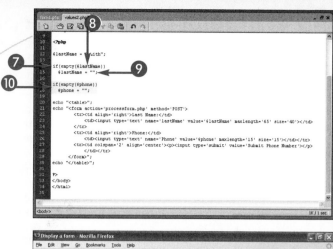

11 View the script in a browser.

The blank fields are displayed without notices.

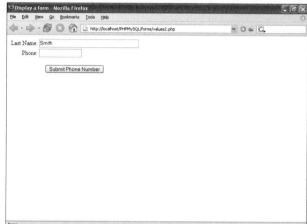

Extra

You can specify the amount of characters a user can type into a text field with the maxlength attribute. For security reasons, you should limit the number of characters whenever possible, to make it more difficult for a person with bad intentions to type damaging code into your form. The size attribute specifies the width of the text field that is displayed. If the size is less than the maxlength, the field scrolls.

You need to include quotes around a value for the form to ensure that the entire value in the variable is assigned to the form field. Without the quotes, only the first word of the value is read into the field.

<table>
<tr><td>TYPE THIS</td><td></td><td>RESULT</td></tr>
<tr><td>

```
$address = "123 Pine St.";

echo "<input type='text'
name='address' value='$address'
maxlength='15'
```

</td><td></td><td>

Displays a text field on the form. The form is displayed with a default width, often 40, but the user is only allowed to type 15 characters into the field. The address is displayed in the field. If there were no quotes around $address, only 123 would be displayed on the form.

</td></tr>
</table>

Add a Multiline Text Area

A *text area* is a text box with multiple lines available for text entry. The user can type an almost unlimited number of lines of text. A text area field has the following format:

```
<textarea name="name" cols="n1" rows="n2">

</textarea>
```

The `name` attribute is required. The parameter $n1$ specifies the number of columns wide the text area should be; the parameter $n2$ specifies the number of rows deep the text area should be. The columns and rows specified refer to the size of the text area displayed on the Web page. These parameters do not limit the amount of text the user can enter. If the user enters more rows

than specified, the text box automatically adds a scroll bar so that the user can enter more text. If you do not specify columns or rows, the browser sets the text area size, often too small for user readability.

Any content that you add between the `<textarea>` and `</textarea>` tags is displayed inside the text area on the Web page. The content can be strings or variables but cannot include tags or other special elements. If no content is included, the text area is blank on the Web page.

When the user submits the form, the contents of the text area are sent, with new line characters between the lines, to the next program, which can access the entire content by the `name` specified in the `<textarea>` tag.

Add a Multiline Text Area

1. Create a variable containing some content.

2. Add a statement that echoes a `form` tag.

3. Add a `textarea` tag with columns and rows specified.

4. Add the variable created in step 1.

5. Add a closing `textarea` tag.

6. Add a submit button.

7. Add the closing `form` tag.

8. View the script in a browser.

   The form with the text area is displayed.

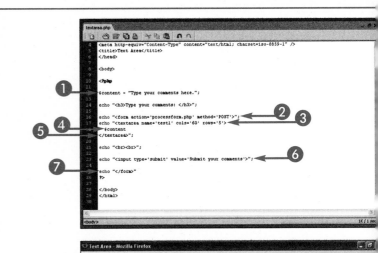

Add a Hidden Field

Y ou can add a hidden field to a form to pass information to the processing program. The field is not displayed on the Web page, and the information is not provided by the user. The field is programmed into the form and passed when the form is passed. The general format of a hidden field is as follows:

```
input type="hidden" name="name"
value="value">
```

The name and value can be assigned a string or a variable. When the user submits the form, the field is passed with the form. The processing program can access the field as an array element with the key "name" and the value "value".

You can include as many hidden fields in a form as you need. Hidden fields are often used to pass information from previous forms. For example, you may have a long form that requires two Web pages. The user submits the first part of the form, and a second part is displayed. If the user fills in and submits the second form, the information from the first form is not available to the third program, the processing program. You need to add the information from the first form to the second form in hidden fields. Then, the processing program has access to the data from both parts of the form.

Add a Hidden Field

1. Create a variable with the value for the hidden field.

2. Echo the `form` tag.

3. Add one or more fields to the form.

4. Add a submit button.

5. Add a hidden field to pass the value created in step 1.

6. Echo `</form>` to end the form.

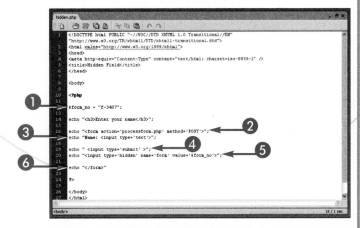

7. View the script in a browser.

   The hidden field does not appear in the form.

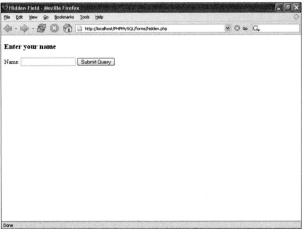

Add a Dynamic Selection List to a Form

Y ou can use selection lists in your forms, instead of text fields. The user selects one item from a drop-down list, instead of typing information into a text field. The HTML code for the field is similar to the following:

```
<select name='listname'>

  <option value='item'>Item name

  . . .

</select>
```

The select tag begins a selection list, providing the name of the field. An option tag is provided for each item in the list. The string in the value parameter is passed to the next script when the user selects the item. The string after the option tag is the string that is displayed in the list on the Web page. The closing select tag ends the list.

The value can be assigned from a variable, providing the ability to create a dynamic list. You can store a group of values in an array and use a foreach loop to echo an option tag for each element in the array. You can select a field from a database and build an option tag for each item retrieved from the database with a while loop.

You can specify that one item is selected by default. If the user does not select any item, the default item is sent to the next script. The word selected is added to the default item, as follows:

```
<option value='item' selected>Item name
```

If no item is appropriate as the default, you can add an item "none" to the list and select it as the default.

Add a Dynamic Selection List to a Form

① Include the file that contains the database connection variables.

② Add a statement that connects to the MySQL server.

③ Create the SQL statement that selects the items for the list.

④ Send the query, assigning the outcome to $result.

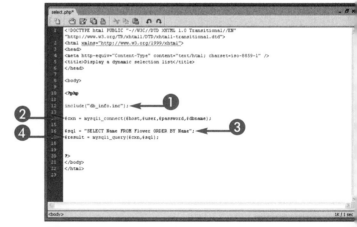

⑤ Echo the form tag.

⑥ Type **<select name='listname'>\n";**.

⑦ Add a while statement that reads the rows from the result set.

⑧ Add the statements that echo the option tag.

⑨ Add the select closing tag.

⑩ Add a submit button.

⑪ Add the closing form tag.

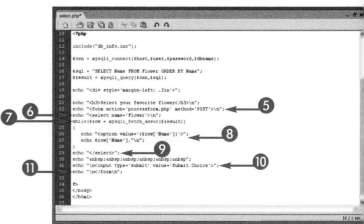

② View the script in a browser.

The list and submit button are displayed.

③ Click the down arrow to see the drop-down list.

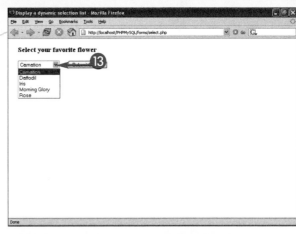

④ View the source code from your browser.

Note: In Firefox, you click View ➪ Page Source to view the source code.

The source is well-formatted and easy to read because of the `\n` characters in the script.

The single quotes specified in the `echo` statement appear in the `option` tag source.

Apply It

You can add a `label` tag that displays a label for a field. You can apply the label to the field using the `id` attribute on the field tag.

TYPE THIS

```
echo "<label for='fl'>Flowers: </label>";
echo "<select name='Flower' id='fl'>\n";
    options
echo "</select>";
```

RESULT

The label — Flowers: — is displayed in front of the selection list.

Add a Date Selection List

Forms frequently need to collect dates — today's date, a birth date, the date of an event, and so on. Providing a selection list of dates avoids the spelling and typing errors that can happen when users type a date into a text field.

A date field consists of three selection lists — the month, the year, and the day. The day is the simplest list to build — a list of 31 numbers. You can use a for loop that repeats 31 times, echoing an option tag for each number. The option value and the name displayed are the same.

The year is a list of numbers. You can start the list with an arbitrary year and add one for each entry — 2005, 2006, 2007, and so on — in a for loop. However, you can make a more useful, perpetual list if you obtain the

current year with the date() function and use the year for the starting value of your loop. Chapter 2 discusses dates and times.

For the month selection list, you want the name of the month to appear in the list, but the number is best for the value. You can create an array of month names. You can use a for loop to echo an option tag for each month, inserting the number for the value and the month name for the display value.

In many cases, you want a date to be selected by default, such as the current date. You can get the current date, using the date() function, and compare the current date with the date in the loop. When the loop date and the current date match, you add the word selected to the option tag.

Add a Date Selection List

① Create an array of month names.

② Create a variable containing the current date.

③ Echo the form tag.

④ Assign the number of the current month to a variable.

⑤ Echo the select tag.

⑥ Add a for loop that echoes the option tags.

⑦ Add an if statement that adds selected to the option tag for the current month.

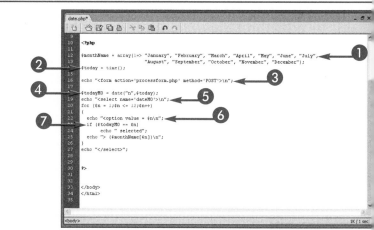

⑧ Assign the number of the current day to a variable.

⑨ Echo the select tag.

⑩ Add a for loop that repeats 31 times.

⑪ Add statements that echo an option tag for each day.

⑫ Add an if statement that adds selected to the option tag for the current day.

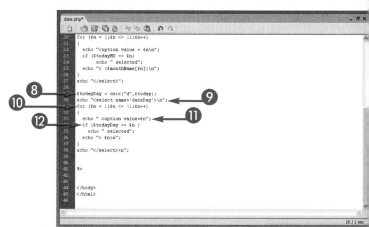

③ Assign the current year to a variable.

④ Echo the `select` tag.

⑤ Add a `for` loop that echoes an `option` tag for each year.

⑥ Add an `if` statement that adds `selected` to the `option` tag for the current year.

⑦ Echo closing tags for the `select` tag and the `form` tag.

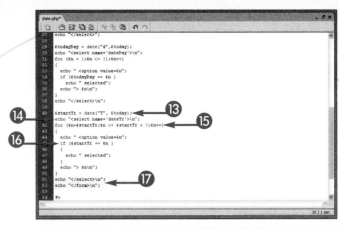

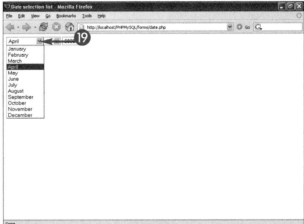

⑧ View the script in a browser.

The three selection lists are displayed.

⑨ Click the down arrow by the month.

The month selection list drops down.

Extra

Starting with PHP 5.1.0, you can set a time zone that PHP uses in any date functions. If you do not set a time zone, PHP guesses a time zone. In some cases, its guess may be UTC (coordinated universal time). You can set date.timezone in your php.ini file or set the time zone in your script, which applies only to the script. A list of time zone codes is available at www.php.net/manual/en/timezones.php.

TYPE THIS

```
date_default_timezone_set
("America/Los_Angeles");
```

RESULT

The default time zone is set to the U.S. west coast time. All date and time functions will produce output using this time zone.

Add Dynamic Radio Buttons

You can add a set of radio buttons to a form. The user can select only one option from the set. The general format of a radio button tag is as follows:

```
<input type="radio" name="name"
value="value">
```

The name of the field should be the same for all the radio buttons in the set. The value should be the value that you want to pass to the next script when the user clicks this radio button. You can assign the value as a string or from a variable. Each radio button needs a text label beside it. You display the label with your HTML code, not inside the radio button input tag.

You can build a set of radio buttons from your database. You can retrieve the values from a column in a table and

use the field values in a set of radio buttons echoed in a while loop.

If no item is checked, no value for the set of radio buttons is sent to the next script. If you want a value sent whenever the submit button is clicked, you can specify that one item is checked by default. To specify a default, the word checked is added to the item, as follows:

```
<input type="radio" name="name"
value="value" checked>
```

If no item is appropriate as the default, you can add an item "none" to the set and select it as the default.

Add Dynamic Radio Buttons

1 Add a statement to include the file that sets $host, $user, $password, and $database.

2 Add a statement that calls mysqli_connect() to connect to the server.

$cxn contains the connection information.

Note: Connecting to the MySQL server from PHP is discussed in Chapter 7.

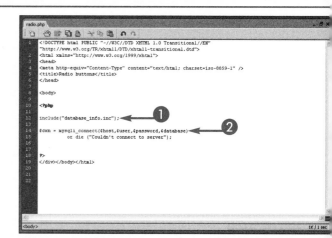

3 Create a variable that contains a SQL query.

$sql contains the query.

4 Add a statement that calls the mysqli_query() function to send the query.

5 Add or and a die() statement to stop the program and display a message if the query fails.

Note: Executing a query from PHP and handling MySQL errors are discussed in Chapter 7.

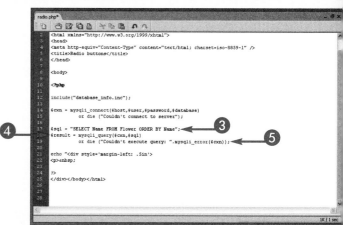

⑥ Add a statement to echo the `form` tag.

⑦ Add a `while` loop that fetches all the rows of data from the result set, one row at a time.

⑧ Add the statements that echo an `input` tag for each radio button.

⑨ Add a submit button to the form.

⑩ Echo `</form>` to end the form.

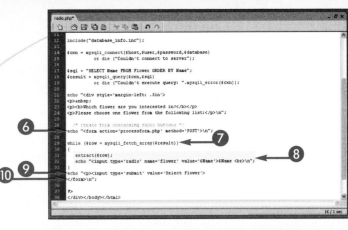

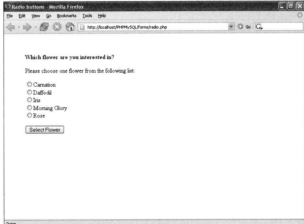

⑪ View the script in a browser.

The list of radio buttons is displayed.

In this example, no radio button is checked because the source code does not specify any radio button as the default.

Extra

If the user does not click a radio button, no element for the set of radio buttons is included in the array that is sent to the processing program. You can specify a default button that is selected when the set of buttons is displayed. Then, if the user does not click a radio button, the default value is sent when the form is submitted.

TYPE THIS

```
<input type='radio' name='flower'
value='none' checked>I don't like
flowers
```

RESULT

When the form is displayed, the radio button for "I don't like flowers" is checked. If the user does not click another radio button, this default value is sent to the processing program when the form is submitted.

You can add a list of check boxes to a form. The user can select as many check boxes as he or she wants from the list. The general format of a check box tag is

```
<input type="checkbox" name="name"
value="value">
```

In order to pass more than one check box, you need to use an array for the name. You can set the array as `interest[]`, which will use a number as the key. Or you can use a string for a key, using a different key for each check box, such as `interest['rose']`, `interest['daffodil']`, and so on.

The value should be the value you want to pass to the next script when the user clicks this check box. Often the check box is assigned a value of `yes` or `1`,

which is passed to the next script when the user checks the check box.

You can assign the name and the value as a string or from a variable. Each check box needs a text label beside it. You display the label with your HTML code, not inside the radio button `input` tag.

You can build a list of check boxes from your database. You can retrieve the values from a column in a table and use the values in a list of check boxes echoed in a `while` loop. You can use the value as the key in the name array, as the value, and/or as the text label.

The script creates an element in the array with a key/value pair for each check box that is selected. The array is passed to the program that processes the form.

Add Dynamic Check Boxes

1 Add a statement to include the file that sets `$host`, `$user`, `$password`, and `$database`.

2 Add a statement that calls `mysqli_connect()` to connect to the server.

    `$cxn` contains the connection information.

Note: Connecting to the MySQL server from PHP is discussed in Chapter 7.

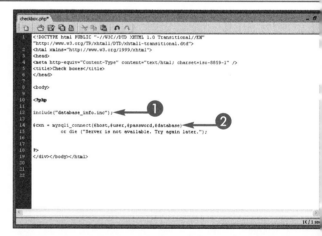

3 Create a variable that contains a SQL query.

    `$sql` contains the query.

4 Add a statement that calls the `mysqli_query()` function to send the query.

5 Add `or` and a `die()` statement to stop the program and display a message if the query fails.

Note: Executing a query from PHP and handling MySQL errors are discussed in Chapter 7.

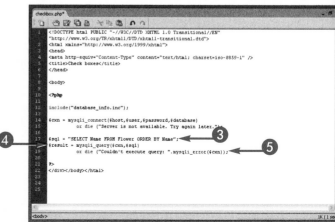

6️⃣ Add a statement to echo the `form` tag.

7️⃣ Add a `while` loop that fetches all the rows of data from the result set, one row at a time.

8️⃣ Add the statements that echo an `input` tag for each check box.

9️⃣ Add a submit button to the form.

🔟 Echo `</form>` to end the form.

🔟 View the script in a browser.

The list of check boxes is displayed.

Extra

You can use a `<label>` tag to display a label beside a check box. You can enclose each check box field in `<label>` tags that display a text string before or after the check box.

TYPE THIS

```
echo "<label><input type='checkbox'
name='flower[$Name]' value='yes'
>$Name </label><br>\n";
```

→

RESULT

The check box is displayed, followed by the value of $Name.

By default, a check box is displayed unselected. If the user does not click the check box, it is not passed to the processing program. You can specify that a check box be checked when it is displayed. If the user does not uncheck the check box, it is sent to the processing program.

TYPE THIS

```
echo "<input type='checkbox'
name='flower[$Name]' value='yes'
checked>$Name\n";
```

→

RESULT

The check box is checked when it is displayed. The user must click it to uncheck it.

Create One or More Submit Buttons

A form must have at least one submit button. When the user clicks the submit button, the information in the form is sent to the program designated in the `form` tag in the `action` attribute. The format of the submit button tag is

```
<input type="submit" name="name" value="value">
```

The tag creates a submit button, with *value* displayed on the button. If you do not include a `value` attribute, the text "Submit" is displayed. When the user clicks the button, the information from the form is sent to the specified program, where the information is available in an array. The array contains an element for the button, with *name* as the key and *value* as the value. If the `name` attribute is not included in the tag, no array element is added for the button. The `name` and `value` parameters can be assigned a string or a variable.

You can add more than one submit button to your form. For example, a sales order may provide two buttons — one that displays "Submit Order" and one that displays "Cancel." The processing program can then perform different actions based on which button the user clicks.

You can give different names to multiple buttons, or you can give the same name to the button but different values, as follows:

```
<input type="submit" name="button1" value=
"Submit Order">
```

```
<input type="submit" name="button1" value=
"Cancel">
```

The processing program can write a conditional statement, as follows:

```
if( $arrayname['button1'] == "Submit Order"
```

Processing information from forms is discussed in Chapter 10.

Create One or More Submit Buttons

---

① Echo the `form` tag to start the form.

Note: This form is formatted with an HTML table.

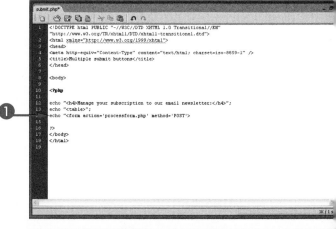

② Add one or more fields to the form.

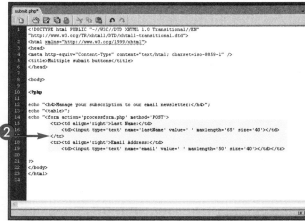

3 Add two or more submit buttons to the form.

In this example, the buttons have the same name but different values.

4 Echo `</form>` to end the form.

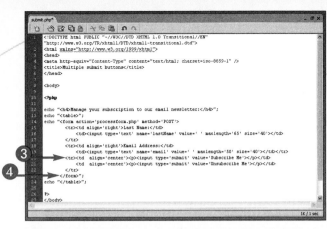

5 View the script in a browser.

The form is displayed with two or more submit buttons.

Note: The processing problem designated in the `form` tag can detect which button was clicked and process the information accordingly.

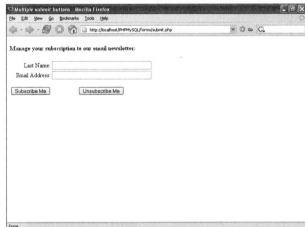

Extra

You can add a reset button to your form, as well as one or more submit buttons. When the user clicks the reset button, the form fields are reset to their default values. No other action is performed. The form is not submitted, the information in the form is not passed on, and the processing program designated in the `form` tag is not started.

TYPE THIS

```
echo "<input type='reset'
value='Reset Defaults'>";
```

→

RESULT

A button with the text "Reset Defaults" displayed on it appears on the form. When the user clicks this button, the default values are reset in the form fields.

Choose the POST or GET Method for a Form

In the `form` tag, you define a method, which determines the way the information that the user types in the form is passed to the next program. You can specify the POST method or the GET method.

With the GET method, the form data is passed by adding it to the URL that calls the form-processing program. For instance, the URL may look like this:

```
processform.php?fname=Joe&lname=Smith
```

The data from a field named `fname` and a field named `lname` are passed by adding the field name and value to the URL.

The disadvantages of the GET method are that less data can be passed and that the information is displayed in the browser where the user can see it, which can be a

security problem in some situations. The advantage is that the GET method is faster. When you are using some other languages, such as CGI, the GET method can be simpler to process in the next program, but this is not th case when you are using PHP.

With the POST method, the form data is passed as a package in a separate communication with the processin program. One advantage of the POST method is that ther is no limitation on the amount of information that can b passed, allowing very large, complicated forms. A secon advantage is that the information being passed cannot b seen by the user, providing greater security.

In most cases, the POST method is preferred for user forms.

Choose the POST or GET Method for a Form

THE POST METHOD

1. Create a form that specifies the POST method.

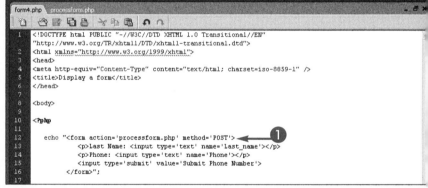

2. View the script in a browser.

3. Fill in the form fields.

4. Click the submit button.

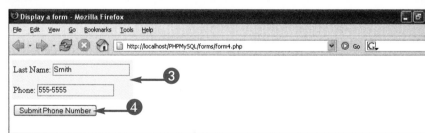

● No values are added to the URL.

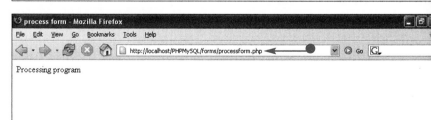

THE GET METHOD

1 Create a form that specifies the GET method.

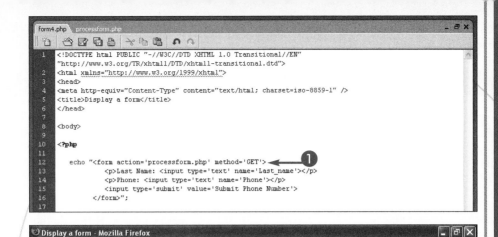

```
<!DOCTYPE html PUBLIC "-//W3C//DTD XHTML 1.0 Transitional//EN"
 "http://www.w3.org/TR/xhtml1/DTD/xhtml1-transitional.dtd">
<html xmlns="http://www.w3.org/1999/xhtml">
<head>
<meta http-equiv="Content-Type" content="text/html; charset=iso-8859-1" />
<title>Display a form</title>
</head>

<body>

<?php

    echo "<form action='processform.php' method='GET'>
            <p>Last Name: <input type='text' name='Last_name'></p>
            <p>Phone: <input type='text' name='Phone'></p>
            <input type='submit' value='Submit Phone Number'>
         </form>";
```

2 View the script in a browser.

3 Fill in the form fields.

4 Click the submit button.

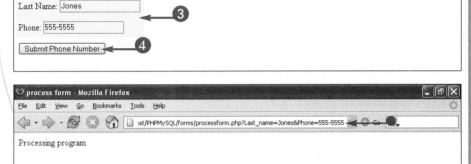

Last Name: Jones

Phone: 555-5555

Submit Phone Number

● The form values are added to the URL.

Processing program

(URL: ...st/PHPMySQL/forms/processform.php?Last_name=Jones&Phone=555-5555)

Extra

Forms using the GET method pass the form information by adding it to the URL. You do not need to create a form to pass information in the URL. You can add information manually to any URL that will then be available to the next script.

TYPE THIS		RESULT
`<a href="prog2.php?fname=John&lname=Smith>Click Here</a>`		When the user clicks the Click Here link, the script named prog2.php runs, and the values fname=John and lname=Smith are passed to prog2.php. Accessing and using variables passed in the URL are discussed in Chapter 10.

Create a Form That Uploads a File

You can allow users to upload a file to your Web server. The user uploads the file with an HTML form designed for that purpose. The <form> tag for uploading files includes an enctype attribute, as follows:

```
enctype="multipart/form-data"
```

The input field that uploads the file specifies the input type, file, as follows:

```
<input type="file" name="name">
```

The information is sent in an array element with the key name.

The form must also include a hidden field with the name MAX_FILE_SIZE that specifies a size for the file to be uploaded. If a user tries to upload a file that is larger than MAX_FILE_SIZE, the file will not upload.

MAX_FILE_SIZE is limited by the setting upload_max_filesize in php.ini. By default, upload_max_filesize is 2MB. If you need to load a file larger that 2MB, you first change upload_max_filesize to the larger size and then send the hidden field with MAX_FILE_SIZE set to the larger value.

The form displays a field into which you can type the path/filename of the file that you want to upload. A Browse button is displayed along with the field. You can browse to the file to select it, instead of typing the filename.

When the user submits the form, the file is uploaded to temporary location. The processing program copies the file to a permanent location. The temporary file is deleted as soon as the processing program ends. Processing an uploaded file is described in Chapter 10.

Create a Form That Uploads a File

① Open php.ini in a text editor.

② Scroll down to the File Uploads section.

③ Set upload_max_filesize to a larger size.

In this example, it is set to 5M.

④ Save the file.

⑤ Restart the Web server.

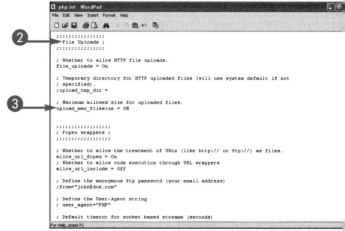

⑥ Echo a <form> tag.

⑦ Include the attribute enctype='multipart/form-data' in the form tag.

⑧ Add a hidden field that sets MAX_FILE_SIZE.

In this example, MAX_FILE_SIZE is set to 3000000.

9 Type **<input type='file'**.

10 Add a `name` attribute to the `input` tag.

11 Add a `size` attribute to the `input` tag.

Note: This size is the width of the field, not the size of the file to be uploaded.

12 Add a submit button.

13 Type **</form>** to end the form.

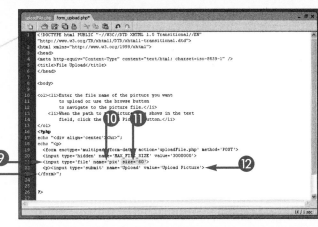

14 View the script in a browser.

A field for entering the filename is displayed.

A Browse button lets the user browse to the file.

Extra

You can allow the user to upload more than one file in a form by including more than one `<input>` tag. The two tags need to provide different names so that the processing program receives both files.

TYPE THIS		RESULT
```<input type="file" name="pix1" size="60"> <input type="file" name="pix2" size="60">```		Two fields are displayed, with Browse buttons beside them. You can select different files in each field.

Process Information from a Form

The `<form>` tag specifies, with the `action` attribute, which script to run when the form is submitted. When the user clicks the submit button, the specified program runs and receives the information from the form. The form data is available in the processing program in built-in PHP arrays.

The program can use the array elements in PHP statements. The program can display the form information, use the information in conditional statements, store the information in a database, or use the information in any manner.

The Superglobal Arrays

PHP provides three built-in arrays, called *superglobal arrays,* that contain the information submitted in a form: `$_POST`, `$_GET`, and `$_REQUEST`. `$_POST` contains information submitted in a form using the `POST` method. `$_GET` contains information submitted in a form using the `GET` method. `$_REQUEST` contains the information in both the `$_POST` and `$_GET` arrays.

The array keys are the names of the fields. For example, the form may contain the following field:

```
<input type='text' name='first_name'>
```

The text that the user types into this field is available in the processing program in the following array element:

```
$_POST['first_name']
```

You can use the array element in any PHP statement.

Converting the Arrays to Variables

A PHP configuration setting, called `register_globals`, converts the arrays to variables automatically when it is on. Variables named for the array keys are created when the processing program runs. Although this automatic conversion is convenient, it adds a security risk. Good programming practice dictates that this setting is not turned on.

In PHP 4.1 and earlier versions, `register_globals` was turned on by default. Beginning with PHP 4.2, `register_globals` is turned off by default. In PHP 6, the `register_globals` setting is removed. The automatic conversion feature is no longer provided.

You can convert the array to variables by using the `extract()` function at the beginning of the processing program. This provides a similar security risk. You need to check the information that you receive before using it.

The Long Built-in Arrays

The superglobal arrays were added to PHP 4.1. Prior to the superglobal arrays, long predefined arrays were used: `$HTTP_POST_VARS` and `$HTTP_GET_VARS`. Older programs may use the long arrays. If you are using a version of PHP prior to 4.1, you need to use the long arrays.

Beginning with PHP 5, a configuration setting determines whether the long arrays are built or not. If you set `register_long_arrays` to off, PHP does not build the long arrays. Currently, long arrays are turned on by default, but this may change in the future. If you do not need to use the long arrays, you should change the setting to off, to prevent wasting the resources used to create the long arrays when they are not being used.

Checking Form Information

A program should never use or store information from an outside source without checking whether it contains the expected information. This is the single, most important rule for the usefulness and security of your Web site.

The information received from forms comes from an outside source. Although the majority of visitors to your Web site are customers with no intentions beyond using the services you offer, not all people are honest and well-intentioned. Some have nefarious purposes, such as stealing information, damaging your Web site, or harming the visitors to your Web site. In addition, your well-intentioned visitors can sometimes cause problems unintentionally with errors and typos that produce incorrect or missing information. Consequently, you must check the information from forms, called *validation*.

Checking for Empty Fields

When you create a form, you can decide which fields are required and which are optional. In the processing program, you check the fields that are required. If a required field is blank, you send a message to the user, indicating that the field is required, and you redisplay the form so that the user can type the required information.

Checking the Format of the Information

The data that is sent from forms usually has an expected format. For instance, abcxyz is not the expected format for a zip code. A zip code should be in a numeric format, such as 12345 or 12345-1234. If you check each field for its expected format, you can catch most typos and prevent most malicious content.

You check the form data using regular expressions, which are patterns. You compare the information in the field against a pattern to see whether it matches an expected format. For example, you can build a pattern that matches the format of a zip code — five numbers or five numbers plus four numbers. You can then compare the information in the zip code field of the form to the pattern. If it does not match, the information in the field is incorrect, and the user must type it again. See Chapter 4 for more on regular expressions.

Trimming the Data

Users often accidentally add spaces at the beginning or end of a text string. You can remove these extra spaces with PHP functions. The spaces are unnecessary, and sometimes cause problems when you are comparing strings. A string with a space at the end does not match the same string without the space.

PHP provides three functions that trim empty spaces: The function ltrim() removes spaces from the beginning of a string; rtrim() removes spaces from the end of a string; and trim() removes spaces from both the beginning and the end.

Handling HTML Tags in Form Fields

In most cases, you would not allow HTML tags in a field because tags are a security risk. Particularly, someone could enter <script> in a field and possibly damage your Web site. You can remove all HTML tags from strings or specify that only certain tags are allowed with the strip_tags() function.

However, in some cases, you need to allow users to enter the < and > characters. For example, the user may need to include formulas that require the characters or may want to discuss the use of particular HTML tags in a forum. You can allow users to enter these characters and then convert them to characters that HTML displays without any special meaning. For instance, < is converted to <, which HTML displays as a < on a Web page but does not treat as the start of a tag. You can convert the characters using the htmlspecialchars() function or the htmlentities() function.

Display Data from a Form

PHP provides the data from a form in the superglobal array $_POST or $_GET. In the program that receives the data from the form, you can get and use the data from these arrays as you would data from any other array. The key for each array element is the name of the input field in the form. Information that the user selects from selection drop-down lists or radio buttons is similarly available for use.

During development, you often just want to see what information is passed to your program, to determine whether the information is passed as you expect it. You can use var_dump() to display the data, as follows:

```
echo "<pre>";

var_dump($_POST);

echo "</pre>";
```

This is troubleshooting code, not code that you would use in a public Web site.

You can display the form data using a foreach loop that walks through the $_POST array, as follows:

```
foreach($_POST as $field => $value)

{

    echo "$field = $value<br>\n";

}
```

You can display the form data on your Web page in any format. You can display it using any HTML tags, in an HTML table, in headers, in form fields, or any other valid HTML use. You just echo the appropriate HTML code with the array elements in the locations that you want.

Display Data from a Form

① Create a form.

Note: Creating forms is described in Chapter 9.

② Specify the program to process the form.

In this example, the program processform.php is specified to receive the information from the form.

③ Create a script with the name specified in step 2.

④ Add a var_dump() statement to see the contents of $_POST.

⑤ Add a foreach loop to display the contents of $_POST.

Note: Working with arrays is discussed in Chapter 3.

6 View the form in a browser.

7 Fill in the form fields.

8 Click a submit button.

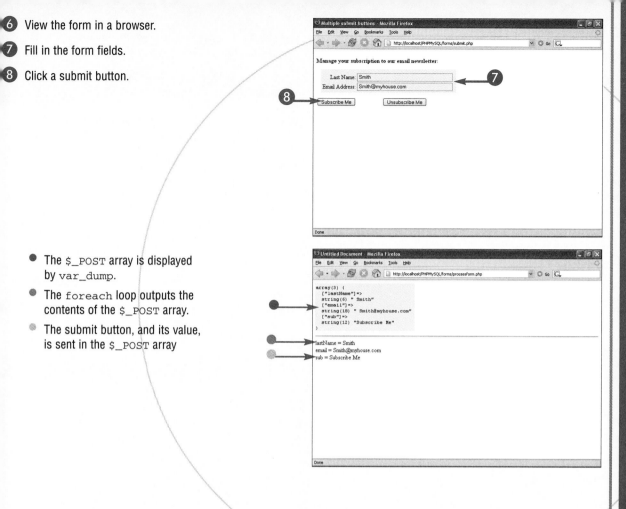

- The $_POST array is displayed by var_dump.

- The foreach loop outputs the contents of the $_POST array.

- The submit button, and its value, is sent in the $_POST array

Apply It

If your form includes a set of check boxes, the form information is in an array, as shown in Chapter 9. The check box array is an element in the $_POST array. For example, you may have named your check boxes with the following attributes: name='flower[rose]' and name='flower[carnation]'. The check boxes that the user checks are passed in the $_POST array.

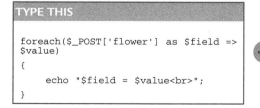

TYPE THIS

```
foreach($_POST['flower'] as $field =>
$value)
{
    echo "$field = $value<br>";
}
```

RESULT

A list of the checked fields and their values is displayed. If the user did not check any of the boxes, the array named flower will not exist in the $_POST array.

Display and Process a Form in One Script

You can simplify your Web site by using a single script to display a form and process it, called a *self-processing* page. When the script is first accessed, it displays the empty form. When the user submits the form, the script processes the form information. The script tests for a hidden field to determine whether the script is running the first time or whether a user submitted the form.

You can include a hidden field in your form and test for the hidden field with a conditional statement, as follows:

```
if(isset($_POST['hiddenfieldname']))

    process form

else

    display form
```

If the hidden field exists in the $_POST array, the form was submitted, so the script processes the form information. If the hidden field is not present, the form was not submitted, so the script displays the form. Hidden fields are described in Chapter 9.

In some cases, the code that presents and displays the form can be quite complicated, as can the code that processes the form information. To make the script simpler to understand for maintenance and upgrading, you can store the presentation and content in a separate file from the script logic, making the logic simpler to follow. For example, you can store the code that displays the form in a separate file and include the file when the script needs to display the form. This organization enables you to display the same form in different scripts with an `include` file, rather than adding the form code to several different scripts.

Display and Process a Form in One Script

1. Open a file in a text editor.

2. Add the code that displays a form.

Note: Displaying forms is discussed in Chapter 9.

3. Specify the current file as the file to run when the form is submitted.

4. Add a hidden field.

5. Save the file as an `include` file.

Note: `include` files are explained in Chapter 5.

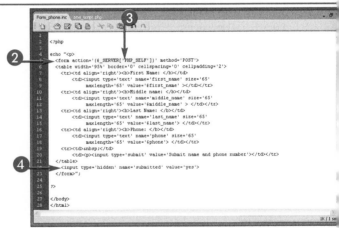

6. Open a separate script file in a text editor.

7. Add an `if` statement that tests for the hidden variable created in step 4.

8. Add a block of statements that processes the form when it is submitted.

   In this example, the form information is displayed with a `var_dump()` statement.

9. Type **else**.

10. Add a statement that sets field values to blank.

11. Include the file that contains the form code.

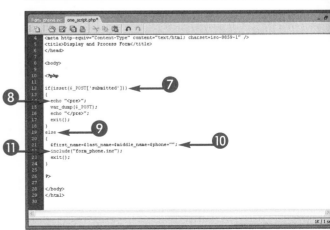

12 View the script in a browser.

The form in the include file is displayed.

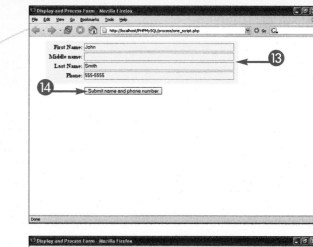

13 Fill in the form fields.

14 Click the submit button.

The script code processes the form information.

In this example, the $_POST array is displayed with a var_dump() statement.

● The hidden field is included in the $_POST array.

Apply It

In some cases, you may provide more than one submit button in your form. If you give the submit button a name, it will be included in the $_POST array. You can give the buttons the same name and different values and then test the buttons in your processing program.

TYPE THIS

```
if($_POST['mybutton'] == "Submit Order")
{
    statements that process the order;
}
elseif($_POST['mybutton'] == "Cancel")
{
    statements that cancel the order;
}
```

RESULT

→ Your program performs different actions, depending on which button the user clicked.

Check for Blank Fields

The script that processes form information needs to check that the information is correct. You can check whether any required fields are blank and whether the data in the form fields is in an expected format. This section discusses blank fields. The field format is discussed in the next section. In most cases, your script should check both.

You can check whether any required fields are blank with an if statement. In most cases, you want to check all the fields in the form. You can do this by looping through the $_POST array and testing whether each field is blank, as follows:

```
foreach($_POST as $field => $value)

{

    if($value == "")
```

```
    {

        block of statements;

    }

}
```

What tasks you perform in the block of statements depends on your form. Usually, you want to display a message, telling the user that a required field is blank, and then redisplay the form so that the user can enter the missing information. You generally need to store the names of the fields that are blank so that you can inform the user which fields are missing. Often, the missing fields are highlighted by color, or a list of the missing fields is displayed. You can add an if statement that skips the fields that are not required, leaving them out of the array of blank fields.

Check for Blank Fields

1. Add an if statement that tests whether submitted is not set, using !isset().

2. Add statements that display a blank form.

3. Type **else** to start a block of code that processes the form data.

4. Add a foreach loop that traverses $_POST.

5. Add an if statement to test for blank fields.

6. Add an if statement to skip nonrequired fields.

7. Add the field name to the array of blank fields.

8. Add an if statement that tests whether any elements were added to the array of blank fields.

9. Add statements that echo an error message.

10. Extract $_POST.

11. Redisplay the form.

12. Add an else block to execute when no fields are blank.

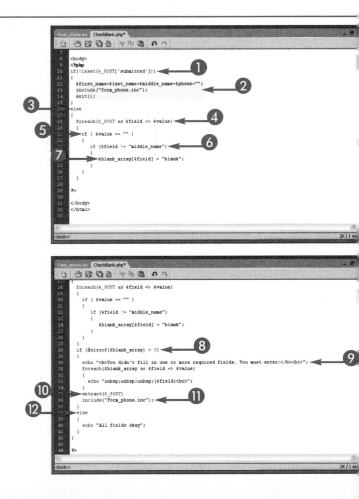

13 View the script in a browser.

The blank form is displayed.

14 Fill in the form, leaving some required fields blank.

15 Click the submit button.

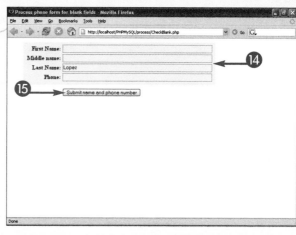

The error message is displayed.

The form is redisplayed with the correct information still in the fields.

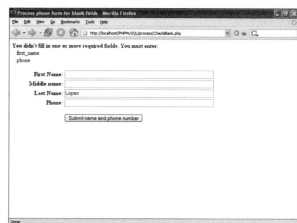

Apply It

In some cases, you may have many fields in your form, with many fields that are not required. Rather than write an `if` statement for every nonrequired field, you can create an array of fields that are not required and test whether the current field is in the array.

TYPE THIS

```
$not_required = array("middle_name","fax");
foreach($_POST as $field => $value)
{
  if( $value == "" )
  {
      if(!in_array($field,$not_required))
      {
          $blank_array[$field] = "blank";
      }
  }
}
```

RESULT

The array of blank fields does not include any fields that are not required.

Verify Form Data

The script that processes form information needs to check that the information is correct. You can check whether any required fields are blank and whether the data in the form fields is in an expected format. This section discusses checking the field format.

You can check the format of the text in a field by comparing the text to a pattern, called a *regular expression,* as discussed in Chapter 4. You can check each field in turn by looping through the $_POST array. For each field, you can compare the value to an appropriate regular expression, as follows:

```
if($field == "fieldname")

{

    if(!ereg("pattern",$value))

    {
```

```
        block of statements;

    }

}
```

In the block of statements, you can display a message and then redisplay the form so that the user can correct the information. You generally need to store the names of the incorrect fields so that you can inform the user which fields need correction. You can store the correct field values for display or storage in the database. You want to be sure to redisplay the correct information in the form so that the user does not need to type the correct information again. You need to add an if condition for any fields that are allowed to be blank.

Verify Form Data

1. Add an if statement that displays the blank form.

2. Type **else** to begin the block that processes form data.

3. Add a foreach loop to loop through $_POST.

4. Add an if statement for one or more fields.

5. Test the field text with a regular expression.

6. If the field does not match the regex, add the field name to an array.

7. If the field matches the regex, add the value to an array of good values.

8. Repeat steps 4 to 7 until all fields are tested.

9. Add an if statement that executes if any bad formats were found.

10. Display an error message.

11. Extract the values from $_POST.

12. Display the form.

13. Add an else block that executes when all the data is correct.

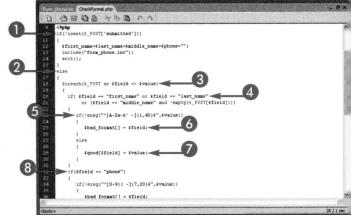

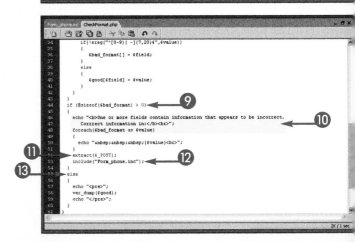

⑭ View the script in a browser.

The blank form is displayed.

⑮ Fill in the form fields, typing incorrect information into at least one field.

⑯ Click the submit button.

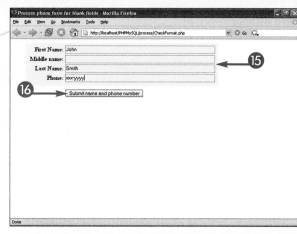

An error message is displayed.

The form is redisplayed with the information still displayed in the fields.

Apply It

You need to check the multiple-choice fields, as well as the text fields. People with malicious intentions can send unwanted values in these fields. You can check the fields using a regex that matches the specific values allowed.

TYPE THIS

```
if(!ereg("(yes|no)",$value))
{
   $bad_format[] = $field;
}
else
{
   $good[$field] = $value;
}
```

RESULT

If $value contains any value other than yes or no, the field is added to the $bad_format array.

Clean Form Data

Users can type data into a text field, either accidentally or maliciously, that can cause problems for your application, your database, or your users. Checking the data and accepting only the characters expected for the information requested, as described in the previous section, can prevent most problems. However, you can miss something. Also, in some cases, the information that the user enters needs to allow pretty much anything. For instance, you normally would not allow the characters < and > in a field. However, there may be a situation in which the user needs to enter these characters — perhaps the user needs to enter a technical formula or to discuss HTML tags.

Users can type blank spaces before or after text when typing in a text field. If you need to compare the text to another string or store it in a database, the extra spaces can cause a problem. You can remove the spaces from the beginning of a string with `ltrim()`, from the end of a string with `rtrim()`, and from both the beginning and end with `trim()`.

You can remove HTML tags from the data users type into a text field using the `strip_tags()` function. You can remove all tags from the text, or you can specify a set of tags to be allowed, removing all other tags.

If you need to allow users to enter < and >, you can convert the characters to HTML special characters, rendering them harmless. The < character is changed to `&lt;`, and > is changed to `&gt;`. Browsers will display the special characters in the Web page but will not treat them as the characters that define a tag. You can use the function `htmlspecialchars()` or `htmlentities()` to convert < and >.

Clean Form Data

1. Add an `if` statement to display a blank form that includes a text area field.

2. Add an `else` statement that processes the form data when the form is submitted.

3. Add a statement that cleans the data with the `trim` and `htmlspecialchars` functions.

4. Echo the cleaned data.

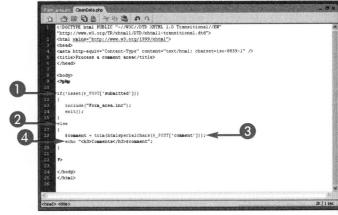

5. View the script in a browser.

   The blank form is displayed.

6. Type in the text area, including one or more HTML tags in the text.

7. Click the submit button.

The comment is displayed, showing
the HTML tag from the form.

8 View the source code for the Web
page.

Note: In Firefox, you click View ➪ Page
Source to view the source code.

- The HTML special characters
  are in the source code, not the
  HTML tags.

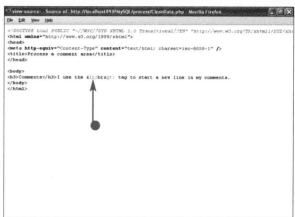

Extra

You can remove some HTML tags and allow others with the `strip_tags()` function. Since PHP 4.3, the
`strip_tags()` function removes HTML comments, as well as HTML tags. The `<!--` tag and the `-->` tags
are removed, along with everything between them. You cannot prevent `strip_tags()` from removing
comments, as you can with other HTML tags.

TYPE THIS	RESULT
`$cleaned = strip_tags ($_POST['comments'], "<b><i>");`	Any HTML tags in `$_POST[comments]` are removed, with the exception of the `<b>` and `<i>` opening and closing tags. `<b>` and `<i>` are included in the text stored in `$cleaned`. The `strip_tags()` function does not validate the HTML code, so missing or incorrect tags can cause more text to be removed than expected.

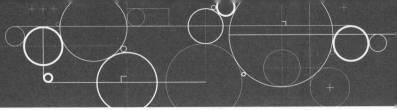

Add Form Data to a Database

You can store data from a form in a database. To do so, you build a SQL query using the data from the form fields after the data is cleaned and validated. However, a malicious user can enter data into your form that can cause damage when sent to the MySQL server. Therefore, you need to protect against an attack that modifies your query into a damaging query, called a *SQL injection* attack.

Building a Query

The data from the form is passed in the $_POST array. You can use the data in a query by using the array elements in the query, as follows:

```
$sql = "INSERT INTO User (Last_name,First_name,Phone)
VALUES ('$Last_name','$First_name','$phone')";
```

You can then execute the query with the appropriate function, such as the following:

```
$result = mysqli_query($cxn,$sql);
```

Building and executing queries is discussed in Chapter 7.

Protecting against SQL Injection

The techniques discussed earlier in this chapter — verifying form data and cleaning the data — provide some protection against SQL injection. However, in many cases, you need to allow quotes to be stored in your database, leaving your Web site vulnerable to a SQL injection attack.

You can escape all the quotes in form data by inserting a backslash (\) in front of quotes. A quote is then treated as any other character, not as a special character with special meaning, rendering the query harmless.

SQL Injection

A *SQL injection* means that a user enters text into your form that, when used in your query, changes your query so that it operates differently than you expect. For instance, suppose that you have a login form in which the user types a username and a password. The query you create using the form data might be similar to the following:

```
SELECT * FROM User WHERE username = '$user'
          AND password = '$password'
```

Suppose that a malicious user types the following into the user field in your login form and leaves the password field blank:

```
xx' or 'in'='in' --
```

The query built from that data would look like the following:

```
SELECT * FROM User WHERE username = ' xx' or
'in'='in' --'
          AND password = ''
```

Because 'in'='in' is always true and -- starts a comment, so the rest of the query is ignored, the query would log the user in to the Web site.

Another type of SQL injection takes advantage of the multiple query feature of SQL by adding a semicolon and a second, damaging query in a form field. This type of query is less of a danger in MySQL than other databases because multiple queries are executed using a special function, not the query function. If multiple functions are sent to a mysql query function, the function fails.

Automatic Escaping (Magic Quotes)

PHP provides a feature that automatically escapes all strings in the $_POST and $_GET arrays, called *magic quotes.* Single quotes, double quotes, backslashes, and null characters are escaped. This feature, designed to help beginning users, is controlled by the

magic_quotes-gpc setting in php.ini, turned on by default in PHP 4 and PHP 5 and turned off by default in PHP 6. Using magic quotes has advantages and disadvantages. Most experienced users turn magic quotes off and escape quotes using PHP functions.

Advantages

Magic quotes protect users from many SQL injection attacks that beginning users may be unaware of. All data is escaped, preventing most damaging injections.

Magic quotes are convenient. You do not need to add code that escapes the quotes.

Disadvantages

All $_POST and $_GET data is escaped, even if it is not going to be stored in a database. This unnecessary escaping causes a loss in performance. It is much more efficient to escape only the strings that are going to be stored in the database. In addition, if you just display the form data or use it in an email, the backslashes in front of the quotes are displayed or added to the email, unless you remove them first.

Portability

If you plan to use your scripts on other computers, it may not be safe to assume that magic quotes are turned on or off. To write portable code, you need to test whether magic quotes are on or off in the script and then use the code that fits the status. You can use the PHP escape functions if magic quotes are turned off or just store the data as is if magic quotes are turned off. You can test whether magic quotes are on or off using the get_magic_quotes_gpc() function in a conditional statement. The function returns 0 if magic quotes are off and 1 if magic quotes are on.

Setting Magic Quotes

Magic quotes are controlled by the magic_quotes-gpc setting in php.ini. You can see whether magic quotes are on or off in the output from phpinfo().

You can change the setting in php.ini. Look for the following setting:

```
; Magic quotes for incoming GET/POST/Cookie data.
magic_quotes_gpc = On
```

You can change the setting to Off if you want them off.

If you do not have access to the php.ini file, if the Web server is Apache, you can change the setting with an .htaccess file. Add the following directive to a file in your Web site directory named .htaccess:

```
php_flag magic_quotes_gpc Off
```

You cannot use the function ini_set() to change the magic quotes setting. Some settings can be changed by using this function in your script, but magic quotes cannot be. If you use this statement, you will not see an error message, but the setting does not change.

Escaping Form Data with PHP Functions

PHP provides the mysql_real_escape_string() and mysqli_real_escape_string() functions to escape form data for use in a MySQL query. The function is used after a connection is made to the MySQL server. The connection is passed to the function, along with the unescaped string, and the function escapes the string with respect to the connection.

If magic quotes are on, the string will already be escaped. Using this function will escape the string that is already escaped, making a double escaped string. If you are storing binary data, you must use this function.

When you select escaped text from the database, you must unescape the string before using it. PHP provides the stripslashes() function to remove the backslashes.

Insert Form Data into a Database

Y ou can store the form data that is passed in the $_POST or $_GET array in a database by building an INSERT query that includes the array elements. You first must validate and clean the form data, as described in the earlier sections "Verify Form Data" and "Clean Form Data." You build a query using the clean data, with the following general format:

```
INSERT INTO Tablename
(colname1,colname2,...) VALUES
('$good_data[colname1]','$good_data
[colname2]',...)
```

The INSERT query is described in more detail in Chapter 7.

The INSERT query requires a list of column names and a list of values, in the same order. If you want to store all the data from the form and have created an array of the validated, cleaned values from the form, you can use the

implode() function, described in Chapter 3, to create the lists you need from the array. The following statements create the needed lists:

```
$field_array = array_keys($good_data);

$fields = implode(",",$field_array);

$values = implode('","',$good_data);
```

Notice that the list of fields is created by separating the array elements by a comma only. The column names in the query are not enclosed in quotes. The values string is created by separating the array elements by both quotes and a comma. The values need to be surrounded by quotes in the query.

You can then build the query as follows:

```
$sql = "INSERT INTO Phone ($fields)
VALUES (\"$values\")";
```

Insert Form Data into a Database

① Add an if statement to display the empty form.

② Type **else**.

③ Connect to the database.

④ Add a foreach loop that processes each field.

⑤ Skip the hidden field.

⑥ Add the field name to an array.

⑦ Clean and escape the field content.

⑧ Add the value to an array.

⑨ Create the field string with implode().

⑩ Create the values string with implode().

⑪ Build the INSERT query.

   In this example, the query is INSERT INTO Phone ($fields) VALUES (\"$values\").

⑫ Execute the query.

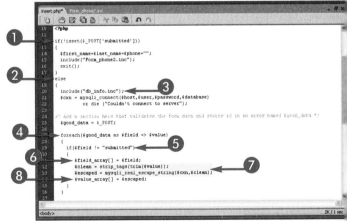

⑬ View the script in a browser.

⑭ Fill in the form fields, including an apostrophe in a field.

⑮ Click the submit button.

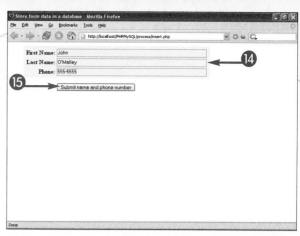

The query is displayed.

● The apostrophe in the query is escaped.

The data is stored successfully.

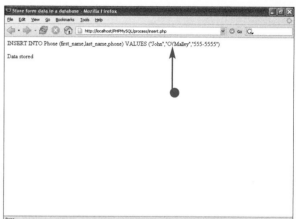

Extra

In some cases, you want to change the data before storing it into the database. For example, users type phone numbers in different formats, using blank spaces, parentheses, hyphens, and so on. You may want to store only the numbers in the database and format the phone number with your preferred format when you retrieve and display the phone number.

TYPE THIS

```
if($field == "phone")
{
  $good_data['phone'] = ereg_replace
("[^0-9]","",$_POST['phone']);
}
```

RESULT

All characters that are not numbers are removed from the string.

Update or Remove Database Data

You can update existing information in a database with the form data that is passed in the $_POST or $_GET array by building an UPDATE query that includes the array elements. You first validate and clean the form data. You then build a query using the clean data, with the following general format:

UPDATE *Tablename*

   SET *col1*='*$good_data[col1]*', *col2*='*$good_data[col2]*',...

   WHERE *condition1* AND|OR *condition2* AND|OR *condition3* ...

If you do not use a WHERE clause to specify rows, the values are set into the columns in all the rows. The UPDATE query and WHERE clause are described in more detail in Chapter 7.

You can remove a row from a database by building a DELETE query. If you do not include a WHERE clause to specify which row to delete, all the data is removed from the database. In most cases, the information to use in the WHERE clause is the information submitted in the form. You can use the information from the $_POST or $_GET array to build the DELETE query, after the form information has been validated and cleaned, as follows:

DELETE FROM *Tablename*

   WHERE *col1*='*$good_data[col1]*' AND|OR *col2*='*$good_data[col2]*'

   AND|OR *col3*='*$good_data[col3]*' ...

The DELETE query is described in more detail in Chapter 7.

You need to validate and clean the data used in the WHERE clause, as described earlier. You store the data in an array of good data. You can then use the data from the good data array to build the appropriate query.

Update or Remove Database Data

① Add an if statement to display the empty form.

② Type **else** to begin the section that processes form data.

③ Add statements that connect to the database.

④ Add a section that validates the form data.

Note: Validating the data is discussed in the section "Verify Form Data." In this example, $_POST is copied, as is, into $good_data. This is for brevity and should never be done in a real script.

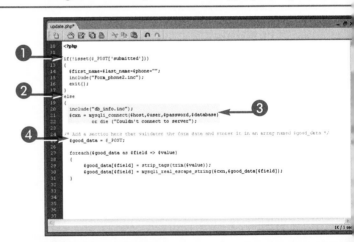

⑤ Add a foreach loop that processes each field.

⑥ Clean and escape the field content.

⑦ Build a query to update the data.

⑧ Add a statement that executes the query.

⑨ Build a query to delete a row.

⑩ Add a statement that executes the query.

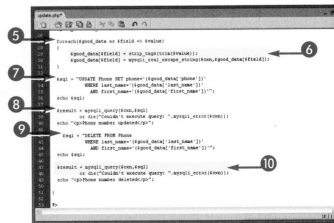

1 View the script in a browser.

2 Fill in the form data.

3 Click the submit button.

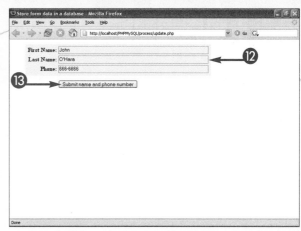

The first query is displayed.

The data is updated.

The second query is displayed.

The data is deleted.

Note: This script updates a row and then deletes it for demonstration purposes. It is unlikely that a real script would perform both tasks in the same script.

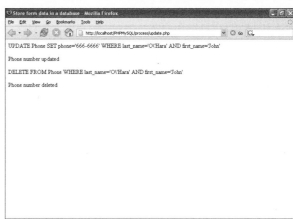

Apply It

In most cases, magic quotes should be turned off, as they are by default. However, if you are writing a script to run on many different computers, magic quotes may be turned either on or off. You need to test whether magic quotes are on or off.

TYPE THIS

```
if (!get_magic_quotes_gpc())
{
    $lastname = mysqli_real_escape_string
($cxn,$_POST['lastname']);
}
else
{
    $lastname = $_POST['lastname'];
}
```

RESULT

If magic quotes are not turned on, `mysqli_real_escape_string` is used to escape the text in the field. If magic quotes are turned on, the function should not be used.

Process an Uploaded File

You can provide your users with a form that allows them to upload a file from their local computer to your server. A form that uploads a file is described in Chapter 9. When the user submits the form, the file uploads to a temporary location, and the processing script runs. The processing script must move the uploaded file to a permanent location because the temporary file is deleted when the processing script finishes running.

Information about the uploaded file is stored in the superglobal array $_FILES. $_FILES is a multidimensional array. The higher-level key is the name of the field in the input tag, such as the name usrfile1 in the following file field:

```
<input type="file" name="usrfile1">
```

For each file field, the following elements are included: name, type, tmp_name, and size. name is the name of the uploaded file; type is the type of file, such as

text/plain or image; tmp_name is the path and filename of the temporary file; and size is the size of the file. Notice that name contains only the filename, but tmp_name includes the path, as well as the filename. If the file is too large to upload, tmp_name is set to none, and size is set to zero.

Your processing script needs to move the uploaded file to a storage location with the function move_uploaded_file(), using the information in $_FILES, as shown here:

```
move_uploaded_file($_FILES['usrfile1']
['tmp_name'], 'path\file');
```

The path\file is the path and filename to the target location where you want to move the file. The directory must already exist; the function will not create the directory.

Process an Uploaded File

1. Add an if statement that displays the blank form.

2. Type **else** to begin the statement that processes the uploaded file.

3. Create a variable that contains the destination path/file for the file and echo it.

4. Type **move_uploaded_file( )**.

5. Pass the temporary location from $_FILES.

6. Pass $destination.

7. Echo information to the user when the file is stored.

8. View the script in a browser.

9. Type the path/filename of the file to be uploaded.

10. Click the submit button.

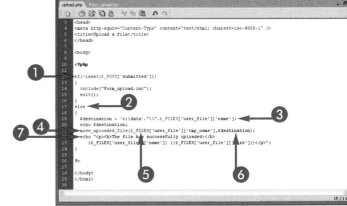

The destination path/filename is displayed.

The information statement is displayed.

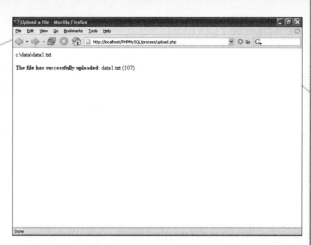

⑪ Change to the destination directory.

● The uploaded file is now stored in the destination directory.

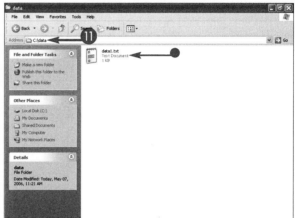

Apply It

You can improve the security when allowing users to upload files onto your computer by checking as many parameters as possible, such as size and file type.

TYPE THIS

```
if(!ereg("image",$_FILES['user_file']
['type']))
{
  echo "<p>Only image files can be
uploaded.</p>";
  include("Form_upload.inc");
}
```

RESULT

If the file type of the uploaded file is not an image type, a message is displayed, and the blank form is redisplayed.

Understanding User Sessions

Most Web sites consist of more than one Web page, with users moving from one Web page to the next. A user *session* is the time that a user spends at a Web site, from the first Web page viewed until the user leaves the Web site. Information from one Web page is not available on another Web page, but you can pass information from one Web page to the next or store information that is available to all the Web pages in a session by using PHP features.

Moving from One Web Page to the Next

Users can move from one Web page to the next by one of several methods. One common method is HTML links, created by <a> tags. When the user clicks the link, a new page is opened. In PHP, you can provide links by echoing the HTML code for the links.

HTML forms are another method for moving a user from one page to the next. Using forms in PHP is discussed in Chapters 9 and 10.

Links and forms require an action from the user — click a link or click a submit button. In some situations, you want to send a new Web page to the user's browser without requiring the user to perform an action. The PHP header() function enables you to do this.

The PHP header() function sends an HTTP header to the Web server. HTTP is the language that Web servers and browsers use to communicate, and an HTTP header is a message in the HTTP language. You can send a new Web page to a user by sending a Location header to the Web server, which instructs the Web server to send a specified Web page back to the browser.

Statelessness

HTML pages are *stateless*, which means that when users move from one page to the next, each new page that is sent to the user's browser is independent of any other pages that the user may have seen previously. No information from any previous pages is available to later pages.

When building dynamic Web sites, you often want information to be available to more than one page. In some cases, you want to pass information from one page to the next. In other cases, you want a particular piece of information, such as the user's ID, to be available to all the Web pages in the current user session. PHP provides several methods for sharing information among Web pages.

Forms

Forms are a common method for passing information from one Web page to the next. In PHP, the information in the form is passed to a script specified in the <form> tag and made available in PHP built-in arrays. Chapters 9 and 10 described the use of forms.

Passing Information in the URL

If you have a small amount of information, you can pass the information to the next Web page by attaching it to the end of the URL of the next page. You can add the information to the URL in the `<a>` tag for links and in the `action` attribute for forms. This information is then available to the next page in the PHP built-in array called `$_GET`.

When information is added to the URL, the information appears in the address window of the browser. The user can see the information. In some cases, you may not want the information to be displayed publicly. For example, if you are moving a password from one page to the next, you do not want it displayed in the browser address window. In addition, the URL can be bookmarked by the browser. You may not want the information that you added to the URL to be saved.

There is a limit on the length of the URL. The limit differs for various browsers and browser versions, but there is always a limit. If you are passing a lot of information, you may not be able to pass it in the URL.

Storing Information in Cookies

Cookies are small amounts of information stored by the user's browser on the user's computer. PHP provides features that enable you to store information in cookies and retrieve the information from the cookie from any Web page in the user session. The cookie information is available in a PHP built-in array called `$_COOKIE`.

Cookies were originally designed to store small amounts of information for a short time period. Unless you specifically set the cookie to last a longer period of time, the cookie disappears when the user closes his or her browser.

The main disadvantage of cookies is that users can set their browsers to refuse cookies. If your Web site depends on cookies to pass needed information, it will not function correctly when the user has cookies turned off.

PHP Session Features

PHP provides session features that you can use to make information available to all the Web pages in your Web site. You can set up a session and store information in a session variable on a Web page. Then, you can open the session on any other Web page, and the variable is available in a PHP built-in array called `$_SESSION`.

PHP assigns a long, unique number as the session ID, stored in a system variable named `PHPSESSID`. All session variables are stored in a session file named with the session ID. The session ID number is passed to every Web page in a cookie. You can also tell PHP to pass the session ID in the URL if cookies are turned off. When you start a session in the new page, the `$_SESSION` array is created, and any variables stored in the session file — the file with the session ID in its name — are stored in `$_SESSION`.

The session files are stored in a directory that is not in your Web space, so the files are not accessible from the Web. PHP stores the files in a default location, but you can change the location by changing a setting in the php.ini file. The session file directory must already exist. PHP will not create the directory, only the files.

Send a New Web Page to the Browser

You can use the PHP `header()` function to send a new page to the user's browser. Unlike a link or a form, the `header()` function can send a new page without the user being required to perform any action. When the `header()` statement is executed in the PHP script, the new page is displayed. The format of the `header` function that requests a new page is

```
header("Location: URL");
```

The URL can be a filename, relative to the script execution, or a complete URL.

The `header` function can only be used before any other output is sent. You cannot send a header requesting a new page after you have echoed some output to the Web page. If you use the statement after sending output, you may see the following message:

Warning: Cannot modify header information - headers already sent by (output started at C:\Program Files\Apache Group\Apache2\htdocs\PHPMySQL\test_header.php:6) in **C:\Program Files\Apache Group\Apache2\htdocs\PHPMySQL\test_header.php** on line **7**

The warning message shows that the `header` statement on line 7 failed because output was already sent on line 6.

Any HTML before a PHP section in the script sends a header. Therefore, to use a `header()` function, the `php` tag must be the first text in the script. Even a single blank space before the PHP section is viewed by the browser as output, resulting in a header being sent.

Send a New Web Page to the Browser

① Type a space and then **<?php**.

② Create a variable containing some text.

③ Add a `header` statement that requests a new Web page.

④ Add the closing `php` tag.

⑤ Create the Web page specified in step 3.

⑥ Echo some text to display when the Web page is opened.

⑦ Echo the variable created in step 2.

8 View the script in a browser.

A warning message is displayed, stating that output has already been sent.

Note: The space before the opening PHP tag in the script constitutes output.

9 Open the script for editing.

10 Remove the space in front of the PHP tag.

11 Save the edited file.

12 View the edited script in a browser.

The echo statement displays the specified text.

The script cannot display the variable because it does not exist.

Note: The variable was not passed to the new script because Web pages are independent of each other.

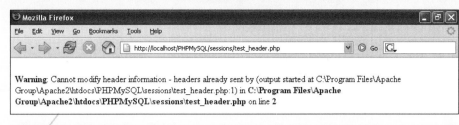

Warning: Cannot modify header information - headers already sent by (output started at C:\Program Files\Apache Group\Apache2\htdocs\PHPMySQL\sessions\test_header.php:1) in C:\Program Files\Apache Group\Apache2\htdocs\PHPMySQL\sessions\test_header.php on line 2

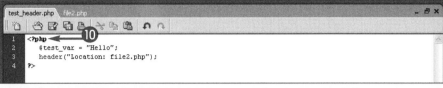

```
1  <?php
2     $test_var = "Hello";
3     header("Location: file2.php");
4  ?>
```

This file was displayed by the header function

Notice: Undefined variable: test_var in C:\Program Files\Apache Group\Apache2\htdocs\PHPMySQL\sessions\file2.php on line 11

Extra

You sometimes need to specify an absolute URL, such as http://www.myserver.com/page1.php. When specifying the URL, either absolute or relative, you can use variables.

TYPE THIS

```
$host="www.agoodplace.com";
header("Location:
http://$host/file1.php");
```

RESULT

The program file1.php, located at the host specified in $host, is sent to the browser.

You can create a URL from information available in PHP built-in arrays. The output from phpinfo() shows you the information available.

TYPE THIS

```
$host=$_SERVER['HTTP_HOST'];
header("Location:
http://$host/file1.php");
```

RESULT

The program file1.php, located at the host specified in $host, is sent to the browser. For example, if the current script is on localhost, $host contains localhost, and the URL sent in the header is http://localhost/file1.php.

Add Information to a URL

When building dynamic Web sites, you often want to pass information from one page to the next. If you have a small amount of information, you can pass the information to the next Web page by attaching it to the end of the URL, as follows:

```
<a href="nextpage.php?name=value">Link
Text</a>
```

In this case, the information has been added to the URL in a link. The information is added in `name=value` pairs. A question mark separates the URL from the name/value pairs. You can add information to the URL in the `action` attribute of a form and to the HTTP header sent by the `header()` function, as well as to the URL in an `<a>` tag.

You can add more than one piece of information, separated by an ampersand (`&`), as follows:

```
?name1=value1&name2=value2&...
```

There is no specific limit on the number of name/value pairs you can add to the URL. However, there is probably a limit to the length of the URL, depending on the browser and browser version. For example, the URL length limit for Internet Explorer is 2,083 characters. Therefore, the information users on your Web site using IE can pass to the next page is limited.

The information passed in the URL is available to the script specified in the URL in the `$_GET` built-in array. You can access the information in an array element as `$_GET['name']`.

When the user moves from one page to the next, the URL of the destination page is displayed in the browser address window. If information is added to the URL, the information is also displayed. In some cases, this may be a security risk.

Add Information to a URL

1. Create a new PHP file.

2. Add a form that collects at least one item of information from the user.

Note: See Chapter 9 for information on creating forms.

3. Save the file.

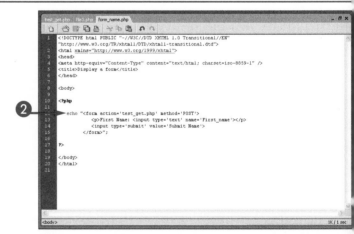

4. Create a file with the name specified in the `<form>` tag in step 2.

5. Type **header("Location:** .

6. Add the name of the Web page file that the `header` function is to send.

7. Add a name for the information to pass to the program in step 6.

8. Type **=**.

9. Add the variable name containing the value to be passed.

10. Type **");**.

11. Save the file.

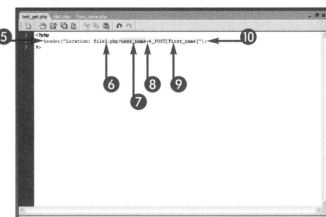

⑫ Create a new PHP file with the name specified in step 6.

⑬ Add an echo statement that displays the information passed in the URL, as added in steps 7 to 9.

⑭ Save the file.

⑮ Display the script created in step 1 in a browser.

The blank form is displayed.

⑯ Fill in the form.

⑰ Click the submit button.

The header statement displays the script created in step 12.

The information typed into the form is displayed.

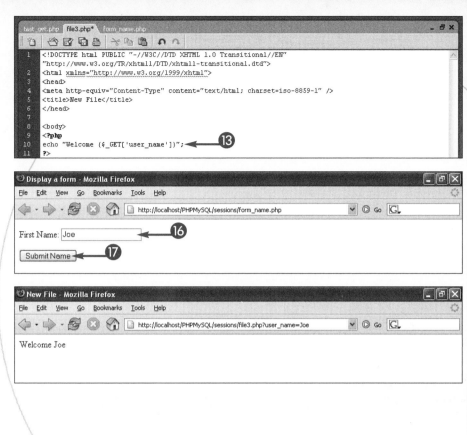

Extra

$_GET is a superglobal array, as are all the built-in arrays that begin with an underscore, such as $_POST and $_COOKIES. Superglobal arrays are available throughout your program, regardless of scope. Chapter 5 describes the use of the global statement with respect to the use of variables in functions. The global statement is not necessary when you use the superglobal arrays. The superglobals are available throughout the script, regardless of scope.

TYPE THIS

```
function add_get()
{
    $total = $_GET['num1'] + $_GET['num2'];
    return $total;
}
```

RESULT

→ This function can access the elements of $_GET without needing to use the global statement.

Store Information in Cookies

You can store information as cookies, which can be accessed by any Web page in the user's session. Cookies are small amounts of information, consisting of name=value pairs, that are stored in a file on the user's computer.

PHP provides a function that stores cookies, as follows:

```
setcookie("name","value",expiretime);
```

The information is stored in the cookie as name=value. The values can be strings or variables.

When the cookie has been stored, any Web page in the user session can access the cookie in the built-in superglobal array $_COOKIES. An array element can be used as $_COOKIE['name'].

The third parameter, expiretime, is optional. If no expiretime is included, the cookie is removed when the user closes his or her browser. The expiretime is usually set using either the time() or mktime() function, similar to the following:

```
time()+3600
```

```
mktime(12,0,0,,,)
```

The time() function returns the current time, so the first expression expires the cookie in 3600 seconds — one hour. The mktime() function returns a date and time, so the second expression expires the cookie at noon on the current day.

The setcookie() function sends an HTTP header, so it cannot be used in a script after some output is sent.

Users can set their browser to reject cookies. If your Web page depends on using cookies to function properly, users who have cookies turned off will not be able to use your Web site. Cookies are most useful in environments in which you know that users will have cookies turned on.

Store Information in Cookies

① Create a variable containing information to store in the cookie.

② Type **setcookie( )**.

③ Insert the name in the function call.

④ Insert the value to store in the cookie.

⑤ Add a line that echoes a link to another PHP file.

⑥ Save the file.

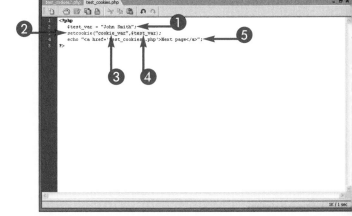

⑦ Open a second PHP file in an editor.

⑧ Add a line that echoes the information stored in the cookie in steps 2 to 4.

⑨ Save the file with the name specified in step 5.

10 View the file saved in step 6 in a browser.

The link is displayed.

11 Click the link.

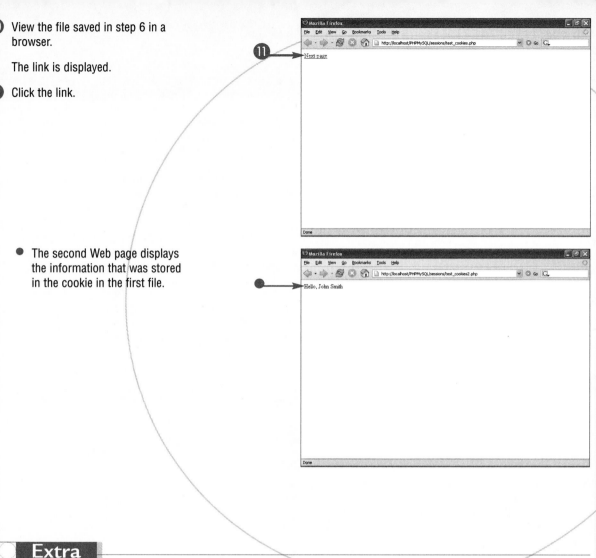

● The second Web page displays the information that was stored in the cookie in the first file.

Extra

You can use an output statement before the setcookie() function if you send the output to a buffer using the output buffering functions, rather than send it to the Web server. You start buffering output with the ob_start() function. The buffered output is sent when you use the ob_end_flush() function or when the script ends.

TYPE THIS

```
ob_start();
echo "Hi";
setcookie("first_name",$first_name);
ob_end_flush();
```

RESULT

→ The setcookie function executes, and no warning message is displayed. The text "Hi" is echoed on the Web page when the ob_end_flush() function executes.

Store Information in a PHP Session

With PHP, you can set up a session on one Web page and save variables as session variables. You can then open the session in any other page, and the session variables are available for your use in the built-in array $_SESSION.

You open a session with the PHP function session_start(). The function opens the current session or, if no current session exists, starts a new session. Because session_start() may use a cookie, it must come before any output is sent from the script. See the section "Store Information in Cookies" for more information.

To store a session variable, you assign the value to the $_SESSION array, using the variable name as the key, such as $_SESSION['first_name']. You can then use the session variable in the $_SESSION array in any other Web page, as long as you open the session on the page.

When you start a new session, a session ID is assigned to the session, the $_SESSION array is created, and a session file is created with a name that begins with sess_, followed by the session ID — a long string of letters and numbers. The session file stores the session variables. The file is located in a default directory, but you can change the session directory with session.save_path in the php.ini file.

In order to access the session variable in a Web page, the session ID must be available. If the user has cookies turned on, the session ID is automatically stored in a cookie, with the name PHPSESSID. Any Web page that needs to access session variables can access the session ID. However, if the user has cookies turned off, the session ID must be handled differently. See the section "Using PHP Sessions without Cookies" to use a session when users have cookies turned off.

Store Information in a PHP Session

① Start a session.

② Create a variable containing information to store in the session.

③ Store the variable in the $_SESSION array.

④ Add a line that echoes a link to another PHP file.

⑤ Save the file.

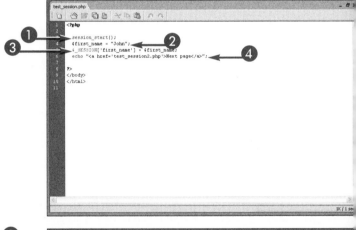

⑥ Open a second PHP file in an editor.

⑦ Add a line that echoes the session ID that is automatically stored in the cookie.

⑧ Add a line that echoes the information stored in the session in step 3.

⑨ Save the file with the name specified as the link target in step 4.

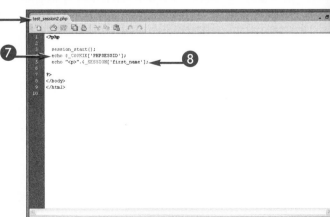

(10) View the file saved in step 5 in a browser.

The link is displayed.

(11) Click the link.

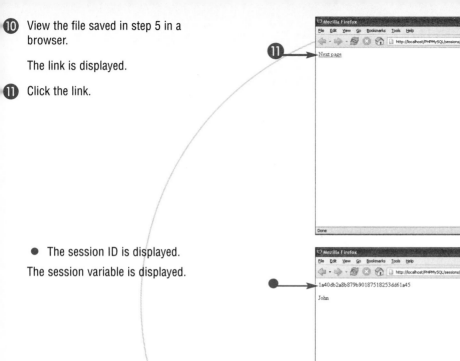

● The session ID is displayed.

The session variable is displayed.

Apply It

You can close a session at any time with the function session_destroy(). This destroys all the data in the session but does not unset $_SESSION or destroy the session cookie. To totally destroy the session and the session data, you need to empty $_SESSION and destroy the session ID in the cookie.

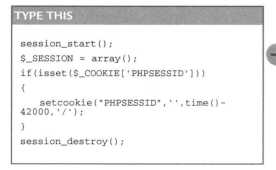

TYPE THIS

```
session_start();
$_SESSION = array();
if(isset($_COOKIE['PHPSESSID']))
{
    setcookie("PHPSESSID",'',time()-
42000,'/');
}
session_destroy();
```

RESULT

→ The session and all its data is gone. The time set in the past in the cookie changes the cookie immediately.

Using PHP Sessions without Cookies

By default, the session ID, created when a new session is started, is stored in a cookie. All the Web pages in the session can access the session ID, which is needed to access the session variables stored in the session file. However, if a user has cookies turned off in his or her browser, the session ID is not available, and the session variables cannot be accessed. If you think users may have cookies turned off, you need to pass the session ID by another method.

PHP provides a mechanism for passing the session ID automatically, even when cookies are off. You can turn on the setting `session.use_trans_sid` in your php.ini file. This has PHP send the session ID to the next page in the URL or as a hidden form field. If the user moves to

the next page via a form with POST, the session ID is passed as a hidden field; if the user moves to the next page via a link, a `header` function, or a form with GET, the session ID is added to the URL.

If your users move from one page to the next using forms, you can pass the session ID manually to be sure that the session ID never appears in the URL. You can pass the session ID in a hidden field by first storing the session ID in a variable and then using the variable in the form field, as follows:

```php
$sessid = session_id();

echo "<input type='hidden' name='PHPSESSID value='$sessid'>";
```

WITH TRANS_SID TURNED ON

1. Type **session_start();**.

2. Store a variable in the `$_SESSION` array.

3. Add a form that displays a submit button, but no fields.

4. Save the file.

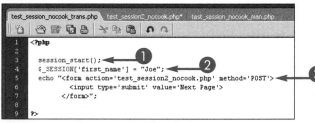

WITH TRANS_SID TURNED OFF

1. Type **session_start();**.

2. Store a variable in the `$_SESSION` array.

3. Create a variable that contains the session ID.

4. Add a form that displays a submit button.

5. Add a hidden field with the name PHPSESSID.

6. Specify the variable from step 3 as the value for the hidden field.

7. Save the file.

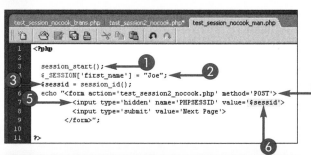

ACCESS THE SESSION VARIABLE

1. Create a second PHP Web page file.

2. Type **session_start();**.

3. Add a statement that echoes the session variable created in step 2 when creating the first file.

④ Set `session.use_trans_sid` to on in your php.ini file.

Note: On is 1, and off is 0.

⑤ Restart the Web server.

⑥ View the first script that you created in this section in a browser.

Note: The first script expects `trans_sid` to be on.

The submit button is displayed.

⑦ Click the submit button.

The session variable is displayed.

⑧ Set `session.use_trans_sid` to off in the php.ini file and restart the Web server.

⑨ Repeat steps 6 to 7 for the second file.

Note: The second file expects `trans_sid` to be turned off.

The same Web pages are displayed.

Extra

You can also pass the session ID in the URL manually, rather than by turning `session.use_trans_sid` on and allowing PHP to add the URL automatically. When a session is started by a browser with cookies turned off, PHP creates a constant called `SID` that contains the session ID formatted as `name=value`. You can add `SID` to a URL to pass the session ID.

TYPE THIS

```
<a href="nextpage.php?<?php echo SID ?>"
>Next page</a>
```

RESULT

The URL that is sent is similar to

```
nextpage.php?PHPSESSID=874c22163c8df9deb342c7
333cfe38a7
```

Understanding
Object-Oriented Programming

Object-oriented programming is in widespread use today. Object-oriented programming, with a limited feature set, is possible in PHP 4. With PHP 5, the object-oriented capabilities of PHP were greatly improved, resulting in both more speed and added features. The information and sample programs in this chapter are written using features added in PHP 5. Features that are not available in PHP 4 are noted.

Object-Oriented Programming

Object-oriented programming is not just a matter of using different syntax. It is a different way of analyzing programming problems. The program is designed by modeling the programming problem. For example, a programmer designing a program to support a company's sales department may look at the programming problem in terms of the relationships between customers and sales and credit lines.

In object-oriented programming, the elements of a program are objects, which represent the elements of the problem your program is meant to solve, such as customers and products. Objects have properties and can perform actions.

Object-oriented programming developed new concepts and new terminology to represent those concepts. Understanding the terminology is the road to understanding object-oriented programming.

Classes

A class is the code that is used to create an object — the template or pattern for creating the object. The class defines the properties of the object and defines the actions that the object can perform. For instance, a `bike` class might define a bike with two wheels and a frame and define its actions as "move forward" and "change gears." When you create a `bike` object, using the `bike` class, the object is created using the blueprint defined in the class. When you use the bike in a program, you may find that something is missing, such as handlebars or the ability to stop.

One of the goals of object-oriented programming is to write classes that can be used in any program that needs the object defined by the class. The user should not need to know how the class works. The user only needs to know the interface to use the class. The class designer can change any or everything inside the class, but as long as the interface remains the same, the changes do not affect the person using the class.

Objects

The basic elements of object-oriented programs are objects. It is easiest to understand objects as physical objects, such as a car. A car has *properties,* such as color, model, engine, and tires. A car can perform actions, such as move forward, move backward, park, and so on. However, objects can be more conceptual, such as a bank account, a computer account, or a mortgage. In general, objects are nouns.

Properties

Objects have *properties*, also sometimes called *attributes.* For example, a customer has a name, an address, and a phone number. Or, a car has a color, a make, and a model. The properties are stored inside the object.

The properties are defined inside the class as variables. For example, the class may include `$color=red` or `$wheels=2`. The class may set default values for properties. The object may or may not have the ability to set or change its properties. For instance, a bike probably will not be able to change the number of wheels but may be able to change its color.

Methods

The actions that an object can perform are sometimes referred to as *responsibilities.* Each action is programmed into the class and called a *method.* In PHP, methods use the same syntax as functions. Although the code looks like the code for a function, the distinction is that methods are inside a class.

The methods are the interface between the object and program using the object. The object needs methods for all its responsibilities. Objects should interact with the program only through their methods. A program should not be able to change the properties of an object directly. If the program needs to change a property, a method should be provided for the purpose. For example, if the program needs to change the color of the bike, a changeColor method should be defined.

A good object should contain all it needs to perform its responsibilities, but not a lot of extraneous data. It should not perform actions that are another object's responsibility.

Abstraction

Abstraction is an important concept in object-oriented programming. When you are designing a class, you need to abstract the important characteristics of the object to include in your class, not include every possible property and responsibility. You abstract the characteristics that are important for your application and ignore the characteristics that are irrelevant for your task.

Constructor

A *constructor* is a method that automatically executes when an object is created from the class. You can use a constructor to set default property values or to perform actions that need to be performed for every object when it is created. The constructor is optional.

Inheritance

Objects should contain only the properties and methods that they need. One way to accomplish this is to share properties and methods between classes by using inheritance. For example, suppose that you have two Car objects: a Sedan and a Convertible. You could write two classes: a Sedan class and a Convertible class. However, many of the properties and responsibilities are the same for both objects. Both have four wheels, and both move forward in the same way. You can use inheritance to eliminate the duplication.

You can write one class called Car, which stores the common information, such as the number of wheels, and provides common methods, such as moveBackward. You can then write two subclasses: Sedan and Convertible. The Car class is called the *master class* or the *parent class.* Sedan and Convertible are subclasses, also referred to as *child classes.*

Child classes inherit all the properties and methods from the parent class but can also have their own individual properties, such as color, and methods, such as lowerTop for the Convertible class.

Exceptions

PHP provides an error-handling class called Exception that you can use to handle undesirable conditions in your script. When the undesirable condition occurs, a routine that you have written is performed, called *throwing an exception.*

Create and Use an Object

bjects are the foundation of object-oriented programming. A program creates the objects it needs, and the objects perform the actions required. This section provides an overview of the process of creating and using an object. Details for the individual steps are provided in the remainder of this chapter.

Objects are created based on patterns, or blueprints, contained in classes. Before you can create an object, you must write a class that defines the object — its properties and the actions that it can perform. The `class` statement begins with the following line:

```
class className
```

This line is followed by a block of code that defines the properties and methods. You can use any valid PHP identifier for the class name, except reserved words. PHP uses the names `stdClass`, `Iterator`, and `IteratorAggregate` internally, so you may not use these names.

After you have written the `class` statement, you can create an object and use its methods with statements similar to the following:

```
$object1 = new
className(value1,value2,...);

$object1->methodName();
```

Creating the object may not require passing values. If values are included, they are passed to the constructor — the method that runs automatically when an object is created. You can use any method defined in the `class` statement to perform actions.

Objects can generally be copied, stored, stored in arrays, and so on. However, in some cases, you need to convert the object into a string representation, called *serialization,* using the `serialize()` function. When you store an object in a session, PHP serializes the object automatically.

Create and Use an Object

① Type **class**.

② Type the class name.

③ Type {.

④ Add any properties for the object.

   In this example, the property is $content, which is assigned the value "Hello".

Note: See the section "Set Properties in a Class" for further information on properties.

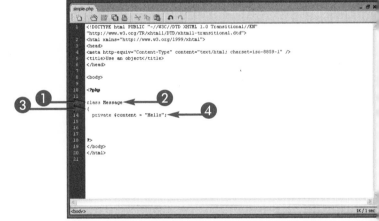

⑤ Add any methods needed for the class.

   In this example, one method is added that displays the message.

Note: See the section "Add Methods to a Class" for more information on adding methods.

⑥ Type } to end the class statement.

7 Create a message object.

In this example, a message object is created and stored in $my_message.

8 Add a statement that uses a method available in the class statement for the object.

In this example, the method displayMessage is called.

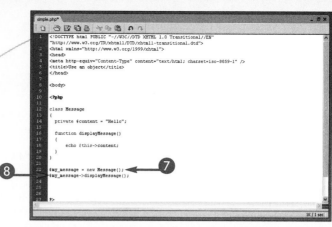

9 View the script in a browser.

The method executes.

In this example, the method displayMessage executes and displays the message in the object $my_message.

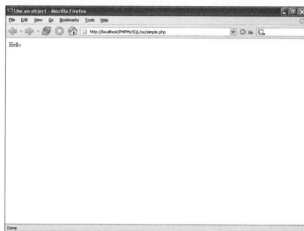

Extra

You cannot redefine a class in a script. If you use a class name that PHP already uses, an error message is displayed.

TYPE THIS		RESULT

`class stdClass`
`{`
`}`
		The following fatal error is issued.
		
		`Fatal error: Cannot redeclare class stdclass in C:\Program Files\Apache Group\Apache2\htdocs\PHPMySQL\oo\simple.php on line 13`

In most cases, class statements are stored in separate files that are included when needed. For large, complicated programs, you can need many include statements at the beginning of the program. Beginning with PHP 5, PHP provides a function, named __autoload (with two underscores), that runs automatically when you call a class that is not defined. In the function, you can include the file containing the missing class.

TYPE THIS		RESULT

`function __autoload`
`($class_name)`
`{`
`    require_once`
`$class_name.".inc";`
`}`
`$my_hat = new Hat();`
		When the last line runs, if PHP does not find a class definition for the Hat class, it runs the function __autoload, passing Hat as the class name. The function executes a statement that looks for a file named Hat.inc in the include directory(s) specified by the include_path setting in php.ini. Chapter 5 discusses include files. If the file is found, the require_once statement includes the file and the new object, $my_hat, is created.

263

Set Properties in a Class

P
roperties are stored as variables in the object. Good programming practice requires you to declare all the properties in the top of the class. PHP does not require you to declare variables in a class, but classes are much easier to understand if the properties are all listed at the top of the class.

As of PHP 5, you must define a property to be public, private, or protected. Public properties can be accessed from the script, outside the class. The script can change the property directly. This is rarely a good idea. Private properties cannot be accessed from outside the class, either by the script or from another class. Only methods inside the class can access or change the property. Protected properties cannot be accessed from outside the class either, except from a class that is a child of the class with the `protected` attribute. In PHP 4, `var` was used to declare all properties. PHP 5 and later accepts `var` but displays an `E_STRICT` error.

Properties are declared with the following format:

```
private $color;
```

You can set a default value for a property, but the values allowed are restricted. You can declare a simple value but not a computed one. That is, you can set `$gas = 10`, but you cannot set `$gas = 5+5`. You can set an array as the default value, as long as the values are simple, such as `$doors=array("front","back")`.

You can also use constants as properties, with the following format:

```
const SALESTAX = .05;
```

To access a property from inside a class, you use the keyword `$this`, such as `$this->color`.

Set Properties in a Class

① Add a statement that defines a class.

② Add at least one private property.

③ Add a method that displays the private property.

Note: The section "Add Methods to a Class" describes methods.

④ Create an object from the class.

⑤ Add a statement that assigns a new value to the private constant.

⑥ Call the method to display the value of the constant.

⑦ View the script in a browser.

An error message is displayed because you cannot assign a value to a private property from outside the class.

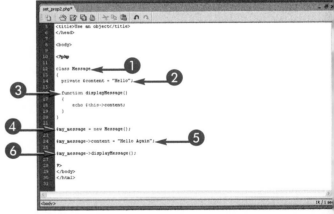

⑧ Open the script for editing.

⑨ Add a method that changes the value of the property.

⑩ Comment out the statement that assigns a value to the property.

⑪ Add a statement that calls the method to change the value of the property.

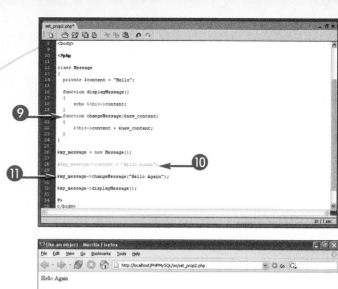

The changed value is displayed.

Apply It

Beginning with PHP 5, you can iterate through the properties of an object with a `foreach` loop. You can use the `foreach` loop either inside or outside the class. If you iterate with a `foreach` loop outside the class, the loop only processes the properties that it has access to.

TYPE THIS

```
$my_list = new List();
foreach($my_list as $itemNo => $item)
{
    echo "{$itemNo} $item<br>\n";
}
```

RESULT

Assuming that a List object has a set of properties named $item1, $item2, $item3, and so on, this code outputs the list, in the following format:

```
item1 itemcontent
item2 itemcontent
```

and so on.

Add Methods to a Class

Methods specify what an object can do. Methods are included inside the class statement and are coded in the same format as functions. You can make methods private or protected with the appropriate keyword. Only methods inside the class can use a private method. Only a child method can use a protected method of its parent. If you do not use any keyword, a method is public by default. Good programming practice requires you to hide as much of your class as possible. Only make methods public that absolutely need to be public.

You can access one method in a class from another method inside a class. To do so, use the keyword $this to specify that the method is in the same class, in the following format:

$this->methodname()

PHP provides some special methods, called *magic methods,* with names that begin with _ _ (two underscores), such as _ _construct, which runs automatically when an object is created; _ _destruct, which runs automatically when an object is destroyed; and _ _clone, which copies an object. These methods are handled differently by PHP internally. Do not begin the names of your own methods with two underscores unless you are taking advantage of a PHP special method.

PHP provides a type of method that can be accessed directly from a script, without creating an object first, called a *static* method, which is specified with the keyword static. Because no object is created when using a static method, the keyword $this cannot be used, and the method has no access to the properties. You can access a static method with the statement classname::methodname;.

Add Methods to a Class

① Create a class.

Note: See "Create and Use an Object" to create a class.

② Add a private property with a default value.

Note: The section "Set Properties in a Class" explains properties.

③ Add a private method.

④ Add a statement that changes the value of the private property.

⑤ Echo the changes.

⑥ Add a public method.

In this example, buyGas is a public method.

⑦ Add a statement that uses the private method created in steps 3 to 5.

In this example, buyGas uses the private method addGas.

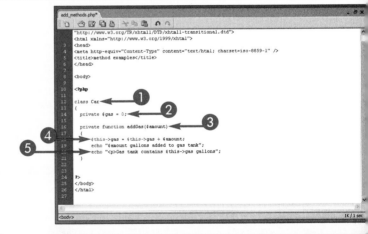

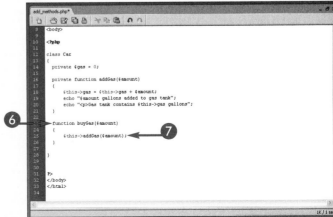

8 Create a new object from the class.

9 Add a statement that changes the property using the public method.

In this example, the script calls buyGas to change the amount of gas in the gas tank.

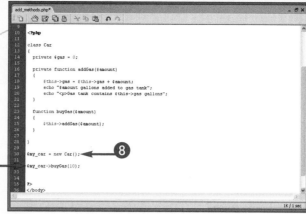

10 View the script in a browser.

The Web page shows the change to the object property.

In this example, ten gallons of gas are added.

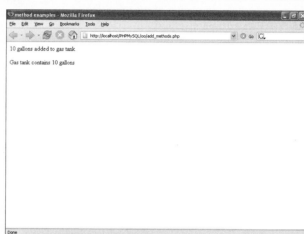

Apply It

PHP provides a magic method named __call that executes whenever you call a method that does not exist in the class. The method is passed two parameters — the name of the method that cannot be found and an array containing all the arguments that are passed to it.

TYPE THIS

Assume a class called Test containing the following __call() method, with no method named Test20.

```
private function __call($name, $arguments)
{
    echo "<p>Method $name was
called.</p>\n";
    var_dump($arguments);
}
$my_test = new Test ();
$my_test->Test20("a","b","c");
```

RESULT

The method __call() executes because PHP cannot find Test20. The method __call() displays the message Method Test20 was called. It then displays the var_dump() output of the array arguments, which contains three elements with the values a, b, and c.

Write a Constructor or a Destructor Method

PHP provides two methods with special purposes: the constructor and the destructor. The constructor, named __construct (with two underscores), runs automatically when an object is created. The destructor, named __destruct, runs automatically when an object is destroyed. Methods that begin with __ are special functions, handled differently by PHP.

The constructor is used to assign any properties or perform any actions that are required for every object when it is created. The constructor often sets up properties or sets up conditions needed by the object, such as a connection to the database. A constructor is not required in a class. Only one constructor is allowed in a class.

If the constructor requires any values, the values are passed when the object is created, as follows:

```
$objectname = new
classname(value1,value2,...);
```

The __construct() method was added in PHP 5. PHP recognized and handled constructors, but constructors were named with the same name as the class. Currently, PHP looks first for a method named __construct(). If it does not find one, it looks for a method with the same name as the class to serve as the constructor. If it does not find one, it does not run a constructor. Thus, classes created using PHP 4 constructor syntax will run in PHP 5 and newer versions. If your class contains both a __construct() method and a method named with the class name, an E_STRICT message is triggered.

The destructor is used to perform any actions that are required when the object is destroyed. The __destruct() method was introduced in PHP 5.

Write a Constructor or a Destructor Method

1. Add a `class` statement.

2. Add one or more properties.

3. Type **function __construct( )**.

4. Add any values that the constructor needs.

5. Add a block of statements to execute when an object is created.

   In this example, `$gas` is initialized with a value passed when the object is created or set to `0` if no value is passed.

6. Add a method that displays the value of one or more properties.

   In this example, the value of `$gas` is displayed.

7. Type **function __destruct()**.

8. Add a block of statements that need to execute when an object is destroyed.

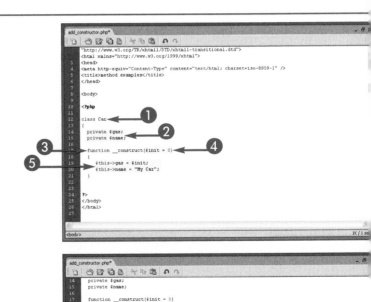

9 Create a new object.

In this example, 5 is passed to the constructor.

10 Add a statement that displays the value of a property using the method added in step 6.

11 Add a statement that destroys the object.

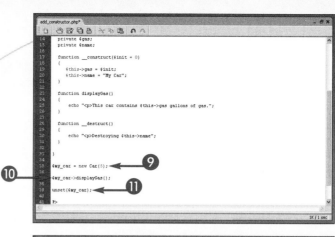

12 View the script in a browser.

The property value is displayed by the method.

- The statements in the destructor are executed.

In this example, a notice that the object is being destroyed is displayed.

Extra

A child class has access to all methods in its parent class. See the section "Using Inheritance in a Class" for more information on parent/child classes. If a child class has a constructor, it is executed when an object is created. If the child class has no constructor, the parent constructor is executed when an object is created from the child class. In some cases, you may have a constructor in both the child and parent classes and want both constructors to execute. If so, you must explicitly execute the parent constructor, which will not execute if the child contains a constructor.

TYPE THIS

```
class Child extends Parent
{
    function __construct($amt)
    {
        echo "$amt";
        parent::__construct($amt);
    }
}
```

RESULT

The child class constructor automatically executes, which calls the parent constructor to execute also.

Using PHP Magic Methods to Get or Set Properties

In your class definitions, properties should be private. If the script attempts to access a private property, an error message is displayed. Access to properties should be provided only through methods. You can add specific methods that access specific properties, or you can add PHP magic methods that display or change any property.

The PHP method that retrieves a property value is `__get()` (with two underscores), which has the following format:

```
private function __get("name")
```

The PHP magic method that changes a property value is `__set()` (with two underscores), which has the following format:

```
private function __set("name","value")
```

When one of these methods is included in the `class` statement, the method is automatically called whenever the script attempts to access a private property. For example, suppose that a script attempted to access a private property with the following statement:

```
$objectname->propertyname = value;
```

If the class used to create `$objectname` does not contain a `__set()` method, an error message is displayed. However, if a `__set()` method is included in the `class` statement, the `__set()` method executes automatically, performing the actions specified in the `__set()` method. The `propertyname` and `value` are passed to the `__set()` method.

Because the class methods are always allowed to access private properties inside the same class, accessing private properties from inside the class does not trigger the execution of the magic methods.

Using PHP Magic Methods to Get or Set Properties

① Create a `class` statement.

② Add one or more private properties.

③ Add a constructor that sets the properties.

④ Type **private function __set($name,$value)**.

⑤ Add an `if/else` statement that changes the value for some properties but refuses to change the values of other properties.

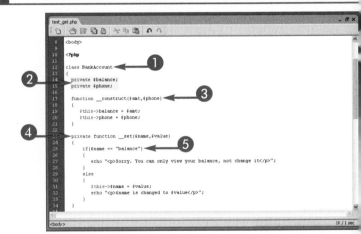

⑥ Type **private function __get($name)**.

⑦ Add an `if/else` statement that checks whether the property exists, changing existing properties and displaying a message if it does not exist.

⑧ Type **private function __isset($name)**.

⑨ Add a statement that echoes a message.

⑩ Use the PHP function `isset` to test whether the property exists.

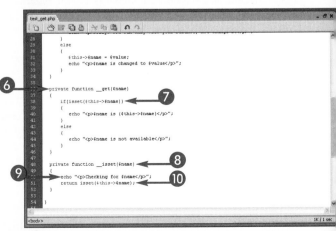

11 Create an object using the `class` statement and echo a property.

12 Add a statement to change the property.

13 Add a statement to change a different property.

14 Store the new value in a variable and echo the variable.

15 Add an `if` statement that tests whether a property exists.

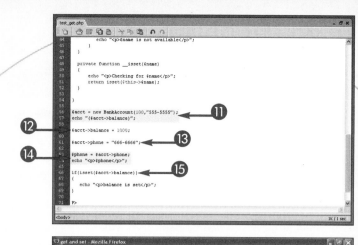

16 View the script in a browser.

The property is displayed because the `__get` method displays any property that exists.

- The property cannot be changed because the `__set` method prevents it.

- The second property can be changed, because the `__set` method allows it.

- The `if` statement checks whether the property exists, using the `__isset` method, and finds that it does exist.

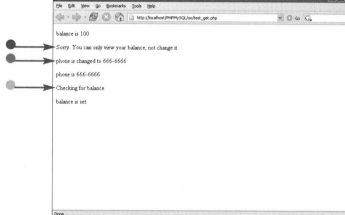

Extra

As of PHP 5, PHP provides magic methods that you can use to check whether a private property exists or to unset a private property. These magic methods have the same name as PHP built-in functions, `isset()` and `unset()`. When the magic methods — `__isset()` and `__unset()` — exist in the `class` statement, they will run automatically when the script uses the PHP built-in functions of the same name.

TYPE THIS

If your class contains the function

```php
private function __isset($name)
  {
      echo "<p>Checking for $name</p>";
      return isset($this->$name);
  }
```

and your script contains the following `if` statement:

```php
if(isset($acct->balance))
{
    echo "<p>balance is set</p>";
}
```

RESULT

When the PHP function `isset` is used in the script, the `__isset` method runs. It echoes the text and then executes the `isset` function, returning the Boolean result.

Using Inheritance in a Class

A class can be a subclass that inherits properties and methods from a parent class. When you have two or more classes that have properties and methods that are the same and properties and methods that are different, you can use inheritance to avoid redundant properties and methods. You can create a *master,* or *parent,* class that contains all the methods and properties that are the same for both classes. Then, you can create two or more *subclasses,* also called *child* classes, to contain the properties and methods that are unique to the subclass. The object created from the child class contains both the properties and methods from the parent class and its own properties and methods. However, an object created from the parent class does not contain the properties and methods of the child class.

When you create a child class, you specify the parent class as follows:

```
class childclassname extends
parentclassname

{

    add the property statements

    add the methods

}
```

The object created from this class has access to all the properties and methods of both the child class and the parent class. In the child class, you can access a property of the parent class using either $this->parentpropertyname or parent::parentpropertyname.

If you add a method to a child class with the same name as a method in the parent class, an object created from the child class will run the child method by default.

Using Inheritance in a Class

① Create a parent class.

② Add one or more properties to the parent.

③ Add a constructor that sets the property.

④ Add a method that displays the property.

⑤ Create a child class.

⑥ Add a property with a default value.

⑦ Add a method that changes the value of the property.

⑧ Add a method that displays the value of the property.

Note: Because the child does not include a constructor, the parent constructor will run when a child object is created.

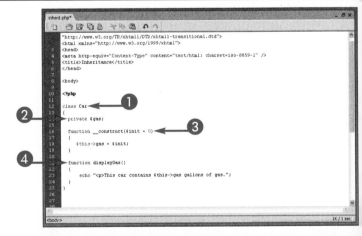

- Create a child object.

Note: A value is passed that will go to the parent constructor.

- Display the parent property value, using the method in the parent class.

- Change the child property, using the method in the child class.

- Display the child property value, using the method in the child class.

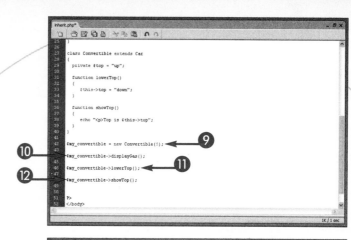

- View the script in a browser.

  • The method in the parent class displays the value of the parent property.

  • The method in the child class displays the value of the child property.

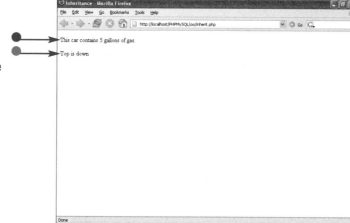

Extra

You can specify that a class cannot be extended by using the keyword `final` with the class. You can also prevent a child class from overriding a method in the parent class by using the `final` keyword.

TYPE THIS	RESULT
`final class Rules` `final function changeRules()`	No child class can inherit from the class Rules. No child class can include a function named changeRules(). If the method changeRules() is inside the final class Rules, it does not need the final keyword because no child class can be created from the class Rules.

Using Exceptions

PHP provides an error-handling class called `Exception`. You can use this class to handle undesirable conditions in your script. For example, in your `Car` class, `$gas` should never become a negative amount. The code will accept a negative number, but it does not make sense. Therefore, you want your script to test for a negative number and perform specified actions if the value of `$gas` goes below zero.

You create an `Exception` object with the following statement:

```
throw new Exception ("message");
```

The *message* is stored in the `Exception` object and can be retrieved with the `getMessage()` method.

You can test conditions in your class methods and throw an exception when an undesirable condition occurs. For example, you might check the gas in your `Car` as follows:

```
if($gas < 0)
```

```
    throw new Exception("Gas amount is less than zero");
```

To handle exceptions, you write two blocks together — a `try` block and a `catch` block. The `try` is included first, followed by the `catch` block. The `try` block contains the statements to be executed, including one or more calls to methods. The `catch` block contains the statements to be executed if an exception is thrown in the `try` block. The `catch` block statement begins with the statement `catch(Exception $e)`.

This statement catches an exception from the immediately preceding `try` block and assigns the object to the variable `$e`. The statements in the `catch` block are executed. One of the statements usually echoes the message stored with the exception, using `$e->getMessage()`.

If an exception is thrown, it must be caught, or an error message is displayed. If no exception is thrown in the `try` block, the `catch` block is ignored.

Using Exceptions

① Add a `class` statement.

② Add a property with a default value.

③ Add a method that changes the value of the property.

④ Add an `if` statement that throws an exception when a specific value is set.

⑤ Create an object from the class.

⑥ Change the property to an acceptable value.

⑦ Change the property to a value that triggers an exception.

⑧ View the script in a browser.

The values of the property are changed.

The change to an unacceptable value produces an error message.

Note: When the unacceptable value was set, an exception was thrown, but no `catch` block exists to catch the exception, resulting in the fatal error.

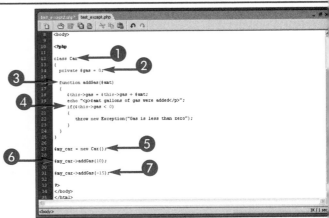

9 Open the file in a text editor for editing.

10 Type **try**.

11 Put the two calls to the method that changes the value of the property into the `try` block.

12 Type **catch (Exception $e)**.

13 Type **echo $e->getMessage();** to display the `Exception` message.

14 Add any additional statements to be executed when an exception is thrown.

5 View the edited script in a browser.

The property value was changed twice.

● The exception message is displayed.

The program ends gracefully.

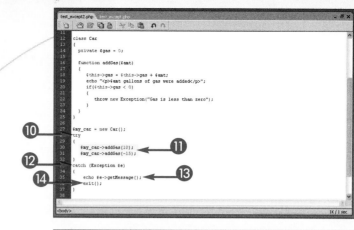

Extra

You can distinguish between various types of errors that you want to handle differently by creating a subclass of the `Exception` class and handling the separate subclasses differently by providing different `catch` blocks. You can create a class that extends `Exception` with an informative name, such as `FileException` or `DatabaseException`. You can throw the subclass when the error condition occurs, resulting in a `FileException` object, rather than an `Exception` object.

TYPE THIS

```
catch (FileException $e)
{
    statements to handle errors of this type;
}
catch (DatabaseException $e)
{
    statements to handle errors of this type;
}
```

RESULT

→ Each `catch` block catches errors of the specific type and handles them.

Copy and Compare Objects

Beginning in PHP 5, PHP provides a magic method, named __clone (with two underscores), that you can use to copy an object. PHP's __clone() method copies an object with all its properties, as is, from the current object to the new object. You can include a __clone() method in your class that runs on the cloned object after the PHP __clone() method executes. Your __clone() method can change any of the properties in the new object.

Because the __clone() method is a magic method, you call it differently than normal methods, as follows:

```
$objectname2 = clone $objectname1;
```

If your class does not contain a __clone() method, $objectname2 is an exact copy of $objectname1, as it exists when the clone statement executes. If property values have changed in $objectname1 since it was

created, the changed property values are stored in $objectname2.

If your class statement includes a __clone() method, the property values in $objectname2 are changed, based on the statements in your __clone() method.

You can compare objects using either the equal operator (two equal signs) or the identical operator (three equal signs). Using the equal operator, two objects are equal if they are created from the same class and have the same properties and values. However, using the identical operator, two objects are identical only if they refer to the same instance of the same class. In other words, two objects created with two different new statements are equal, but not identical; an object created using the clone statement and the object it is cloned from are equal, but not identical; but an object created with an assignment statement is both equal and identical to the object assigned to it.

Copy and Compare Objects

① Create a class statement.

② Add one or more properties with defaults.

③ Type **function __clone()**.

④ Add a statement that changes one of the properties.

⑤ Create an object from the class.

⑥ Create a clone.

In this example, the clone statement is $my_car_clone = clone $my_car.

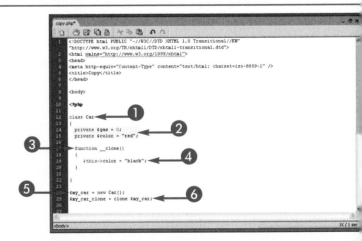

⑦ Add an if statement that compares the original object with the clone and echoes the result.

Note: The clone is not equal to the original because the __clone method changes the $color.

⑧ Create a second object from the class.

⑨ Add an if statement that compares the two objects.

Note: The two objects created with new from the same class are equal.

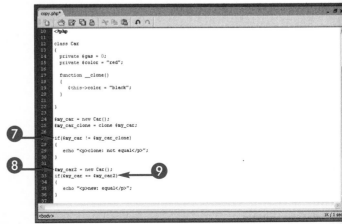

10 Create a new object with an assignment statement.

11 Add an if statement that compares the object with the object that it was assigned to.

Note: The two objects are both equal and identical.

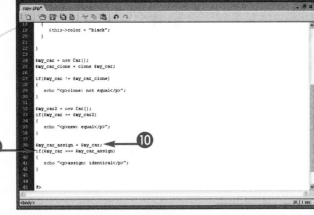

12 View the script in a browser.

The results of the if statements are displayed.

Apply It

Cloning an object takes a snapshot of the object at a given time, including all the current settings of the properties. This makes a rollback of an object possible. You can clone the object and, at any later time point, return to the object as it was when it was cloned.

TYPE THIS

```
$database_Sunday = clone $database;
statements that change database;
if($dberror == "yes")
{
    $database = $database_Sunday;
}
```

RESULT

If an error occurs, the $database object returns to its condition as of Sunday.

Get Information about Objects and Classes

PHP provides several functions that you can use to get information about objects and classes. You can check whether a class exists with `class_exists("classname")`. You can test whether a property exists in a specific class with `property_exists("classname","propertyname")`. The function returns TRUE if the property exists, even if its value is NULL.

You can find out the properties, with their defaults, and the methods defined in a class using the `get_class_vars("classname")` and `get_class_methods("classname")` functions. The functions return an array. The properties array contains the property name as the key and the default as the value. The methods array contains numeric keys and the names of the methods as values. If a property or method is private, the function will not return its name unless it is executed from inside the class.

You can find out the class, the parent class, and the properties of an object with the functions `get_class($objname)`, `get_parent_class($objname)`, and `get_object_vars($objname)`. `get_class()` and `get_parent_class()` return a string that is the name of a class. `get_object_vars()` returns an array containing the current values of the properties, with the property names as keys.

You can test whether an object, its parents, or their implemented interfaces were created by a specified class using the `instanceof` operator added in PHP 5, as follows:

```
if($objectname instanceof "classname")
```

In PHP 4, you can use the functions `is_a($objectname,"classname")` and `is_subclass_of($objectname,"classname")`. You can test whether a specific method has been defined for a specific object with the function `method_exists($objectname,"methodname")`.

Get Information about Objects and Classes

1 Add a `class` statement.

2 Add one or more properties, at least one private and one public.

3 Add at least one method.

4 Create an object from the class.

5 Change one of the public properties.

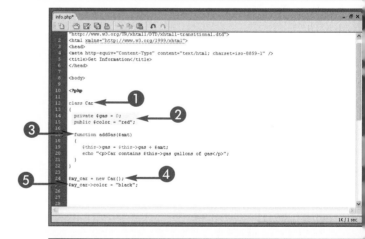

6 Get and echo the class name of the object created in step 4.

7 Add a statement that gets the properties with `get_class_vars()` and echo the properties array.

Note: The array will contain the default values from the class.

8 Add a statement that gets the properties with `get_object_vars()` and echo the properties array.

Note: The array will contain the current values from the object.

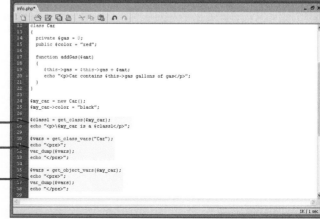

Add an if statement that tests whether a
method exists before executing the
method.

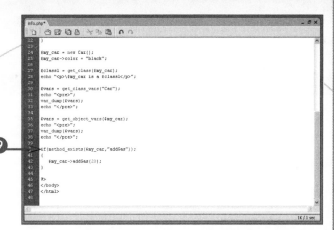

View the script in a browser.

● The class name is displayed.

The first array contains the default values.

The second array contains the current
values of the properties.

The if statement containing the method
call executed because the method exists.

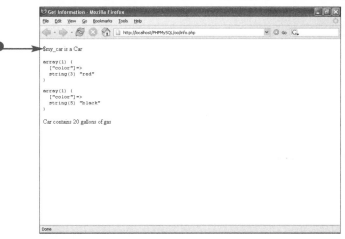

Extra

The function class_exists() triggers __autoload() if it does not find the named class. You can use a
second parameter to prevent the execution of __autoload(). The function interface_exists(), added
in PHP 5, has similar behavior when used with an interface.

TYPE THIS

```
if(class_exists("Car",false))
{
    $new_car = new Car();
}
```

RESULT

→ If PHP cannot find the class Car, it will not execute
__autoload().

Using Abstract Classes

You can use methods called *abstract methods* that specify the methods to be used and the information to be passed, but do not contain any code. Abstract methods were added in PHP 5.

Any class that contains an abstract method must be declared abstract. An abstract class can contain both abstract methods and methods that are not abstract.

You cannot create an object from an abstract class. The function of an abstract class is to serve as a parent for one or more child classes. The abstract class specifies the methods, including abstract methods that contain no code. The child classes must implement the abstract methods that are defined in the parent class, although each child class can implement the abstract method differently, with different code. If an abstract method is not included in a child class, a fatal error occurs. The child must define the method with the same or less

visibility. For example, if the abstract class is declared protected, the child class must be protected or public.

Abstract classes and methods are defined with a keyword, as follows:

```
abstract class classname

{

    abstract public function
methodname(value1, value2, ...);

}
```

The class is defined as abstract because it contains an abstract method. The abstract method is defined with the keyword `abstract`. The name and the values expected by the method are defined, but no code block is included.

Using Abstract Classes

① Type **abstract class**.

② Type the class name.

③ Add a protected property.

④ Add a constructor that initializes the property.

⑤ Type **abstract public function**.

⑥ Type the class name.

⑦ Add variable names for the values that the abstract class expects to be passed.

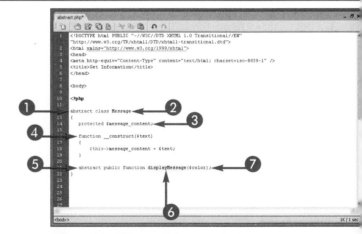

⑧ Add a `class` statement that extends the class created in steps 1 to 2.

⑨ Add a method with the same name as the abstract method added in steps 5 to 7.

⑩ Add a second `class` statement, with a different class name, that extends the abstract class.

⑪ Add a method with the same name as the abstract method, but with different code.

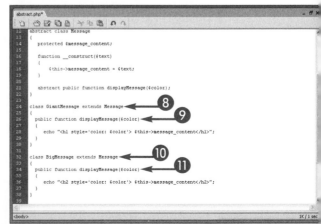

② Create an object from the child class created in steps 8 to 9.

Because the child class contains no constructor, the constructor in the abstract class executes.

⑬ Add a statement that executes the method in the child class.

⑭ Create an object from the second child class.

⑮ Add a statement that uses the class method.

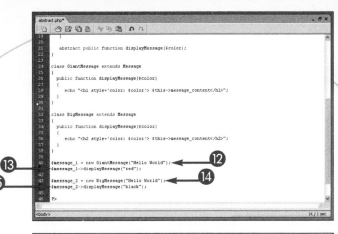

⑯ View the script in a browser.

The first child class executes its implementation of the abstract method.

The second child class executes its implementation of the abstract method.

Extra

You must implement all abstract methods in a child class that are included in the parent class or declare the child class to be abstract, which means that you cannot create an object from the class. If you do not implement all the abstract classes in the child, PHP issues a fatal error. The error message is very helpful, stating exactly how many abstract classes are not implemented and their names.

TYPE THIS		RESULT

Assume a class named `Mom` that is an abstract class containing two abstract methods.
 	
``
class Child extends Mom
{
}
$child_1 = new Child;
``
	→	The following error message:
		
		Fatal error: Class Child contains 2 abstract methods and must therefore be declared abstract or implement the remaining methods (Mom::feedChild, Mom::pickupChild) in **C:\Program Files\Apache Group\Apache2\htdocs\PHPMySQL\oo\abstract.php** on line 31

Using Interfaces

An *interface* contains only abstract methods, which are discussed in the preceding section, "Using Abstract Classes." You cannot create an object from an interface. The function of an interface is to enforce a pattern on a class by specifying the methods that must be implemented in the class. If a method included in the interface is not included in the class that implements the interface, a fatal error occurs.

An interface has the following format:

```
interface interfacename

{

    methods

}
```

An interface cannot have the same name as a class used in your script. All methods specified in an interface must be public. Do not use the abstract keyword for methods in an interface.

You implement an interface in a class with the following format:

```
class classname implements interfacename
```

You can implement more than one interface in a class, as follows:

```
class classname implements
interfacename1, interfacename2, ...
```

Multiple interfaces implemented by a single class may not contain methods with the same name. You can specify inheritance and an interface in the same class, as follows:

```
class classname extends parentname
implements interfacename
```

Using Interfaces

1. Type **interface**.

2. Type a name.

3. Add a block containing the methods.

   Do not add abstract in front of the methods.

4. Create a class that contains one or more protected properties and a constructor that sets a property.

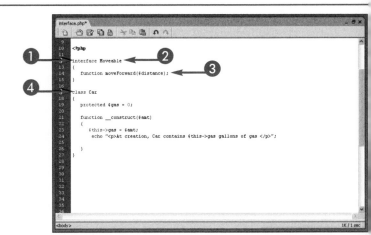

5. Create a child class of the class created in step 4.

6. Implement the interface.

7. Add a property.

8. Add a method with the same name as a method in the interface.

9. Add code that performs the action for the method.

10. Repeat steps 8 to 9 until the child contains all methods specified in the interface.

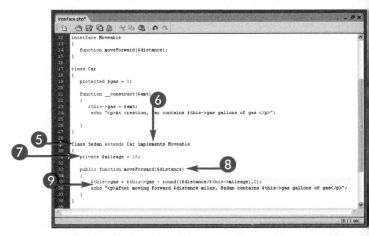

1 Create an object from the child class.

2 Add a statement that calls a method in the child class.

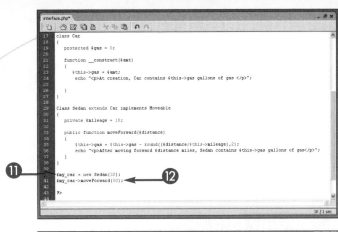

3 View the script in a browser.

● The constructor in the parent class executes, setting a property.

● The method in the child class executes.

Apply It

When you define an abstract method, you specify the values to be passed. If you define an object as the value to be passed, you can specify the class of the object as well, called *type hinting*. If the object passed is not of the specified class, a fatal error occurs. You can use type hinting when defining any type of method, but it is particularly useful in interfaces where the goal is to enforce a pattern.

TYPE THIS

```
abstract class Test
{
    abstract function storeMessage(Message
$my_message)
}
class Test2 extends Test
{
    function storeMessage($my_message)
    {
        statements that store the message;
    }
}
$my_message = new Message("Hello");
$test_message = new Test2();
$test_message->storeMessage($my_message);
```

RESULT

→ A fatal error occurs because the method in the class Test2 does not specify Message in the type hint, as specified in the abstract class.

Programming Editors and IDEs for PHP

PHP scripts are text files that can be created and changed using any text editor. You can use your favorite tool for writing text files to write PHP scripts, including vi, Notepad, or WordPad. However, programming editors or integrated development environments (IDEs) offer features that can save you time during development. You can find information about many editors, including reviews, at www.php-editors.com

This appendix describes some popular programming editors and IDEs that you can use with PHP. Some are free or cost very little. Those with a higher price tag provide trial versions that you can download and try out for free.

Programming Editors

Programming editors offer many features specifically for writing programs. The following features are offered by most programming editors:

Color highlighting: Highlight parts of the script — such as HTML tags, text strings, keywords, and comments — in different colors so that they are easy to identify.

Indentation: Automatically indent inside parentheses and curly braces to make scripts easier to read.

Line numbers: Add temporary line numbers. This is important because PHP error messages specify the line where the error was encountered.

Multiple files: You can have more than one file open at once.

Easy code inserting: Buttons for inserting code, such as HTML tags or PHP statements or functions.

Code library: Save snippets of your own code that can be inserted by clicking a button.

Available Programming Editors

Some popular programming editors that support PHP include the following:

ARACHNOPHILIA

Platform: Windows

Cost: Free (CareWare)

Web site: www.arachnoid.com/arachnophilia/

PHP Support: Sends PHP code to the Web server, so you can preview the Web page produced by a PHP script.

Arachnophilia is a programming editor with some special HTML production and editing features. The built-in FTP service assists with Web site management. Arachnophilia is written in Java, so you need to install the Java runtime system on your computer.

BBEDIT

Platform: Mac

Cost: $179.00

Web site: www.barebones.com/products/bbedit/index.shtml

PHP Support: Can send PHP code to the Web server. You can view the Web page produced by a PHP script by clicking a button.

BBEdit is a professional HTML and text editor for the Mac. It provides spell-checking and CSS support. HTML Tidy, a tool for cleaning HTML source code, and an HTML Syntax Checker are included with BBEdit. BBEdit provides support for the Subversion and Perforce source control management systems.

Programming Editors *(continued)*

EDITPLUS

Platform: Windows

Cost: $30.00

Web site: www.editplus.com

PHP Support: Provides customizable syntax highlighting for PHP source code.

EditPlus is an Internet-ready text editor, HTML editor, and programming editor. It can serve as a replacement for Notepad, but offers many features for Web page authors and programmers. It provides syntax highlighting for HTML, CSS, PHP, JavaScript, and other languages. You can preview HTML Web pages in its browser. It has built-in FTP commands to manage Web page files.

EMACS

Platform: Windows, Linux, UNIX

Cost: Open source/free

Web site: www.gnu.org/software/emacs/emacs.html

PHP Support: Provides customizable syntax highlighting for PHP source code.

Emacs works with Windows, Linux, and UNIX, and it is free.

HTML-KIT

Platform: Windows

Cost: Free

Web site: www.chami.com/html-kit/

PHP Support: Syntax highlighting for PHP source code. The Preview window displays output from PHP code.

HTML-Kit is a full-featured, highly customizable editor that can be used to create, edit, validate, preview, and publish Web pages and scripts. Its features include code highlighting, auto-save and backup, spell-checking, built-in FTP, block indenting, and many others. Many plug-ins are available for HTML-Kit.

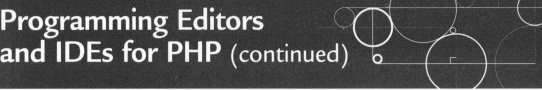

Integrated Development Environments

An *integrated development environment* (IDE) is an entire workspace for developing applications. It includes a programming editor as well as other features. Some features included by most IDEs are the following:

Debugging: Have built-in debugging features.

Previewing: Display the Web page output by the script.

Testing: Have built-in testing features for your scripts.

FTP: Have the built-in capability to connect and upload/download via FTP. They keep track of which files belong in which Web site and keep the Web site up-to-date.

Project management: Organize scripts into projects; manage the files in the project; include file checkout and check-in features.

Backups: Make automatic backups of your Web site at periodic intervals.

IDEs are more difficult to learn than programming editors. Some are fairly expensive, but their wealth of features can be worth it. IDEs are particularly useful when several people will be writing scripts for the same application. An IDE can make project coordination much simpler and make the code more compatible.

Available IDEs

The following are popular IDEs:

DREAMWEAVER

Platform: Windows, Mac

Cost: $399.00

Web site: www.macromedia.com/dreamweaver

Dreamweaver provides visual layout tools so that you can create a Web page by dragging elements around and clicking buttons to insert elements. Dreamweaver can write the HTML code for you. It includes the HomeSite editor, so you can write your own code. It also supports PHP dynamic Web sites with MySQL databases.

KOMODO

Platform: Windows, Mac, Linux

Cost: $29.95 for personal or educational use, $295.00 for commercial use

Web site: www.activestate.com/Products/Komodo

Komodo is an IDE for open-source languages, including Perl and Python, as well as PHP, providing a powerful workspace for editing, debugging, and testing programs.

Integrated Development Environments *(continued)*

MAGUMA

Platform: Windows

Cost: Depends on package and operating system selected

Web site: www.maguma.com

Maguma is an IDE for Apache, PHP, and MySQL. It comes in two versions at different costs: Maguma Workbench and Maguma Studio, which offer features for huge sites with multiple servers. Maguma Open Studio is the open-source version of Maguma Studio. It is a PHP IDE that includes features for class browsing, FTP support, snippets, debugging, and project management.

PHP DESIGNER

Platform: Windows

Cost: Open source/free

Web site: www.mpsoftware.dk/phpdesigner.php

PHP Designer is an IDE for coding PHP for both professional and novice designers. It provides tools for editing, debugging, analyzing, and publishing PHP scripts.

ZEND STUDIO

Platform: Windows, Mac, Linux

Cost: Standard edition, $99.00; Professional edition, $299.00

Web site: www.zend.com/store/products/zend-studio.php

Zend Studio is an IDE that was developed by the people who developed the Zend engine, which is the engine under the hood of PHP. Zend Studio provides editing, debugging, analysis, optimization, and database tools.

Troubleshooting Tips

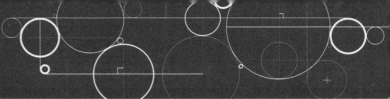

Typos and minor mistakes are inevitable when writing a script. Appendix A discusses programming editors and IDEs that can be tools to assist with programming. This appendix lists and explains the most common PHP scripting errors.

Understanding Error Messages

PHP error messages try to provide as much information as possible to assist with troubleshooting a problem. The program name and line number where the problem was encountered are included in the error message. Chapter 2 discusses runtime error messages.

PHP also provides parse error messages. Parse errors, identified at compile time, prevent PHP from beginning to execute the script. A parse error message looks similar to the following:

Parse error: parse error, unexpected '{', expecting '(' in **C:\test.php** on line **12**

The message identifies what it encountered — a curly brace — and what it was expecting — a parenthesis, including the program and the line where the problem was encountered.

The parse error message cannot always identify the entire problem. Sometimes it just identifies the unexpected character that causes the problem, without specifying what character should actually be there, as follows:

Parse error: parse error, unexpected ')' in **C:\test.php** on line **12**

Although the parse error message sometimes displays the exact character, it often displays tokens that represent parts of the PHP language, as follows:

Parse error: parse error, unexpected T_ STRING in **C:\ test.php** on line **13**

In this case, the token T_STRING represents a string. The message means that PHP encountered a string where it does not belong.

The token, T_STRING, has an informative name. Not all tokens are as clear, such as T_DEC, which means the decrementing operator (--) or T_AS, which means foreach. You can find a list of the tokens and what they reference at www.php.net/manual/en/tokens.php.

Common Errors

This section discusses the most common errors in PHP.

Error: Missing semicolons

Every PHP statement ends with a semicolon (;). PHP does not stop reading a statement until it reaches a semicolon. If you leave out the semicolon at the end of a line, PHP continues reading the statement on the following line.

Result: Usually a parse error because the two lines, read as one statement, are not a statement with acceptable syntax.

```
Example:
$test = 1
echo $test;
```

Parse error: parse error, unexpected T_ ECHO in **C:\ test.php** on line **13**

Error: Using = instead of == or ===

In a comparison statement, you test whether two values are equal with two equal signs (==) or whether two values are identical with three equal signs (===). Using one equal sign is a common mistake. When you use one equal sign, the comparison statement becomes an assignment statement, which is always true.

Result: Usually an infinite loop or an `if` statement that never executes, rather than an error message.

```
Example:
$test = 0;
while($test = 0)
{
    $test++;
}
```

Results in an endless loop because `$test` is reset to 0 each time the `while` loop executes.

Error: Misspelled variable names

If you misspell a variable name, PHP treats it as a new variable.

Result: PHP handles the misspelled variable as a new variable and executes the statement. This error often does not result in an error message.

```
Example:
$test = 0;
while($test == 0)
{
    $Test++;
}
```

Results in an endless loop because `$Test` (with an uppercase *T*) is not the same variable as `$test` (with a lowercase *T*). The `$test` variable is never incremented inside the loop; the value remains 0.

Error: Missing dollar signs

If you leave out the dollar sign in a variable name, PHP does not recognize the string as a variable.

Result: In most cases, the variable name has no meaning to PHP as a string and a parse error results.

```
Example:
test = 0;
```

Parse error: parse error, unexpected '=' in **C:\test.php** on line **12**

Error: Using quotes incorrectly

When PHP reads a quote, either single or double, it continues to read the script as a quoted string until it encounters a matching quote. If you leave out the closing quote, PHP continues to read the PHP language commands as part of the string. If you include a matching quote inside the string without escaping it, PHP ends the quoted string at that point and reads the next text as PHP language.

Result: In most cases, when quotes are not matched correctly, the result is incorrect syntax, which results in a parse error.

```
Example:
$test = "Hello World;
echo "$test";
```

Parse error: parse error, unexpected T_VARIABLE in **C:\test.php** on line **13**

Common Errors *(continued)*

Error: Output in the script before a header is sent

A `header` statement sends a header to the Web server. The `setcookie()` and `session_start()` statements also send headers. Headers must be the first statements sent in a PHP script. You cannot send output from your script and than send a header after the output. Any characters, even one blank space, preceding the PHP tag are sent as HTML output.

Result: An error message stating that a header has already been sent.

Example:
```
<html>
<?php
    header("Location: http://company.com");
?>
```
Warning: Cannot modify header information - headers already sent by (output started at **C:\test.php:1**) in **C:\test.php** on line **3**

Error: Incorrect numeric keys when accessing arrays

The first value in a numeric array created by PHP is 0. Attempting to access the first value with the key 1 is a common error.

Result: The expected array element is not the actual array element accessed.

Example:
```
$test = 1;
while($test <= 3)
{
    $array[] = $test;
    $test++;
}
echo $array[3];
```
Notice: Undefined offset: 3 in **C:\ test.php** on line **18**

The array is actually:
```
$array[0] = 1
$array[1] = 2
$array[2] = 3
```
There is no `$array[3]`.

Error: Missing PHP tags in `include` files

When PHP executes an `include` statement and reads in a file, the contents of the `include` file are read in HTML mode, even though the `include` statement is in a PHP section of the script. If the contents of the `include` file are PHP statements, they must be enclosed in PHP tags — `<?php` and `?>`.

Result: If the PHP tags are not included in the PHP file, the content of the file is seen by PHP as HTML. In most cases, the file content is seen as text by the browser, so it is displayed in the Web page, showing the PHP commands. This is often a security risk.

Example:

A file named file1.inc contains the following statement:

```
if($test == 1)
     echo "Hi";
```

The main script contains the following statements:

```
<?php
$test = 1;
include ("file1.inc");
?>
```

The word *Hi* is not displayed on the Web page. Instead, the Web page displays the `if` statement contained in file1.inc. To display the word *Hi,* file1.inc needs to include the PHP tags.

Error: Missing parenthesis or curly bracket

Parentheses and curly brackets must come in pairs. Opening with a (that has no closing) or a { with no } results in incorrect syntax.

Result: An error message

Example:

```
$test = $test2 = $test3 = 0;
while($test < 3)
{
    if($test2 != "yes")
    {
        if($test3 > 4)
        {
            echo "go";
        }
    }
}
```

Parse error: parse error, unexpected $end in **C:\test.php** on line **10**

The indentation in the script assists in locating the missing curly bracket.

Error: Typing a curly brace for a parenthesis and vice versa

A parenthesis and a curly brace sometimes look similar on the screen. Typing one when you mean the other is common.

Result: A parse error

Example:

```
if($test == 0}
     echo "Hello";
```

Parse error: parse error, unexpected '}' in **C:\test.php** on line **11**

INDEX

Symbols

- character, 78, 105, 122
! (exclamation point), 75, 80, 83
!is_string function, 75
signal, 50
$ (dollar sign), 36
$ character, 78
$$ (two dollar signs), 47
$_COOKIE array, 72, 249
$_COOKIES array, 253, 254
$_ENV array, 72
$_FILES array, 72
$_FILES superglobal array, 246
$_GET array, 72, 73, 228, 241, 252, 253
$_POST array, 72, 73, 228, 230, 231, 234, 236, 240, 241, 253
$_REQUEST array, 72, 73, 228
$_SERVER array, 72
$_SESSION array, 72, 249, 256
$age variable, 47
$array_include statement, 99
$array_of_keys function, 55, 62
$arrayname array, 58
$ascii_code variable, 138
$bad_format array, 237
$bool variable, 62
$count function, 124
$GLOBALS array, 72, 109
$HTTP_GET_VARS array, 228
$HTTP_POST_VARS array, 228
$keyname => parameter, 70
$keyname variable, 58
$letters array, 53
$nameOfVariable variable, 47
$num function, 111
$num_large function, 118
$num_small function, 118
$path statement, 100
$result function, 122
$strcage variable, 37
$string function, 130
$sub_string statement, 129
$this keyword, 264
$valuename variable, 58
% (percent sign), 188

% sign, 122
& (ampersand), 111, 252
( ) character, 78
* character, 78
, (commas), 162
. (dot), 42, 178
. character, 78
: (colon), 91
? character, 78
?> (closing tag), 32
[ ] character, 78
[^] character, 78
\ (backslash), 42, 78, 240
\ character, 78
\n character, 42
\t character, 42
^ character, 78
_ (underscores), 38
_ _autoload( ) function, 263, 279
_ _call method, 267
_ _clone method, 276
_ _construct( ) method, 268
_ _destruct( ) method, 268
_ _get( ) function, 270
_ _set( ) method, 270
{n} character, 78
{n1,n2} character, 78
| character, 78
+ character, 78
++ operator, 46
= (equal sign), 77, 94, 95, 174
.= operator, 42
== (two equal signs), 76, 289
== (two equal signs) operator, 74
=== (three equal signs), 76, 289
> character, 238
; (semicolon), 32, 97, 100, 154, 288
< character, 238

A

<a> tag, 248, 249, 252
abstract keyword, 280, 282
abstract methods, 280
abstraction, 261
access level, 148

B

INDEX

INDEX

INDEX

G

H

INDEX

INDEX

INDEX

INDEX

For more professional instruction in a visual format, try these.

All designed for visual learners—just like you!

Read Less–Learn More®

HTML

Your visual blueprint™ for designing Web pages with HTML, CSS, and XHTML

0-7645-8331-X

Excel® Data Analysis
2nd Edition

Data analysis tools on CD-ROM!
• FinOptions XL, Analyse-It™, SigmaXL, and other trial software
• Macro codes, an e-version of the book, and more

Your visual blueprint™ for analyzing data, charts, and Pivot Tables

0-7645-9780-9

JavaScript™
2nd Edition

Your visual blueprint™ for building dynamic Web pages

0-7645-7497-3

For a complete listing of *Visual Blueprint*™ titles and other Visual books, go to wiley.com/go/visualtech

Wiley, the Wiley logo, the Visual logo, Read Less-Learn More, and Visual Blueprint are trademarks or registered trademarks of John Wiley & Sons, Inc. and/or its affiliates. All other trademarks are the property of their respective owners.

Visual®
An Imprint of WILEY
Now you know.

Credits

Project Editor
Dana Rhodes Lesh

Acquisitions Editor
Jody Lefevere

Product Development Supervisor
Courtney Allen

Copy Editor
Dana Rhodes Lesh

Technical Editor
Mark D. Lesh

Editorial Manager
Robyn Siesky

Business Manager
Amy Knies

Permissions Editor
Laura Moss

Media Development Specialist
Laura VanWinkle

Manufacturing
Allan Conley
Linda Cook
Paul Gilchrist
Jennifer Guynn

Book Design
Kathie S. Rickard

Production Coordinator
Adrienne L. Martinez

Layout
Jennifer Mayberry
Heather Ryan
Amanda Spagnuolo

Screen Artists/Graphics
Ronda David-Burroughs
Cheryl Grubbs
Joyce Haughey
Jill A. Proll

Cover Illustration
Rita Marley

Proofreader
Shannon Ramsey

Quality Control
John Greenough

Indexer
Kevin Broccoli

Special Help
Laura VanWinkle

**Vice President and Executive
Group Publisher**
Richard Swadley

Vice President and Publisher
Barry Pruett

Composition Director
Debbie Stailey

PRAISE FOR VISUAL BOOKS...

"This is absolutely the best computer-related book I have ever bought. Thank you so much for this fantastic text. Simply the best computer book series I have ever seen. I will look for, recommend, and purchase more of the same."
 —David E. Prince (NeoNome.com)

"I have several of your Visual books and they are the best I have ever used."
 —Stanley Clark (Crawfordville, FL)

"I just want to let you know that I really enjoy all your books. I'm a strong visual learner. You really know how to get people addicted to learning! I'm a very satisfied Visual customer. Keep up the excellent work!"
 —Helen Lee (Calgary, Alberta, Canada)

"I have several books from the Visual series and have always found them to be valuable resources."
 —Stephen P. Miller (Ballston Spa, NY)

"This book is PERFECT for me — it's highly visual and gets right to the point. What I like most about it is that each page presents a new task that you can try verbatim or, alternatively, take the ideas and build your own examples. Also, this book isn't bogged down with trying to 'tell all' – it gets right to the point. This is an EXCELLENT, EXCELLENT, EXCELLENT book and I look forward to purchasing other books in the series."
 —Tom Dierickx (Malta, IL)

"I have quite a few of your Visual books and have been very pleased with all of them. I love the way the lessons are presented!"
 —Mary Jane Newman (Yorba Linda, CA)

"I am an avid fan of your Visual books. If I need to learn anything, I just buy one of your books and learn the topic in no time. Wonders! I have even trained my friends to give me Visual books as gifts."
 —Illona Bergstrom (Aventura, FL)

"I just had to let you and your company know how great I think your books are. I just purchased my third Visual book (my first two are dog-eared now!) and, once again, your product has surpassed my expectations. The expertise, thought, and effort that go into each book are obvious, and I sincerely appreciate your efforts."
 —Tracey Moore (Memphis, TN)

"Compliments to the chef!! Your books are extraordinary! Or, simply put, extra-ordinary, meaning way above the rest! THANK YOU THANK YOU THANK YOU! I buy them for friends, family, and colleagues."
 —Christine J. Manfrin (Castle Rock, CO)

"I write to extend my thanks and appreciation for your books. They are clear, easy to follow, and straight to the point. Keep up the good work! I bought several of your books and they are just right! No regrets! I will always buy your books because they are the best."
 —Seward Kollie (Dakar, Senegal)

"I am an avid purchaser and reader of the Visual series, and they are the greatest computer books I've seen. Thank you very much for the hard work, effort, and dedication that you put into this series."
 —Alex Diaz (Las Vegas, NV)